C000225776

Kerala

CONTENTS

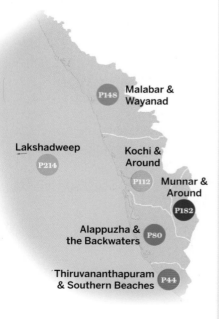

Get to Know Kerala 224

Travellers' Helpdesk 238

HOW TO USE THIS BOOK

1
Plan Your Trip

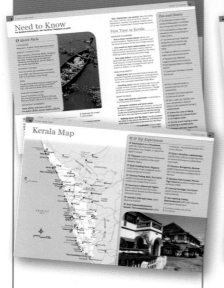

- Written specially by our Indian author who travelled extensively across the state.

- Our suggestions for the best things to do and see.

- Advice on everything you need to travel around, shop, eat and keep the family happy.

- Need to Know: A 'quick reference guide' for all the key information you will need.

2
Kerala's Best Trips

- Highlights of the main regions, covering the best attractions and activities.

- Expert recommendations tell you about not-to-be-missed highlights.

- Reviews of accommodation, restaurants and shopping by Lonely Planet author.

- Easy maps for each region, with clearly marked, numbered highlights.

4 Easy-to-use colour-coded sections:

3
Get to Know Kerala

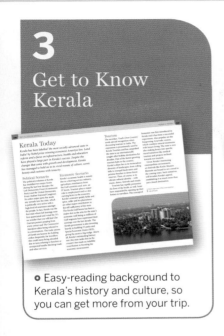

● Easy-reading background to Kerala's history and culture, so you can get more from your trip.

4
Travellers' Helpdesk

● An A to Z of all the vital information you will need.

Special information

Look for these boxes to help you get the most out of your trip:

✓ *Top Tip* – insider advice

♥ *If You Like* – themed suggestions

® *Value for Money* – money-saving advice

◈ *Detour* – off-beat trips

▣ *Snapshot* – interesting facts

⌜TOP CHOICE⌟ *Top Choice* – our top picks

OUR REVIEWS

Lonely Planet writers have visited every hotel, restaurant, shop and activity in this book. They don't accept any freebies and favours, so you can be sure our recommendations are unbiased.

PLAN YOUR TRIP

▌I Sprawling tea plantations offer plenty of green
respite in Kerala

Need to Know

For detailed information, see Travellers' Helpdesk on p240

🛈 *Quick Facts*

LANGUAGES

Malayalam, English, Tamil and some Hindi.

MOBILE CONNECTIVITY

Major operators like Airtel, BSNL, Vodafone, Idea and Aircel provide service through the state. In hilly regions like Munnar, Thekkady and Wayanad, you are likely to get signals sporadically.

INTERNET ACCESS

Internet booths are available in market areas (₹10–20/30min), but most hotels offer wi-fi facilities on the house.

ATMS

Though Federal Bank has the widest reach within the state, you will also find HDFC, ICICI, SBI and Axis Bank ATMs easily.

TOURIST INFORMATION

Tourist Facilitation Centre, Thiruvananthapuram (📞0471 2321132; Museum Road). Offices in all major cities.

IMPORTANT NUMBERS

Police 📞100; ambulance 📞108; fire station 📞101; women helpline 📞1091

When to Go

Waterways are a major form of travel

The weather in Kerala is warm and humid, barring the eastern hilly regions. It rains copiously during the monsoon, and high summer months are intensely hot.

• **October–February; high season:** This is when the weather is at its coolest and prices of all accommodation at their highest. Though still warm in the day, the evenings can get chilly. If travelling to the hills (Munnar and Wayanad) carry a light jacket. You may encounter rain in late October with the retreating monsoon.

• **March–April; mid-season:** These two months get low tourist activity on the coastline, but the higher regions are still packed with travellers as schools close after exams.

• **May–September; low season:** Very hot along the coast, until the rains arrive from June to September. However, the greener eastern parts are at their freshest best. Expect huge discounts.

First Time in Kerala

ADVANCE PLANNING:

• **Two to three months before:** Book your accommodation, flights/trains, as prices swell during peak season. Chalk out a rough itinerary.

• **One month to three weeks before:** You may want to alter your plan after a quick check of national parks (sometimes closed for the rains), trekking routes and festivals at this stage.

• **One week before:** Look out for fabulous deals with flexi pricing resorts. Draw up the final itinerary. Confirm bookings. Stock up on medicines you need. Arrange for pick-ups at airport or station, or car rentals.

HEALTH & SAFETY

• **Medical aid:** Well-stocked medical shops and standard hospitals are present in most big towns, but hard to find in the plantations and forested areas. Carry enough prescribed medication.

• **Travelling alone:** Kerala is fairly safe. If you are a single woman, be alert and follow the rules of safety you would in your own hometown. Though locals are extremely helpful, use your instincts.

WHAT TO PACK

• **Caps, dark glasses, sunscreen:** A necessity in the frequently hot weather.

• **Mosquito repellent and leech socks:** Mosquitoes love Kerala's lush environs, so be sure to carry a repellent. Plantation areas and trekking routes are breeding grounds for leeches during the rains. You may want to invest in leech socks.

• **Walking shoes and flip-flops:** Comfy sneakers are ideal in hilly places like Munnar and Wayanad, while beach destinations demand airy flip-flops.

• **Warm clothing and umbrellas:** Carry a light jacket for evenings in coastal areas; you'll need something heavier in October–February for the hills. A sturdy umbrella in June–September is a must.

Dos and Don'ts

✓ Do attempt to learn a few words of Malayalam. It will take you a long way with the locals.

✓ If confused by a map, take directions from local shops or traffic police.

✓ Try the local food. Seafood along the coast and the veg sadya (p32) are especially tasty.

✓ Make an effort to conserve water and natural resources.

✓ Respect the different religious beliefs and customs. Dress appropriately in religious places.

✓ Leave your footwear outside the house.

✗ Don't ridicule words or accents that you do not understand.

✗ Abstain from loud opinions on food and culture.

✗ Don't walk out midway, use your cell phone or disturb others in the audience during a culture show.

✗ Follow the rules of taking photographs at cultural shows or at religious sites.

✗ Strictly avoid making a noise or littering in wildlife parks.

✗ Bargain with tact, especially with local craftspeople.

This is Kerala

Expect to be mesmerised by Kerala's idyllic environs, laid-back pace and pulsating cultural vibe. The locals take great pride in their traditional roots, and this imbues every aspect of life – be it food, architecture, language or art forms. Visually, Kerala is one of the most scenic destinations in India, attracting thousands every year to its palm-lined beaches, verdant jungles and spice-scented hills.

Diverse Cultures

A long history of spice trade with China, Arabia, Portugal and other parts of the world has influenced the multi-cultural composition of the state in many ways. Synagogues, churches and forts emerged in the port towns and enriched the landscape. Besides the influence from

overseas, Kerala's deep-seated Hindu culture can be seen in innumerable ancient temples – the most important ones being the Guruvayur Sree Krishna Temple and Sree Padmanabhaswamy Temple. For travellers, history continues to live on in a number of traditional Keralite as well as colonial houses, many of which have been converted into museums, heritage homestays or hotels.

Performing Arts

Among the irresistible attractions of Kerala are its performing art forms, which can be easily experienced thanks to shows designed especially for visitors. Reputed schools like Kerala Kalamandalam and Margi Kathakali offer a more in-depth understanding.

Kathakali, with its elaborate ritualised gestures, heavy mask-like make-up, and dramatic stories of love, lust and power struggles based on the *Ramayana*, *Mahabharata* and *Puranas*, stems from temple rituals.

Theyyam, an even earlier art, is a ritual centred around a deity (of which there are 450) and performed in kavus (sacred groves) in northern Kerala. Magnificently attired, the performers engage in frenzied dancing to a wild drumbeat, creating a trance-like atmosphere.

Taking its cue from both of these, kalaripayattu is a form of martial arts, taught and displayed throughout the state in a kalari – an arena combining gymnasium, school and temple. Mohiniyattam is another popular dance form that displays grace and gentle movements.

Kerala also celebrates its festivals with great vigour. Flamboyant elephant parades, elaborate feasts and carnivals add to the revelry during these events.

Home of Ayurveda

Kerala is the best place for an exceptionally peaceful and refreshing Ayurvedic vacation

Ayurveda and Kerala have become almost synonymous, not only due to the state's vast knowledge of this ancient form of medicine, but the hard-sell that delivers what it promises. Herbal remedies and rejuvenation massages are in great demand and countless practitioners make use of the state's herbal resources and traditional expertise. You will find Ayurvedic massage in almost every large resort worth its name. For a more authentic version you can visit the well-established schools and clinics.

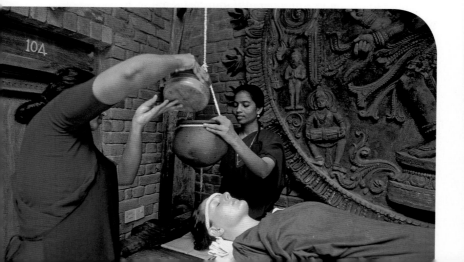

Diverse Cuisine

With a tremendous variety of local cuisines, Kerala is
deliciously rewarding. The cultural and religious diversity of
its people has resulted in a wide repertoire of cuisines that
are distinct from the curries of north India. Ranging from
brilliant Mappila (Muslim) biryanis, sadyas (feasts) served
in Hindu households, lip-smacking non-vegetarian dishes
of Syrian Christian families, to a steady supply of seafood
delights, you will always find something new to try. The
food tastes even better when eaten on banana leaves.

Lush Landscapes

It is difficult to imagine how a small strip of land on India's
southwestern edge can encompass such a varied landscape.
Luminescent paddy fields, fragrant spice gardens and
verdant tea and coffee plantations offer plenty of green
respite. Then there are the waterways where boats cruise
along the slender rivers and glassy lagoons. Azure seas
gently lap crescents of sun-warmed sand. The coastal areas
graduate mildly to the hills of the Western Ghats, which
have a plethora of flora and fauna in the national parks of
Periyar and Parambikulam. In Kerala you can paddle, swim,
join wildlife safaris or simply inhale the fresh country air.

Delicious
red fish
curry
flavoured
with myriad
spices

Kerala Map

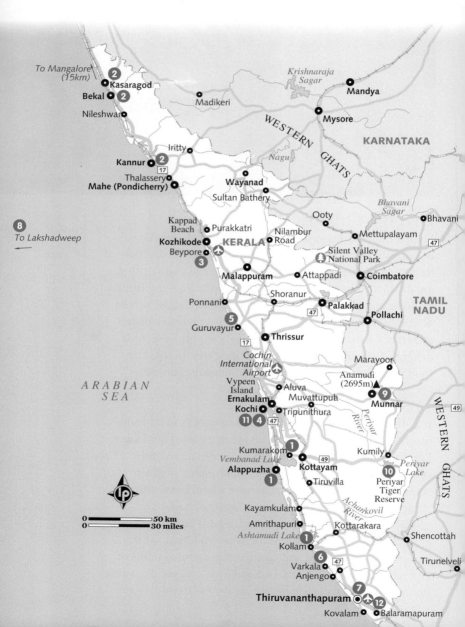

✪ *12 Top Experiences*

❶ Backwaters on a Houseboat (p87, 98, 106) Float past sprawling plantations and villages, or spend the night in a boat.

❷ Theyyam (p153) Watch the ancient dance form practised in the north Malabar region.

❸ Boat-building Yards, Beypore (p155) Have a look at gigantic boats being carved out of wood.

❹ Chinese Fishing Nets, Fort Kochi (p131) A centuries-old legacy of traders from Kubla Khan's court.

❺ Guruvayur's Mammoth Sights (p142) Visit the famous Guruvayur Sree Krishna Temple and the elephant sanctuary nearby.

❻ Varkala's Cliff-side Cafes (p64) Must-try seafood.

❼ Sree Padmanabhaswamy Temple, Thiruvananthapuram (p54) A massive – and extraordinarily rich – Vishnu Shrine.

❽ Diver's Paradise, Lakshadweep (p218) Swim with an embarrassment of marine life living on undisturbed coral reefs.

❾ Planters' Bungalows, Munnar (p194) Experience the grand estate life in the plantation-cloaked hills of Munnar.

❿ Bamboo Raft Cruise, Periyar Tiger Reserve (p200) A unique way of spotting wildlife.

⓫ Colonial Heritage, Fort Kochi (p130) Explore the rich history of colonial Kerala.

⓬ Sari-weaving Colony, Balaramapuram (p57) See weavers spin classic Kerala saris.

❚ Fort Kochi is dotted with colonial-era buildings

12 Top Experiences

1 Backwaters on a Houseboat

It is not every day you come across a place as sublime as Kerala's backwaters: 900km of interconnected rivers, lakes and glassy lagoons lined with lush tropical flora. And if you do, there likely won't be a way to experience it that's quite as serene and intimate as a few days on a teak-and-palm-thatched houseboat. Float along the water – while nibbling on seafood so fresh it's still almost wriggling – and forget about life on land for a while. The distinctive houseboats that cluster around the main hubs of Alappuzha (p87), Kumarakom (p98) and Kollam (p106) are designed like traditional rice barges or kettuvallam ('boat with knots', so-called because the curvaceous structure is held together by knotted coir).

2 Theyyam

Theyyam, Kerala's most popular ritualistic art form, is believed to pre-date Hinduism. The word refers to the ritual itself, and to the shape of the deity or hero portrayed, of which there are more than 450. The costumes are magnificent, with face paint, armour, garlands and huge headdresses. The performance consists of frenzied dancing to a wild drumbeat, creating a trance-like atmosphere. The best areas to see Theyyam performances are in the villages around Kannur (p162), Bekal (p166) and Kasaragod (p166) between October and April.

3 Boat-building Yards, Beypore

The traditional craft of dhow (boat) building is still practised in Beypore (p155), a quaint little village close to Kozhikode. The sheer architectural feat of creating these massive wooden beauties is accomplished without any complex machinery or blueprints – it's through plain ingenuity and practical knowledge passed on from generation to generation. Watch the team piece together these vessels that eventually leave the shores for Middle Eastern countries.

4 Chinese Fishing Nets, Fort Kochi

The captivating sight of local fisherman heaving and tugging at the Chinese fishing nets (p131) is the perfect way to start your day at Fort Kochi (p130). These enormous, spider-like contraptions – a legacy from the AD1400 court of Kubla Khan – scoop up kilos of sea creatures, but need some brawn to get the job done. At least four people are required to operate their counterweights at high tide.

5 Guruvayur's Mammoth Sights

The Hindu-only Guruvayur Sree Krishna Temple (p142), 33km northwest of Thrissur, is the most famous place of worship in Kerala. Said to have

been created by Guru, preceptor of the gods, and Vayu, god of wind, the temple is renowned for its healing powers. Thousands visit the temple each day, many even get married here. While here, you must visit the Guruvayur Anna Kotta (p142) where the temple elephants are kept. Just 3km from the temple, it is one of the largest elephant sanctuaries in India. Children will especially enjoy bathing and feeding the elephants.

6 Varkala's Cliff-side Cafes

Watch the minutes go by from the breezy cliff-side cafes serving to-die-for seafood in Varkala (p64). Most of these cafes offer a mishmash of Indian, Asian and Western fare to a soundtrack of easy-listening reggae. Perched almost perilously along the edge of dizzying cliffs, this breathtaking beach resort town is the perfect destination to soak up the sun, indulge in rejuvenating Ayurvedic treatments and binge on delicious seafood.

7 Sree Padmanabhaswamy Temple, Thiruvananthapuram

An iconic Vishnu temple, Sree Padmanabhaswamy (p54) gets its fair share of blissed-out devotees each day. The temple is not only known for its 18-ft-long reclining statue of Vishnu but also for having one of the richest coffers among Indian temples. The temple gets pretty crowded during the Painkuni festival in the months of March and April.

8 Diver's Paradise, Lakshadweep

With a landscape made up entirely of iridescent waters and powder-white sands, Lakshadweep has plenty of allure on the surface. But go underwater – 12m to be exact – and you will find even greater treasures. The Wall of Wonder at Kadmat (p219) and Kavaratti is an endless underwater cliff made entirely of soft corals. It teems with marine life in all sizes and colours of the rainbow and you can join them too. Experienced as well as novice divers agree that it is one of the top dives of the world.

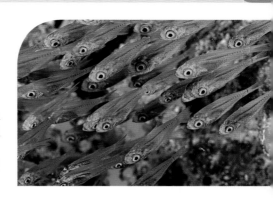

9 Planters' Bungalows, Munnar

In Munnar you'll be engulfed in a sea of a thousand shades of green. The rolling hills all around are covered by a sculptural carpet of tea plantations, and the mountain scenery is magnificent – you're often up above the clouds, watching veils of mist cling below the mountaintops. A stay at one of the many planters' bungalows (p194) here ensures you experience all this and more at close quarters. Look forward to classic colonial-style features – wooden floors, dusty libraries, high ceilings and weathered furniture – in these graceful bungalows.

🔟 Bamboo Raft Cruise, Periyar Tiger Reserve

The best way to experience south India's most popular wildlife sanctuary (p200) is by drifting languidly in the namesake lake on a bamboo raft. These day-long trips can be arranged by the Ecotourism Centre, run by the Forest Department. The massive sanctuary encompasses 925 sq km and has a 26-sq-km artificial lake created by the British in 1895. The vast reserve is home to bison, sambar, wild boar, langur, elephants and tigers.

11 Colonial Heritage, Fort Kochi

Explore the eclectic mix of historic sites that include magnificent Portuguese-era cathedrals and Dutch palaces at Fort Kochi (p130). Of these, the St Francis Church (p131) on River Road is believed to be one of the first European churches (1503) in India. Fort Kochi's heritage buildings are best experienced by walking down or cycling along the narrow streets.

12 Sari-weaving Colony, Balaramapuram

A small colony of weavers spin and ply the warp and weft at the manual looms at Balaramapuram (p56), off Thiruvananthapuram. Gorgeous patterns and designs are woven here on cotton saris – you can watch the process for hours. The famous white cotton sari with a golden border is the region's most famous product and you can pick up one of these much cheaper here.

Kerala's Top Itineraries

Based on the time you have at hand, these suggested itineraries include a variety of experiences for a holiday in Kerala: food, culture, history, landscape and, let's not forget – sheer relaxation.

Historic Sites & Backwaters (3 Days)

This itinerary covers quintessential Kerala, with backwaters, colonial history and culture. Note that you can also begin the trip at Alappuzha (p87), which is well connected by train.

❶ KOCHI (1 DAY)

Arrive in Ernakulam (p120) and head straight to Fort Kochi (p130), Kerala's historic colonial trading centre. Spend a day exploring the **Pardesi Synagogue** (p134) on Jew Street, the **Chinese fishing nets** (p131), **St. Francis Church** (p131) and other monuments here, stopping for food at the atmospheric cafes. End the evening with a cultural show at **Greenix Village** (p140). For dinner, there's fresh seafood at restaurants near Princess Street. Fort Kochi is very small and it's easy to get around. **Tuk-Tuk Odyssey** (p132) can arrange for a quick tour.

Laid-back vacationers on Kovalam Beach ▮

❷ ALAPPUZHA (1 DAY)

Leave for Alappuzha (60km/1½ hr) in the morning for a pre-booked 22-hour stay in a houseboat. Most operators start these trips by 11am so ensure that you are at the dock in time. The houseboat experience allows you to see the countryside in super comfort. Wake up to the sight of fishermen gathering their nets and heading to the villages.

❸ ERNAKULAM (1 DAY)

You will be able to leave Alappuzha by noon and will easily manage to reach Ernakulam to catch an evening flight. If catching a late night bus or train, you can explore the shops and grab a quick bite on the arterial MG Road.

Beaches & Heritage (4 Days)

This trip is about sunny beaches and excellent seafood. It also includes a visit to one of the most famous temples in Kerala.

❶ KOVALAM (2 DAYS)

Arrive in Thiruvananthapuram (p51) and head straight to your hotel at Kovalam (p70) (15km from the airport). Enjoy the seaside and fresh seafood in breezy cafes.

❷ VARKALA (1 DAY)

You can head to Varkala (p64) (58km/1½ hr) for a different experience of the Arabian Sea. The topography of the laterite cliffs plunging into sandy patches below is stunning. The nightlife is vibrant with live music in cafes as you relish some fresh seafood.

❸ THIRUVANANTHAPURAM (1 DAY)

Head back to Thiruvananthapuram to indulge in some sightseeing. Don't miss the **Sree Padmanabhaswamy Temple** (p54), **Puthe Maliga Palace Museum** (p55) and the **Zoological Gardens & Museums** (p52).

Nature Trail (5 Days)

In five days you have ample time to take back memories of historical monuments in Fort Kochi, one of the best wildlife parks of India and scenic views of tea plantations carpeting the hills of Munnar (p189).

❶ KOCHI (1 DAY)

Arrive in Ernakulam and check-in at a hotel in Fort Kochi to spend a day exploring the beautiful monuments and relaxing in cafes serving irresistible seafood (see historic sites & backwaters itinerary).

❷ KUMILY & PERIYAR TIGER RESERVE (2 DAYS)

Kumily (p200) is the base camp for visiting Periyar Tiger Reserve (p200) around 115km from Fort Kochi. You can take a taxi early in the morning and reach in time for lunch. Spend time in the Periyar forest. Activities include a day-long bamboo raft trip through the jungles, jeep rides, nature walks or a boat ride in the evening.

❸ MUNNAR (2 DAYS)

Drive through the thick cardamom plantations of Kumily to the neat tea estates of Munnar (50km). Since the drive is in a hilly region, you will take a good three to four hours with stops to reach Munnar. Check in and relax for the rest of the day. The next morning, go for a plantation walk or make a trip to the **Kanan Devan Tea Museum** (p189) and head out for Ernakulam post lunch. There are many overnight buses from Munnar to the major cities.

Culture & Wildlife (7 Days)

This is a culture-heavy trip, with the added bonus of lush coffee-scaped hills of Wayanad and unusual Mappila food.

❶ FORT KOCHI (2 DAYS)

Embrace the colonial ambience of the town, speckled with atmospheric cafes, art galleries and interesting buildings (see historic sites & backwaters itinerary).

Elephants are a common sight at Periyar Lake

② ALAPPUZHA (1 DAY)
Take a quick trip to Alappuzha and spend a day on the
houseboat or a country boat for a backwaters experience.
Travel back to Fort Kochi for the night.

③ KOZHIKODE & GURUVAYUR (1 DAY)
Leave early for Kozhikode (p155), stopping at the famous
Guruvayur Sree Krishna Temple (p142). Do see the elephant
camp here. Post lunch, start your journey northwards again
and arrive in Kozhikode for the night.

④ BEYPORE & WAYANAD (2 DAYS)
There's not a lot for tourists to see in Kozhikode, though it's
a nice break in the journey and the jumping-off point for
Wayanad (p172). The boat-building village of Beypore (p155)
is an interesting place to visit off Kozhikode. Make a quick
stop here and head to Wayanad on the same day. It is a long
drive and reaching your accommodation in Wayanad will
take some time. Explore the plantations and a few sightseeing
options closest to your place of stay. You must be very aware
of the time and distance ratio in Wayanad, since the roads
are not so good.

⑤ KOZHIKODE (1 DAY)
Head back to Kozhikode to catch your return flight.

Getting Around

There are ample options for travelling in Kerala: trains, buses, taxis and water transport. Road journeys are recommended for the shorter distances to optimise time and comfort. But if you are doing a long stretch along the coast, the views from the train are delightful and the journey convenient.

Trains

The rail line along the coast covers many key destinations from Thiruvananthapuram in the south to Kasaragod up north. You can book train tickets four months in advance on www.irctc.com or take a chance for short trips by booking at the counter a few hours prior to your journey. Trivandrum Express (16348), Malabar Express (16630), Parasuram Express (16649), Maveli Express (16603) and Ernad Express (16605) run daily on the coastal route. For more information on trains that connect you from your city to Kerala, see 'Getting There & Away' at the beginning of each chapter and also visit the IRCTC website (see Quick Facts box).

Buses

You will see plenty of red-and-yellow buses of **Kerala State Road Transportation Corporation** (KSRTC) plying the routes within the state. These are reliable and timely, but overcrowded and not recommended for children and elders. If you are travelling on a budget, then hop onto one and see the countryside while interacting with locals. You can book through www.keralartc.com (although the site gives up pretty often). Else, book your seat at the bus depot an hour in advance of your journey.

✓ Top Tip: Double the fun

Hop aboard a government double-decker bus in Thiruvananthapuram (☎0471 2461013) for a 'heritage' trip around the key sightseeing spots. You can also make a booking for a private tour.

Cars & Taxis

To plan your trip at your own pace, these are your best options.

Roadways connecting cities are fairly decent. If driving yourself, be sure to fuel up whenever possible. Hired taxis will charge you by the km (₹9–12 per km) with an additional amount for the driver's daily allowance (₹200–300), also known as 'bata'. A fair range of cars is on offer. In hilly areas, only day charges are applicable.

Autorickshaws

Autos are easy to hire and make perfect sense if you are sightseeing within a city. The minimum fare in most cities is ₹20, but may increase as night falls. If you're in Munnar or Wayanad, you can always hire an auto to take you to all the sightseeing spots on a pre-decided fare.

Ferry

The backwaters of Kerala are well connected by government ferry services; this includes Alappuzha, Kochi, Kollam and Kumarakom. The journey might be slow, but well worth your time for the picturesque views of the countryside.

Kochi's islands have regular ferries connecting each other and charge only ₹2.50 per head per trip.

❶ *Quick Facts*

TRAIN TICKETS

• **IRCTC** Visit www.irctc.com to book tickets up to four months in advance. The Tatkal (instant) tickets quota opens a day in advance.

TAXIS

• **Oriental Leisure Tours** (☎09400432000; www.taxicarkerala.com)
• **Prepaid Taxi** (☎099952 05828; www.keralaprepaidtaxi.com)

AUTORICKSHAWS

• **Prices** The standard fare for autorickshaws in most Kerala cities is ₹20 (officially the minimum rate is ₹12 for 1.5km; additional fare of ₹7 per km).

Enjoy a scenic train ride through Kerala

Staying in Kerala

Being one of the top tourist destinations of India, Kerala has a wide variety of accommodation options: you will find classy high-end hotels, warm homestays, basic guesthouses, scenic plantation homes and of course, houseboats on the backwaters – the undisputed attraction of a trip to Kerala.

A comfy room at the Harivihar Heritage Homestead, Kozhikode

Hotels & Resorts

In Kerala, you will not only find plush four- and five-star resort chains, but also chic boutique hotels. Good service and facilities can by and large be expected even in far-flung jungles, plantations, backwaters and beaches.

Homestays

Kerala is known for its homestay culture. Many homestays have immense heritage value and ambience. They are highly

✔ Top Tip: Heritage value

Many hotels and homestays in Kerala feature traditional architecture and have heritage value. Houses as old as 100 years have been refurbished into beautiful homestays. Granaries converted into cosy rooms, open courtyards, tiled roofs and spaces endowed with antiques are often found here.

recommended to get the best advice for travel in the region from the hosts and to experience local culture at close quarters. Prices vary according to facilities and location, and there is often no room service. Be sensitive to timings, noise restrictions and rules about alcohol (if any).

Plantation Bungalows

Staying in British-style plantation bungalows with high ceilings, breezy front verandahs and fireplaces can be a truly unique experience. Plantation walks and short hikes are popular.

Houseboats

These make for your very own floating cruise. The larger ones may even have Jacuzzis, business halls and swimming pools. Most travellers tend to do a 22-hour trip (overnight) with a driver and a caretaker/cook to steer them across the watery paths.

Guesthouses and B&Bs

Travellers with low budgets can opt for guesthouses or simple bed and breakfast places. These have basic rooms and only provide breakfast and no other meals.

Rental Villas

Those who are lucky enough to have a long vacation can choose to rent fully furnished villas with a kitchenette, washing facilities and all the comforts of a home. In some cases, you will also be provided with a caretaker and/or cook.

Quick Facts

PRICE RANGES

Throughout this book, reviews of places to stay use the following price ranges, all based on double room with private bathroom in high season. Rates quoted in this guide do not include taxes, unless otherwise specified.

KEY TO RATES

₹₹₹   over ₹7000
₹₹   ₹3000–7000
₹   below ₹3000

ABBREVIATIONS

The following abbreviations are used to describe the room types given in this book.

s single rooms
d double rooms
ste suites

TAXES

Taxes are additionally charged on the room tariff. Hotels charge between 12.5% to 19.92%. Homestays usually add a 5% tax component.

SEASONAL PRICING

The tariffs are sensitive to high traffic tourist seasons. Peak season can command up to 40% higher tariffs.

FLEXI TARIFF

Some hotels do not reveal the tariff in order to keep it flexible; they can then offer the best deal depending on their bookings.

Eating in Kerala

Kerala cuisine is so diverse and distinct from the rest of India that the tantalising flavours are going to keep you raving, long after you've returned from your trip. The less adventurous can find refuge in various multi-cuisine restaurants, though every visitor should try some local fare.

Appam and stew are synonymous with Kerala cuisine

Roadside Eateries

When on the highway, you are likely to find small, almost austere restaurants that get crowded at lunchtime. During these busy hours, lunch tables are shared between complete strangers as each one digs into the 'meals' combos: dollops of white/brown rice, sambar, veggies with an optional side dish of fried fish or chicken.

✓ Top Tip: Water

Do not be alarmed if you are served warm, pinkish water in restaurants and homes – this is sterilised water. The magic ingredient is the aromatic bark of the herbal pathimugam tree. This is the best way to prevent any water-borne infection on your travels, and one can safely have non-bottled water in this form.

Vegetarian Sadya

Traditionally, sadya refers to a large feast in Malayalam. A typical sadya is served on a banana leaf and can have 24–28 dishes in a single meal. These are served in a particular order. Onam sadyas are a rage during the festival. **Sarovaram** (p117) in Bharat Hotel, Kochi, is a good place to try this.

Non-vegetarian Delights

The Syrian Christians (Nasrani) and Muslims (Mappila) have contributed sensational non-veg dishes to Kerala cuisine. Nasrani dishes have variations of beef, lamb, chicken, duck and fish curries. Mappila dishes (p158), found mostly in the Kozhikode region, are also non-veg heavy. The long coastal stretch of the state offers a large array of seafood.

Cakes & Bakeries

With a large Christian community in the state, cakes are a part of the culture. In fact, the first bakery of the state, **Mambally Bakery** (p171), still carries on business in Thalassery. If you are travelling through Kottayam, drop by at Ann's Bakery (p101).

Snack Shops (Chai Kadas)

Small teashops are local hotspots. You will find glass cases stacked with delicious fried snacks like ethakkappams (banana fritters), parippu vada (lentil fritters) and more.

Breakfast Items

Breakfast can be quite elaborate in Kerala. Favourites like puttu (made from rice flour and grated coconut) and kadala (black gram) curry, idiyappams (string hoppers) and the appam-stew combo will leave you licking your fingers.

Beverages

Coconuts are a common sight. The orangy-yellow ones are ripe and sweeter. For those who want a bit of intoxication, fresh toddy from coconut trees tastes great with tapioca snacks. Large restaurants serve alcohol as well.

---

❶ *Quick Facts*

OPENING HOURS

• **Restaurants**: Most restaurants open at 11am for lunch and close at 3.30pm. Dinner timings are 7pm to 11pm.

• **South Indian Cafes**: Most open as early as 7am for breakfast. Lunch, tea and dinner timings should be respected as there is a high footfall during these hours. Such cafes mostly close around 10.30pm.

PRICES

Rnges used in this book are based on prices of mains for two people.

KEY TO RATES

₹₹₹ over ₹500

₹₹ ₹200–500

₹ under ₹200

TIPPING

In larger restaurants, you can check for service charge and choose to tip over and above that. In smaller places, there are no particular rules.

Shopping in Kerala

Kerala has an extravagance of souvenirs, handicrafts, handwoven saris and edible giveaways. You will find it difficult to control your purse strings.

Saris & Textiles

Sari aficionados should positively buy Kerala's typical white cotton saris with golden borders (kasavu). If you are looking for more colourful stuff, Ernakulam and Thiruvananthapuram are full of sari shops. In fact, the small town of Balaramapuram (p57), off Thiruvananthapuram, has streets full of weaver families whom you can visit to watch them at work. For other cotton textiles like durries, bedspreads and towels, weaving cooperatives in Kannur and around are a good bet.

Handicrafts

Local knick-knacks made from coir, wooden elephants and snake boat models, replicas of nettippattom (ornaments worn by elephants during festivals) and Kathakali masks are common in souvenir shops across the state. Uravu (p180) in Wayanad promotes bamboo craft, lamps, earrings, paintings and more. One of the most exotic things to pick up is the Aranmula kannadi (mirror), made from a special mix of metal and alloy. You will find these in **Kairali** branches and the **SMSM Institute** (p63) in Thiruvananthapuram. You can also visit the few families that hand-craft these mirrors in the village of Aranmula, 54 km from Alappuzha. Other

✅ *Top Tip: Ayurveda products*

Kerala has become synonymous with Ayurveda due to the age-old expertise that exists here. Even so, you should consult a physician before buying a not so common Ayurveda item off the shelf. Many Ayurveda clinics manufacture their own products. **Santhigiri** outlets are easy to find across the state.

📷 *Snapshot:*
The myth about gold

While gold shops are a dime a dozen in Kerala, the price of gold is the same as in any other city in India. The only difference may be in the making charges, which differ according to the quality and brand. **The Grand Kerala Shopping Festival** (p49) is a good time to check for the best deals as many brands waive off the making charges. Gold items are so popular here, because of the intricate temple designs typical of the state.

traditional souvenirs, which are worth carrying home, are the bell metal lamps, locally known as nilavilakku.

Kerala jewellery designs are popular all over India

Art & Antiques

You are sure to encounter Raja Ravi Varma's paintings during your trip at galleries and museums across the state. Most handicrafts and antique shops sell copies in varying sizes. Kerala is also a leading shopping destination for antiques; many of the articles may be purposely made to look old, but you are likely to find originals as well. Jew Street in Mattancherry is strewn with antique shops. You are bound to find something that will suit your budget.

Spices, Coffee & Tea

Kerala's aromatic spices, rich coffee, Kozhikode halwa and tea from Munnar are great for gifts, as well as for your own kitchen. These come in easy and attractive packaging, suitable to carry. Kumily, Fort Kochi and Munnar are the best places for spices, especially cardamom and pepper. Coffee will be freshest in Wayanad, and Munnar is best for tea leaves and home-made chocolates. The Kozhikode halwa needs some getting used to, but is a popular gift.

Travelling with Kids

In Kerala, you can expect children to get quickly and surely wooed by nature; the lure of spotting a langur in a national park or splashing around with an elephant in a pool will definitely keep the fun levels up. It is also a good place to introduce them to vibrant dance forms like Kathakali.

Fun for Kids

Here are some recommendations for fun activities to keep children engaged.

- **Periyar Tiger Reserve** (p200) has multiple options for trips into the jungle and waterways within. Try a bamboo-raft trip for a unique experience. Remember to bring warm and waterproof clothing.

- **Boat Rides:** Houseboats can have a lazy pace that may not match the energy levels of children. Instead, opt for a motorboat ride to **Pathiramanal Island (p89)** in Vembanad Lake where they can spot a wide range of migratory birds.

Kovalam Beach is safe for wading and swimming

- **Elephant Interaction:** The **Guruvayur Anna Kotta** (p142) has 63 elephants that can be seen at close quarters. At **Carmelgiri Elephant Park** (p198) in Munnar and **Elephant Junction** (p201) in Kumily, your kids will have a field time feeding and bathing pachyderms.
- **Theme Parks:** Spend a day at **Wonder La** (p124) in Ernakulam or **Vismaya Water Theme Park** (p165) off Kannur to hear some excited squeals.
- **Folk Performances:** Abridged folk performances are easy on children. The brightly painted faces of Kathakali artistes are bound to mesmerise them. **Greenix Village** (p140) in Fort Kochi is perfect for this.
- **Beaches:** Arm the young ones with a pail and a plastic shovel to build sand castles on the flat sandy stretches of **Lighthouse Beach** (p70) in Kovalam.
- **Cycling:** Villages around Fort Kochi can be explored by cycle. Check out **Village Rubble** (p140) that organises trips for kids seven years and above. A back-up vehicle is always close by.

Family Hotels

Ask for family rooms or suites to accommodate extra beds for children. This is an economical option. Most of the larger resorts in Kerala ensure supervised game rooms, easy hikes, sightseeing trips, documentary shows and more.

₹ *Value for Money: Discounts for kids*

Entry tickets to sightseeing spots are at least 50% cheaper for children 12 years and below.

What's New

Though deeply rooted in its traditional culture, Kerala is ever changing. This travel-friendly state is constantly adding tourism attractions cutting across varied interests and age-groups.

Lulu, Kerala's most famous shopping mall

Lulu Mall

A trip here is going to be no less than an expedition. **Lulu (p129)**, India's largest mall, was launched in March 2013 at Ernakulam. The mall offers a skating rink, gaming zone, a 12-lane bowling alley and a 5D cinema experience.

Keralam, Museum of History & Heritage

Relatively new to the list of museums in Thiruvananthapuram, Keralam (p52) was opened in February 2011. It has a range of exhibits – starting from the Neolithic age, including murals, sculptures, coins and more. The museum is well organised and the staff is helpful.

Kochi-Muziris Biennale

A multi-venue three month-long contemporary art festival (p235) showcased the work of 90 artistes from 24 countries across the world, and ended in March 2013. The exhibits were displayed across Ernakulam and Fort Kochi. This is expected to be a regular event (www.kochimuzirisbiennale.org).

Village Rubble

Cycling excursions off Fort Kochi are a great way to experience the village life of Kerala. You will see lush paddy fields, prawn farms and toddy being tapped at close quarters. The day-long trips run by **Village Rubble (p140)** are instructor-led, with well-serviced cycles and a back-up van at your heels.

Get Inspired

Books

God of Small Things
(Arundhati Roy, 1997) Booker winner for the year, Roy's story of seven-year-old fraternal twins is based in Aymanam village off Kumarakom. It grapples with dark social issues like class segregation and forbidden love.

Where the Rain is Born: Writings About Kerala
(edited by Anita Nair, 2002) The book is a compilation of stories, essays and poems written by some of the most esteemed English- and Malayalam-language authors of India. It is a journey about what Kerala has to offer.

| Mani Ratnam's *Dil Se* has songs filmed in Kerala

Films

Karthik Calling Karthik
(2010) This psychological thriller drifts from the bustling urban life of Mumbai to the quiet streets of Kerala. Parts of the movie were shot in Fort Kochi.

Raavan (2010) Mani
Ratnam shot parts of the film at the Athirappally Falls (p123). Abhishek Bachchan, playing a bandit, chooses to capture and torture Aishwarya Rai, a policeman's wife, here.

Nishabd (2007) The
Amitabh Bachchan starrer, *Nishabd*, was shot in Munnar. The neat tea-lined hills are a refreshing backdrop to an unconventional love story.

Guru (2007) The song,
Barso Re Megha Barso Re, with Aishwarya Rai was shot near the Athirappally Falls. Yet another Mani Ratnam film.

Dil Se (1998) Kerala
with its backwaters and houseboats became the location choice for the Shah Rukh Khan-Preity Zinta song *Jiya Jale*.

Bombay (1995) It is at
Bekal Fort where actress Manisha Koirala runs into the arms of Arvind Swamy in the song *Tu Hi Re*.

The Hollywood Connection

Kerala has not broken into the 'exotic location clique' of big Hollywood productions, but some smaller, notable English films have been shot here.

BEFORE THE RAINS (2007) Nandita Das and Linus Roache make an atypical couple as a village woman and a spice baron in this period drama. The movie is set in the 1930s in the Malabar region. It won the Best Theatrical Feature award at the World Fest in Houston.

COTTON MARY (1999) An Ismail-Merchant production, the movie is about a British woman living in India. Fort Kochi was the ideal backdrop for this period film.

Websites

www.keralatourism.org A comprehensive resource to plan your trip.

www.keralaprepaidtaxi. com Look up this site for customised trips and taxi services.

KERALA'S BEST TRIPS

This section takes you through the different regions of Kerala and provides you with planned outings to explore each.

The spectacular snake boat race on Pampa River

Kerala at a Glance

Lush green backwaters, azure seas, surf-kissed beaches and historic trading towns along the coast. Move inland to spice and tea plantations, and forests with wild elephants, exotic birds and the odd tiger. The phrase 'God's own country' is not a mere exaggeration.

P148

KOZHIKODE

LAKSHADWEEP ←

P214

KOCHI •

MALABAR & WAYANAD Explore the unspoiled golden-sand beaches around Kannur and Bekal. Spot herds of wild elephants at Wayanad.

LAKSHADWEEP This string of 36 palm-covered coral islands is a magnet for flipper-toting travellers and divers alike.

KOCHI & AROUND Packed with historical hotspots, Kochi is also a culinary centre. Thrissur and Guruvayur offer a spot of culture and spirituality.

MUNNAR & AROUND This tea-growing heartland is a great place to trek and discover viewpoints across epic mountain scenery.

P112

MUNNAR

ALAPPUZHA & THE BACKWATERS Experience days of languorous drifting on the green maze of backwaters around Alappuzha.

P182

P80

KOLLAM

P44

THIRUVANANTHAPURAM & SOUTHERN BEACHES While the capital city is ideal for visiting off-the-track museums, Varkala and Kovalam are great for some beachside fun.

Thiruvananthapuram & Southern Beaches

Why Go?

Uncharacteristic of a capital city, Thiruvananthapuram (Trivandrum) is surprisingly easygoing. The city is a haven for history lovers with numerous Victorian-styled museums and traditional architecture. The only thing that gives away its capital status are the swanky new high-rises emerging through the red tiled roofs of old houses. Head out to the nearby towns of Varkala and Kovalam for sandy stretches to soak in the sun and sea. Dramatic laterite cliffs and remnants of hippie life in Varkala are a stark contrast to the premier resort-driven Kovalam, further south, but both have a unique charm for visitors – especially the Ayurvedic treatments and brilliant seafood. Those who have the time, can take a detour to Kanyakumari where you can watch the sun set over three oceans at once.

Getting There & Away

Air: Thiruvananthapuram International Airport has air links with all major cities of India. Multiple carriers like Spice Jet, IndiGo and JetKonnect have direct flights through the week. The airport is a convenient 8km from the city centre and 15km from Kovalam; both taxis and autos are easily available.

Bus: The KSRTC bus stand in Thiruvananthapuram connects it with various key cities including Alappuzha, Chennai, Kochi and of course Kovalam and Varkala. These KSRTC buses may not be plush but are great value for money. You can also opt for private Volvo buses that have push back seats and are much more comfy.

Train: The coastal stretch of Kerala is linked very well by trains from across the country. The Kerala Express (12626) from Delhi, Kanyakumari Express (16381) from Mumbai and the Kanyakumari Express (16526) from Bengaluru ply daily. From Thiruvananthapuram there are frequent local trains to Varkala and Kovalam. Check for train timetables and schedules on www.irctc.co.in.

■I The lighthouse overlooking Kovalam Beach

Top Highlights

1 Sree Padmanabhaswamy Temple

This ancient temple (p54) spilling over 2400 sq m is Thiruvananthapuram's spiritual heart. Queue up to meander through a trail that leads up to the sanctum of Lord Vishnu. Enormous walls enclose fantastic architectural and spiritual energy that draws millions each year. Enter through the east nada (door) under the massive yellow 30m-tall gopuram (gateway) looming over the fort area. Inside, the massive 18ft reclining statue of Lord Vishnu can be seen through three different doors. Nearly 12,000 holy stones (saligramams) were used to construct this magnificent statue. Though you will get only a fleeting glimpse as you are ushered past the deity, the experience is memorable.

2 Zoological Gardens & Museums

An enormous green patch, atop a low hill, distinctly marks the centre of Thiruvananthapuram, within which sits the city's zoo and museums complex (p52). Enter through its towering red gates for a day filled with activity for adults and children alike. The park contains art galleries, museums and one of the oldest zoos in the country, beautifully landscaped to recapture natural environments. Amongst the museums, **Napier Museum** (p53) is known for its Gothic architecture and rare collection of artefacts.

3 Sree Chitra Art Gallery

Situated within the Zoological Gardens & Museums complex in Thiruvananthapuram, this gallery (p53) commemorates the work of the master artist Raja Ravi Varma (p55). Though trained in the western style

of painting, Ravi Varma brilliantly portrayed stories from the *Mahabharata*, *Ramayana* and other Indian themes. Other artists like Svetoslav and Nicholas Roerich also share this coveted space with Varma. Established in 1935, the gallery includes works of the Rajput, Mughal and Tanjore schools of art, making this a satisfying trip for art lovers.

4 Seafood at North Cliff, Varkala

Enjoy a picturesque Kerala sunset from a first-floor perch at any of the restaurants that line North Cliff at Varkala (p64). An elaborate choice of fresh catch in the form of snappers, barracudas and swordfish lies temptingly on ice slabs for you to select. A long dinner in the breezy cliff-side cafes of Varkala is an absolute essential, while you take in the scenic ambience of fishing boats silhouetted against the setting sun.

5 Lighthouse Beach, Kovalam

The liveliest stretch of sand on the southern coast of Kerala, Lighthouse Beach (p70) at Kovalam sprawls at the edge of the town in a crescent shape. Brightly coloured beach umbrellas are splashed across the sand, with numerous cafes at an arm's length. Lighthouse Beach ensures that one is never starved of activities, including boat rides. Visit early morning to see the fishermen bringing in the catch.

Local Knowledge
Fairs & festivals

Geetha Mathen Oommen, actor, student counsellor and 'natya-yoga' instructor, recommends some of the annual events and festivals in Thiruvananthapuram and surrounding regions.

- **International Documentary and Short Film Festival of Kerala** (☎0471 2310323; www.iffk. in): A platform that showcases an alternative genre of movies, the IDSFFK is held each year in Thiruvananthapuram. Experimental movies from across the world are entered in this five day festival. The IDSFFK is a part of the annual International Film Festival of Kerala, which was started in 1996 and is hosted by the Kerala State Chalachitra Academy.

- **Kovalam Lit Fest** (☎9811802538; www.kovalamlitfest.com): This is an annual event, held in October at the Kanakakunnu Palace in Thiruvananthapuram. Authors of international repute participate in discussions, readings, book releases and interactions with visitors.

- **Nishagandhi Dance and Music Show:** A seven-day cultural extravaganza is organised in January every year at the Kanakakunnu Palace. During the week, there are dance and music performances by local and international artistes.

- **Swathi Sangeetholsavam:** In January, a 'free for all' music festival brings alive the central courtyard of Kuthiramalika Palace in Thiruvananthapuram. Started by the royal family as a tribute to the Maharaja of Travancore, Sri Swathi Thirunal Rama Varma, the festival is bound to enthrall both connoisseurs of Carnatic music and others.

- **Grand Kerala Shopping Festival:** You can give that bargainer in you a rest as the Grand Kerala Shopping Festival offers plenty of discounts, freebies, gift certificates and more each year. This is one of the largest shopping festivals in Asia.

| Kovalam Lit Fest is an annual affair held at Kanakakunnu Palace

Thiruvananthapuram & Southern Beaches

Best Trips

1. **Thiruvananthapuram**
2. **Varkala**
3. **Kovalam & Around**
4. **Kanyakumari**

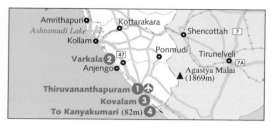

The 60km coastal stretch of Thiruvananthapuram, Kovalam and Varkala allows you to combine a relaxed beach holiday with exploration of history and heritage. Make the capital city your base and explore the museums, art galleries and evocative architecture. Head southwards to Kovalam for a beach holiday, where you will find an array of budget and luxury places to stay and eat. For a bohemian vibe reminiscent of the 70s, travel north to the Varkala cliffside, dotted with cafes, bookshops and Ayurvedic massage parlours, and sunbathers lined up on the beach below.

| A bird's-eye view of
| Varkala Beach

Thiruvananthapuram

The unassuming capital of Kerala, Thiruvananthapuram, is steeped in a strong lineage of art and history. The city's prominent intellectual ambience is hard to miss because of its famous poets and artists. Though the capital is fast transforming into a technology hub, it has managed to retain its old-world charm with large green residential areas speckled with traditional architecture.

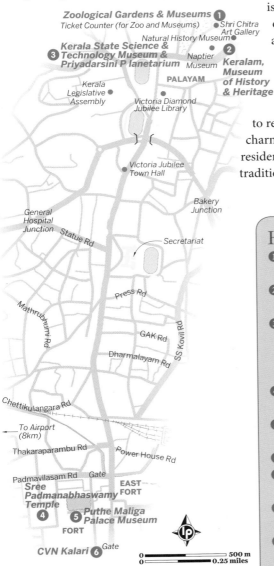

Highlights

1. Zoological Gardens & Museums
2. Keralam, Museum of History & Heritage
3. Kerala State Science & Technology Museum & Priyadarsini Planetarium
4. Sree Padmanabhaswamy Temple
5. Puthe Maliga Palace Museum
6. CVN Kalari
7. Margi Kathakali (off map)
8. Shankhumugham Beach (off map)
9. Veli Tourist Village (off map)

GETTING AROUND

Autorickshaws: Getting around town is not difficult since autorickshaws are easily available. The minimum daytime fare is ₹20. However, at night you will have to depend on your bargaining skills since some drivers expect a surcharge of more than 50%.

❶ ZOOLOGICAL GARDENS & MUSEUMS

Head to the heart of the city for a day full of museums and the city zoo. Over 55-acres of well-manicured land are dotted with interesting attractions: the **Natural History Museum, KCS Panicker's Gallery, Sree Chitra Enclave, Napier Museum, Sree Chitra Art Gallery** and the **Zoo** (see box opposite). Even though the complex is buzzing with visitors, school groups and locals, you will have ample breathing room to absorb the varied offerings of each place.

❷ KERALAM, MUSEUM OF HISTORY & HERITAGE

A recent addition to Thiruvananthapuram's list of museums, this well-organised, bright white repository of history and heritage is a pleasure to visit. Situated just outside the Zoological Gardens & Museums, it elucidates the history of the state with exhibits ranging from the Neolithic age to more recent temple architecture. Intricate palm leaves depicting Vedic scriptures in Tamil and Malayalam are fascinating. The in-house travel information desk is exceptionally helpful. 📞09567019037; Park View; adult/camera ₹20/25; 10am–5.30pm, Mon/public holidays closed

❸ KERALA STATE SCIENCE & TECHNOLOGY MUSEUM & PRIYADARSINI PLANETARIUM

This expansive complex has six sections to explore. When it all gets too serious, a 3D movie or a break at the planetarium will lighten the experience. The simulation of the night sky, both from the past and projected for the future, is one of the best shows to catch here. 📞0471 2306024; www.kstmuseum.com; Vikasbhavan PO; adult/child ₹15/10 (separate charges for all sections); 10am–5pm

TOP CHOICE *Zoological Gardens & Museums: Things to do*

• **Zoo** (Adult/child/family/group/camera/video ₹10/5/25/130/25/75 (group discounts given); 9am–5.15pm, Mon closed) Constructed in 1857, this strictly plastic-free zoo is one of the oldest in the country. Shaded paths meander through woodland and lakes, where animals ranging from tigers to a variety of birds live in massive open enclosures that mimic their natural habitats.

• **Sree Chitra Art Gallery:** Master of the oleograph technique, Raja Ravi Varma's outstanding collection of paintings sits in the Sree Chitra Art Gallery, which you have to enter barefoot. Apart from Varma's art, you also see the Russian artist Svetoslav Roerich's work as well as murals from other parts of Kerala in the wooden-floored gallery.

• **Napier Museum** (☏0471 2316275; www.keralamuseumandzoo.org; Museums Compound; adult/child ₹5/3; 10am-4.45pm, Wed 1–4.45pm, Mon Closed) Built in 1855, the Indo-Saracenic-style museum has an eclectic display of bronzes, Buddhist sculptures, temple carts and ivory carvings. The over 150-year-old structure is considered a masterpiece with its brilliant ornamental roof. In fact, the architecture of the museum takes precedence for some over the artefacts inside. An audio guide can be accessed via phone by dialling ☏9048755555.

• **KCS Panicker Gallery:** Renowned abstract artist KCS Panicker's paintings and exhibits have a separate gallery space in the complex. It is a sure stop for art enthusiasts.

• **Sree Chitra Enclave:** The history of the Travancore royal family and particularly the last king, Sree Chithira Thirunal Balarama Varma, has been crisply presented in this museum. You can leisurely stroll past the regal artefacts such as weapons, coins and even a chariot, which were used by the much-loved king.

• **Natural History Museum** (Adult/child/group ₹5/3/100; 10am–4.45pm, Wed 1–4.45pm, Mon closed; camera allowed only in Natural History Museum) The kids are going to love this one. A vivid display of animal skeletons and stuffed birds is engaging enough for a short stop here.

| Napier Museum is an architectural masterpiece

Wooden horses at the Puthe Maliga Palace Museum

④ SREE PADMANABHASWAMY TEMPLE

References to it in the epics suggest this temple is thousands of years old. It is the spiritual heart of the city ('Thiru' 'Anantha' 'Puram' means sacred abode of Lord Anantha Padmanabha). Expect long queues for a darshan of the sleeping deity, which can be seen only in parts through three doors. Seven yellow-tiered gopurams tower around the complex. If you strain your neck you can see the Methan Mani clock high on the outer wall of the temple, which rings hourly as metallic goats swing into a demon-faced man's cheeks.

🕿 **0471 2464606; www.sreepadmanabhaswamytemple.org;**

📷 *Snapshot: The secret chamber*

Conjecture and controversy have been a part of the Sree Padmanabhaswamy Temple for many years. It is believed to be the world's richest temple with an undisclosed treasure worth ₹90,000 crore. A mysterious secret chamber hoarding this wealth has evoked much debate and speculation within political circles on its rightful ownership. Despite the controversy, the spiritual footfalls have not decreased.

📷 *Snapshot: Raja Ravi Varma*

The 17th-century painter Raja Ravi Varma successfully fused European art techniques with themes from the *Mahabharata* and *Ramayana* to produce an exquisite collection of paintings that won him many accolades both in India and internationally. Prepare to get pretty familiar with his works as people here proudly display prints of them at hotels, restaurants and even their homes. The sheer number of imitations of Raja Ravi Varma's oleographs that are still available in the market in Kerala is evidence of how popular he remains till date.

West Nada, Fort; Darshan: 3.30–4.45am, 6.30–7am, 8.30–10am, 10.30–11.10am, 11.45am–12pm, 5–6.15pm, 6.45–7.20pm

⑤ PUTHE MALIGA PALACE MUSEUM

Walk through a small banana plantation to reach the 200-year-old museum next to the Padmanabhaswamy Temple. The erstwhile palace of the Maharaja of Travancore sports carved wooden ceilings, marble sculptures and even imported Belgian glass. The palace is also called Kuthira Malika (Palace of Horses) after the 122 horse figures in the brackets of the walls. A scheduled guide takes small groups around regaling them with anecdotes and pointing out the highlights (his services are free but you may want to tip him). The annual classical music festival from 6–12 January is held here free for the public.

Museum; Indian/foreigner/ photography outside/video outside ₹15/50/30/250; 8.30am–12.45pm, 3–4.45pm, Mon closed

⑥ CVN KALARI

The prestigious kalari school of Thiruvananthapuram is also a working hospital where Ayurvedic orthopedic treatment is given. For visitors, the daily kalaripayattu

✓ *Top Tip: Temple protocol*

In most temples in Kerala, especially the major ones like Sree Padmanabhaswamy Temple, Vaikom Mahadev Temple (p100) and Guruvayur Sree Krishna Temple (p142), men can only enter bare-chested with legs covered and women have to wear a sari (or tie a mundu around the waist, which can be bought from shops that line the road to the temple). In some cases, foreigners and non-Hindus are not allowed inside inner sanctums.

Stone Pavilion at
Shankhumugham
Beach

(martial arts) training in the traditional rink is the most interesting part.

 0471 2474182; www.cvnkalari.in; East Fort; 7–8.30am, Sun closed

⑦ MARGI KATHAKALI

Barely 200m west of the fort lies this inconspicuous building

---

↱ *Detour: Balaramapuram*

Just 14km south of Thiruvananthapuram, Balaramapuram is a congested bustling town, the lanes of which resonate with the constant rhythm of weaving looms. The traditional weavers, Shaliyars, have settled here on four main streets; Single Street, Double Street, Vinayagar Street and New Street. If you are walking down any of these be sure to seek an invitation into houses to see the weaving process. You can also buy the typical white-and-gold of saris and mundus at a much lower cost than in town.

We recommend **SS Handloom Centre** (0471 2400261; New St; 9.30am–7.30pm), **Kannan** (9895612361; Double St; 10am–10pm) and **R Paramasivan** (0471 2407293; Double St; 10am–6pm).

En route, stop by at a small village called **Punnamoodu**, where almost 200 households engage in making fresh fried snacks like kuzhalappam and churuttu. The road is lined with rows of fresh-from-the-pan savouries.

housing the Margi Kathakali institution. Visitors can peek at informal practice sessions of the dramatic dance form in the main hall every day for two hours.

📞 0471 2478804; Fort; Mon–Fri 10am–noon

❽ SHANKHUMUGHAM BEACH

Watch the fishermen tug at the boats late morning as they bring the catch in, and then enjoy a variety of snacks at the seafront shacks on Shankhumugham Beach. The sandy stretch is not really fit for swimming, though there are lifeguards at short intervals to ensure your protection.

❾ VELI TOURIST VILLAGE

The 12km ride to the Veli Tourist Village is worth your while if you are travelling with children. A Kerala Tourist Development Corporation (KTDC) establishment, the park has swings, boating, enormous and slightly overbearing sculptures and a floating restaurant at the cusp of the sea and Veli Lake.

📞 0471 2500785; Veli Tourist Park; 8am–630pm; adult/child ₹5; boating ₹100–1000

Kalaripayattu is one of the oldest forms of martial art

📷 *Snapshot: Kalaripayattu*

Kalaripayattu is an ancient tradition of martial training and discipline, still taught throughout Kerala. Some believe it is the forerunner of all martial arts, with roots tracing back to the 12th-century skirmishes among Kerala's feudal principalities. Masters of kalaripayattu, called Gurukkal, teach their craft inside a special arena called a kalari. Kalaripayattu movements have roots in Kerala's performing arts, such as Kathakali and Kootiattam, and in ritual arts such as Theyyam.

🛏 Accommodation

Amruthum Ayurvedic
Village Resort   **Ayurveda Resort ₹₹₹**
📞 0471 2484600; www.
amruthamgamaya.com; RKN Rd,
Panangodu, Venganoor PO; d
₹7000–8000 (incl of full board) The
fact that no signboards are brandished
on the highway makes the yoga-and
Ayurveda-inspired Amruthum a hidden
secret in the village of Panangodu.
Amid dense greenery, it has seven
rooms and is perfect for those who
need an intimate holiday with some
simple living, with the luxury of a
swimming pool. You can enjoy the
roof deck over meals or just laze in
the sunny garden between yoga and
massage schedules. It's a good place
to stay even if you don't require any
Ayurveda treatment.

Taj Vivanta   **Hotel ₹₹₹**
📞 0471 6612345; www.vivantabytaj.
com; C V Raman Pillai Road,
Thycaud; d ₹9500–12,000, ste

A well-manicured garden at Amruthum
Ayurvedic Village Resort

₹20,000–30,000 (incl of breakfast)
The never disappointing chain of Taj
hotels has a conveniently located
property in Thiruvananthapuram as
well. In classic Taj style the rooms
are slick and well-furnished. The
usual features such as an in-house
restaurant, gymnasium, swimming
pool and wi-fi complement the warm
hospitality of its staff.

SP Grand Days   **Hotel ₹₹**
📞 0471 2333344; www.spgranddays.
com; Panavila Junction; d ₹4000–
5000, ste ₹7000 (incl of breakfast)
Choose from a selection of four room
types at the comfortable SP Grand
Days. Though centrally located, it is
still pleasantly away from the busy
downtown. Apart from the rather bare
and unused swimming pool area, the
rest of the hotel is filled with action
with an in-house restaurant and coffee
shop. You can also avail of the free
wi-fi facility. Do not hesitate to crack
a better deal on the tariff if you are
booking a room for more than one day.

Maurya Rajadhani   **Hotel ₹₹**
📞 0471 2469469; www.
mauryarajadhani.com; Statue–GH
Road; d ₹3500–4000, ste ₹6000–
7000 (incl of breakfast) Maurya
Rajadhani is just off the main MG
Road which makes it easy to step out
for meals or just walk around the main
street. The cosy rooms are clean,
bright and spacious. Do not opt for
the fourth floor as muffled sounds of
a live band from the restaurant reach
the rooms.

The Residency Tower   Hotel ₹₹
☎0471 2331661; www.
residencytower.com; Press Road;
d ₹4500–5000, ste ₹7000 (incl of
breakfast) The flexi rates policy at
The Residency Tower can get you a
great deal if occupancy is low or the
peak season has not set in. Rooms are
clean, comfortable and reasonably
well decorated. There is also a fitness
centre, curio shop, pool, wi-fi facility
and in-house restaurant.

The South Park   Hotel ₹₹
☎0471 2333333; www.
thesouthpark.com; MG Road; d
₹5000–5500, ste ₹6500–9200 (incl
of breakfast) Stay at The South Park
for its proximity to MG Road and for its
spacious rooms, which can be made
family friendly by adding an extra bed.
There is plenty to do here as there
is a coffee shop, terrace garden, pub
and a restaurant. Do check-out the
incongruous gold-embossed lift in this
over 20-year-old hotel.

The Residency Tower offers beautiful rooms
at reasonable rates

Mascot Hotel   KSTDC Hotel ₹₹
☎0471 2316736; www.ktdc.com;
Mascot Square; d ₹5000–7000,ste
₹9000–15,000 (incl of breakfast)
Period touches, massive hallways
and an imposing reception lend this
KSTDC establishment an aura of old-
world charm. Rooms are extremely
spacious though minimalistic in
decor. Some overlook the enormous
pool. The hotel is also known for its
Ayurvedic Centre and a refreshing
garden cafe, Sahyana (5pm–10pm).

Beach and
Lake Resort   Beachside Resort ₹₹
☎0471 2382086; www.
beachandlakeresort.com; Pozhikara
Beach, Pachalloor PO; d ₹5915–9165
(incl of full board) As the name
suggests, Beach and Lake Resort gives
you the experience of staying both
by the sea and a lake. The property
lies at the edge of the ocean and is

fragmented by a backwater canal which divides the rooms from the restaurant and the yoga house. The in-house canoe is a fun way to get across to these sections. Though the resort is focused on long-stay Ayurveda-inclined guests, rejuvenation massages can be enjoyed by weekend visitors too. Choose the first-floor rooms for a fabulous view of the sea from large breezy balconies. Facilities include wi-fi connectivity and a reasonably sized swimming pool.

Varikatt Heritage   Homestay ₹₹
📞0471 2336057; www.
varikattheritage.com; Punnen Road;
d/ste ₹5500/6500 (incl of full
board) Be sure to read the historical docket put together by Col Roy, the owner, to truly enjoy your stay at this 18th-century British villa in the heart of the city. Though the home is refurbished to include all modern amenities, the ambience exudes an old-world charm. The award-winning

| The courtyard at Villa Maya,
▌ a Kerala-themed restaurant

homestay has three suites and two double rooms, all of which are spacious and aesthetically done up. The villa is tucked away just behind the central MG Road, a convenience much appreciated by tourists.

Windsor Rajdhani   Hotel ₹₹
📞0471 25477755; www.
windsorrajdhani.com; Kowdiar; d
₹4500, ste ₹8000–16,000 (incl
of breakfast) Choose Windsor Rajdhani for elegantly furnished and comfortable rooms, as well as easy access to the city's sightseeing options. If you are travelling with family, choose the well-appointed suite as it can accommodate an extra bed.

Riverside Eco
Homestay   Home to Hire ₹₹
📞09847062392; VP XIII 764,
Shankaramukham, Vellanad; full
house $100 (quoted rate in $ but
they also accept Indian rupee
equivalent) The exquisite Riverside Eco Homestay, overlooking the Karamana River, lies just beyond

the Aruvikara Dam (15km from Thiruvananthapuram). Located behind a rubber plantation, it's set against a lush sloped garden leading down to the river, crossed by a 90-year-old bridge. It is suitable for big groups who can hire the entire house. You can use the kitchenette to fix your meals but you have to carry supplies. There are no restaurants close by.

The Lakewood Retreat   Homestay ₹
☑ 0471 2134053; www. shalimarlakewoods.in; NH Road, Thiruvallam; d ₹1200–1600 (incl of breakfast) Lakewood Retreat offers an escape to the soothing suburbs, where the water from the Karamana River splashes against the front porch. The two guest rooms and a bamboo cottage suite face the idyllic backwaters. Lakewood Retreat is just 5km from Thiruvananthapuram, making it easy to visit Kovalam (6km) or get into the city for sightseeing.

 Eating

TOP CHOICE Villa Maya   Multi-Cuisine ₹₹₹
☑ 0471 2578901; Airport Road; mains ₹1000–1500; 11am–11pm Frangipani trees in the courtyard, water-spewing fountains, lotus ponds, dim lighting and the music of classical instruments give a chic air to the newly opened Kerala-themed Villa Maya. It serves a fusion cuisine of authentic Kerala dishes, Indian grills and continental food. Try the refreshing pineapple shikanji. It is spread over three floors of a restored 19th-century house.

Azad   Indian ₹₹
☑ 0471 3070601; www.azadhotels. com; mains ₹200–500; 7.30am–9.30pm Manoeuver past waiters balancing heaped biryani plates and asking to make way in this legendary joint. Having branched out into six restaurants since its inception in 1940, Azad is hugely popular for its efficient service and delicious biryani. Visit the Overbridge branch and get a seat in the basement for a nostalgic ambience amidst old low doors and windows.

Indian Coffee House, Maveli Cafe   Coffee Shop ₹
☑ 0471 2333517; Thampanoor; mains ₹100–200; 6.30am–10pm Heave yourself up a steep spiral red tower in this one-of-a-kind Indian Coffee House in front of the railway station. Maveli Cafe brings back the nostalgia of uniformed waiters, and the familiar coffee shop menu – with a slightly unique touch of its own.

Sree Arul Jyothi   South Indian ₹
☑ 0471 2470240; TC 26/143, opposite Secretariat, MG Road; mains ₹100–200; 7am–10pm Arul Jyothi has been dishing out both south Indian snacks and Kerala specials for years. One of the most famous vegetarian joints in town, it is particularly packed in the evenings. Piping hot coffee and masala dosas are perfect for an evening snack here.

Ambrosia   Coffee Shop ₹₹
☑ 0471- 2337515; www.theambrosia. com; Bakery Junction; mains

₹200–500; 10.30am–10pm Look out for one of the four branches of Ambrosia for the best baked goodies in town. You can settle in for a quick snack of yummy biscuits and cakes in the brightly lit cafe with the chatter of youngsters in the background, or grab a roll to go.

Suprabhatham South Indian ₹
📞0471 2471723; MG Road; mains ₹100–200; 7am–9.30pm One of the better vegetarian restaurants among similar establishments on MG Road. Decent south Indian fare like thalis and dosas are speedily served here. Lunch hours are busy and packed.

Annapoorna South Indian ₹
Pazhavangadi, MG Road; mains ₹100–200; 5.30am–11.30pm The clean and brightly lit Annapoorna serves the regular south Indian food (idlis, dosas and uthappams) and also local delights like puttu. Since it opens early, you can get here for breakfast if you are visiting the Padmanabhaswamy Temple in the first darshan slots.

Ayswariya South Indian ₹₹
📞0471 3082000; Overbridge, MG Road; mains ₹250–500; 11am–10pm Tired of dawdling around MG Road? Hop into the spic and span Ayswariya restaurant for a quick bite of south Indian specialities and some refreshing juice.

Shopping
Pothys Clothing
📞0471 2574133; www.pothys.com; MG Road, Near Ayurveda College Junction; 9.30am–10.30pm The multi-storey Pothys is easy to get lost in. An extravaganza of colour unfolds in this massive sari shop just off MG Road. Even though Pothys is always spilling over with eager shoppers, well categorised sections make it easy to locate saris of your choice.

Sarwaa Souvenirs
📞0471 3022220; www.sarwaa.com;

📷 *Snapshot: The Indian Coffee House story*

The Indian Coffee House is a place stuck in time. Its India-wide branches feature old India prices and waiters dressed in starched white with peacock-style headdresses. It was started by the Coffee Board in the early 1940s, during the British rule. In the 1950s the Board began to close down cafes across India, making employees redundant. At this point, the communist leader Ayillyath Kuttiari Gopalan Nambiar took up the cause of the workers and began the India Coffee Board Worker's Co-operative Society. The intention was to provide them with better opportunities and promote the sale of coffee. The Coffee House has remained ever since, always atmospheric, and always offering bargain snacks and drinks such as Indian filter coffee, rose milk and idlis. It's still run by its employees, all of whom share ownership.

**Shankar Road, Sasthamangalam;
9.30am–8pm** Get your kitsch fix at
Sarwaa, with its large collection of
bright bags, curios and an assortment
of jewellery and lingerie. Expect
contemporary souvenirs instead of
traditional Kerala-themed articles.

SMSM Institute   Handicrafts
📞0471 2330298; Puthenchanthai;
9am–8pm, Sun closed An elaborate
collection of handicrafts, brass curios,
coir products and paintings makes
this a good stop to pick up souvenirs.
It may take you a while to sift through
the large variety of goodies to suit your
budget and baggage space. Since the
establishment is a Kerala government
undertaking, you can rely on the
quality and pricing.

Khadi Gramodyog Bhavan Souvenirs
📞0471 2331627; Gramodaya, MG
Road; 10am–7.30pm Sun closed

Centrally located, Khadi Gramodyog
is best for Kerala-themed souvenirs,
especially Raja Ravi Varma prints for
as little as ₹200.

Chalai Market   Market
10am–8pm Fruits, clothes, jewellery,
spices, utensils and plenty of local
atmosphere can be found in this busy
market. If you are planning on going
there on a Sunday, expect it to be
slightly quieter than other days.

Connemara Market   Market
MG Road; 8am–8pm For an authentic
local Kerala market experience,
wander around Connemara Market
amidst a sea of vendors selling
vegetables, fish, fabric, clothes and
spices. Established in 1888, the market
is more of a historic landmark than an
essential shopping venue.

| Exotic spices are available at Chalai and
Connemara markets

Varkala

Highlights
1. **Janardhana Swamy Temple**
2. **Beaches**
3. **Anjengo Fort**
4. **Ayurvedic Treatments**

The unusual coastal topography consisting of dramatic red laterite cliffs dropping down to small clean patches of sand will enthrall you at the small seaside town of Varkala. The cliff tops have paved pathways that are lined with colourful shops and restaurants keeping the place abuzz with travellers. The unique blend of a strong Hindu religious influence and a vibrant bohemian beach culture makes Varkala an intriguing destination to explore. You can easily drift between the holy **Papanasam Beach** and the centuries-old **Janardhana Swamy Temple** on one side, and soak up the sun, indulge in Ayurvedic treatments and tuck into fresh seafood on the other.

❶ JANARDHANA SWAMY TEMPLE
This 2000-year-old Vishnu temple stands starkly in contrast to the bikini-clad visitors on beaches just a kilometre away. The temple overlooks a kalyani (pond) which is mostly occupied by youngsters splashing about. It allows non-Hindus, as long as they remain on the temple grounds, and do not try to enter the sanctum. During the annual festival

The Anjengo Fort was used by the East India Company

in March, the temple is decorated in palm fronds as an elephant procession ambles by.

Temple Road; 4am–noon and 5–8pm

❷ BEACHES

Bright beach umbrellas, reclining chairs and baked sunbathers are a permanent fixture in the strand of golden beaches that nuzzle Varkala's cliff edge. Of them, **Papanasam** lies at the far end and is mainly known for its religious connect with Hindus. You can see religious ceremonies for ancestors being performed under beach umbrellas. Walk south towards **Black Beach**, **Odayam** and **Manthara** for a more authentic touristy beach ambience.

> ✅ *Top Tip:*
> *Torrid waters*
>
> Do note that the beaches at Varkala have strong currents; even experienced swimmers have been swept away. This is one of the most dangerous beaches in Kerala, so be careful and swim between the flags or ask the lifeguards to point out the safest places to swim.

❸ ANJENGO FORT

History buffs will love the immaculate, well-preserved Anjengo Fort (1695), 12km from Varkala. The seaside ride takes you through colourful fishing villages and small townships. The fort lies in a village called Anchuthengu, from which it derives its name. This unassuming village was an early trade settlement of the East India Company and the fort an important signalling station for ships coming in from England. Do climb up the windy lighthouse nearby for a bird's-eye view of the surrounding areas.

10am–5pm

❹ AYURVEDIC TREATMENTS

It seems as if everybody has an Ayurveda-related product or treatment to sell, although many aren't qualified practitioners. Ask for recommendations before you go to get herbalised. **Kadaltheeram Ayurvedic Beach Resort** has an intensive programme that lasts for a minimum of 14 days. A simpler rejuvenation package is also available at **Absolute Ayurveda Spa** (www.absoluteayur.com) on Temple Road.

🛏 Accommodation

Varkala, a long-time tourist favourite, gets especially packed from December to February. The prices of hotels spike by 30–40% between mid-December and the first week of January. Some might close down for 2–3 months in the summers. Most places to stay are crammed in along the North Cliff. Less developed Odayam Beach, about 1km further north of Black Beach, is a tranquil alternative.

Taj Gateway Hotel   Hotel ₹₹
🕽 0470 6673300; www.tajhotels. com/gateway; Janardhanapuram Varkala, Near Government Guest House; d ₹6600–7600, ste ₹8600 (incl of breakfast) Rebranded and refurbished, the Taj Varkala is looking hot – especially the new rooms, with beds covered in crisp linen and mocha cushions, and glass shower cubicles in the bathrooms, complete with electric blinds. There's a good pool, but poor access to the beach.

Villa Jacaranda   Bed & Breakfast ₹₹
🕽 0470 2610296; www.villa-jacaranda.biz; Temple Road West; d ₹5175 (incl of breakfast) Away from the North Cliff clutter, Villa Jacaranda is tucked away on the comparatively peaceful Temple Road. A hand-painted signboard ushers you into this relaxing retreat with just a handful of huge, bright rooms, each with a balcony and decorated with a chic blend of minimalist modern and period touches. The delicious breakfast is served on your verandah. The home has wi-fi connectivity.

Hindustan Beach Retreat   Hotel ₹₹
🕽 0470 2604254; www. hindustanbeachretreat.com; Papanasam Beach; d ₹4500–5000, ste ₹5500 (incl of breakfast) Feast your eyes on the blue sea across the Papanasam Beach from the pool area or any of the sea-facing rooms here. Hindustan Beach Retreat has spacious, comfy rooms, all with breezy balconies. The in-house Ayurvedic spa, Turtle Bay, has an impressive menu of rejuvenation massages. The wi-fi service at the resort is fast, just in case you want to keep in touch with the world.

Thanal   Hotel ₹₹
🕽 0470 2604342; www. thanalbeachresort.com; North Cliff; d ₹3500 A pleasant relief from the predictable resort ambience, Thanal is a new and intimate four-roomed property, right in the middle of the North Cliff. The rooms are exceptionally clean though there are no extra services other than wi-fi. Not having an in-house restaurant is hardly a problem, as there are plenty nearby.

🔲 Palm Tree Heritage   Beach Resort ₹₹
🕽 09946055036; www. palmtreeheritage.com; Odayam Beach; d ₹4000–4500, ste ₹6000 (incl of breakfast) Pleasantly away from the packed North Cliff zone,

Palm Tree lies at Odayam Beach. It's a wonder how the management has been able to keep a seaside garden looking absolutely fresh and green at all times. Exemplary service, Kerala-themed cottages, an in-house restaurant, Ayurveda spa and proximity to the swimming area of the beach keeps regulars coming back. The resort also has an annexe with slightly less atmospheric but comfortable rooms.

Woodhouse Beach Resort
Resort ₹
09562454757; www. woodhousebeachresort.com; Thiruvambady; d/cottage ₹2200/2800 Sea-facing breezy cottages and a sunset view to die for make Woodhouse a great option. Situated on the right edge of the North Cliff, the hotel seems slightly cluttered but is in fact quite neat and good value for money. The staff are extremely pleasant and make your stay worthwhile with prompt service.

Clafouti Beach Resort
Resort ₹
0470 2601414; www.clafoutiresort. com; North Cliff; d from ₹1750 If you want to be in the thick of action at the popular North Cliff restaurant zone, this seaside resort offers a medley of options to stay. You can pick from Kerala-style wooden cottages overlooking a bright green garden, bamboo huts or standard rooms. With a clean Ayurveda spa as part of the property, you do not have to walk far for a massage.

La Exotica
Homestay ₹
0470 2608866; www.laexotica.in; Helipad; d with/without AC ₹3500/ 2500 (incl of breakfast) The only homestay option in Varkala, La Exotica lies an earshot away from the sea. Centrally located, it offers basic but clean rooms and a hammock in the garden to relax in. Select a room on the first floor for a view of the sea.

Antique furniture decorates the verandahs of Villa Jacaranda

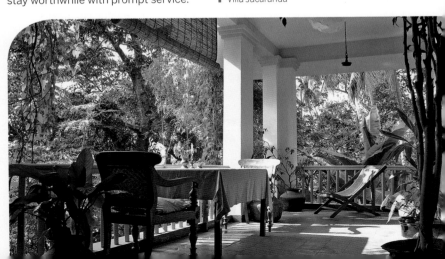

Eating

Most restaurants in Varkala offer the same mishmash of Indian, Asian and Western fare to a soundtrack of easy-listening trance. Join in the nightly Varkala saunter till you find a place that suits you. Those who are unlicensed will usually serve alcohol discreetly. Most restaurants have temporary seasonal licences.

> ## ✓ *Top Tip: Licence to drink*
>
> Beer is served in a clandestine way as most of the restaurants do not have legal permits. Expect to be served in a coffee mug or a bottle wrapped in newspaper.

Hotel Suprabhatham   South Indian ₹
☏ 0470 2606697; NH Rd, Mythanam; mains 100–200; 7am–9.30pm The narrow entrance to Suprabhatham opens into a world of delicious south Indian fare – idlis, uthappams and filter coffee, a relief from the overwhelming foreign cuisines near the beach. If your Indian taste buds need familiar flavours, this is the place for you.

Trattorias   Multi-Cuisine ₹₹
☏ 09746983917; North Cliff; mains from ₹250; 7am–10.30pm Chat away with the friendly waiters at the upper deck of 'Kingfisher' poster-clad Trattorias with 80s pop music as a constant companion. Fresh juices, goodies from the German bakery and a large multi-cuisine spread can keep you here for a whole evening.

Cafe Italiano   Italian ₹₹₹
☏ 08129751097; North Cliff; mains ₹500–750; 7.30am–11pm The thematic wood-floored and tree-scaped Cafe Italiano deserves appreciation for its aesthetic ingenuity; droopy vines hang lazily on a central tree adding to the languorous ambience. Sit on the upper deck and choose from the Italian fare.

Hungry Eye   Multi-Cuisine ₹₹₹
☏ 09633253591; middle cliff; mains ₹500–750; 7.30am–11pm The atmospheric Hungry Eye restaurant, with tiered seating and candle-lit tables, offers a massive Thai-inclined menu to choose from. It's a good place to relax, put your feet up and watch the fishing boats come in after a long sunny day at sea.

Clafouti Restaurant   Multi-Cuisine ₹₹₹
middle cliff, Papanasam; mains ₹500–750; 7am–11pm One of the most popular and well-known places in town, Clafouti seems to have a sizeable fan-base for their fresh salads and pizzas. The place is buzzing with guests from 7.30pm onwards till post 11pm. Take a seat close to the street and watch the tourists pass by on the Middle Cliff.

Milestone Cafe   Multi-Cuisine ₹₹₹
☏ 09995920651; North Cliff; mains ₹500–750; 7am–11pm Watch the

sunset as you gorge on juicy grills and momos at the Milestone Cafe. The lengthy menu offers a variety of cuisines for you to pick from.

🔒 Shopping

Stroll around the North Cliff and you will find the hippest bohemian clothes, jewellery and bags. Next in line are the sewing masters who can whip up self-designed kurtas and pants in hours. There isn't much difference between these shops, so find your own favourites.

Karnataka Shop   Clothing

North Cliff; 7am–10pm Discover a large collection of harem pants, cotton kurtis, spaghetti tops, slippers and jewellery at the well-stocked Karnataka Shop. It will be a surprise if you can leave without lightening your wallet here.

Balaji Handicrafts   Handicrafts

North Cliff; 7am–10pm The assertive and convincing owner of the shop will allow you to leave only after you have gone though the entire collection of Kashmiri shawls, jewellery, psychedelic tees, tops and footwear. Carry an extra duffel bag as you may end up making a substantial addition to your wardrobe.

Acto Tex and
Tailoring Shop   Clothing

North Cliff; 7am–10pm Select your own fabric and design a masterpiece to your taste with the talented 'master ji' at Acto. They have a commendable collection of fabric and you will find some of the previous creations hanging up for inspiration.

❘ Shops along Varkala's bustling
❚ North Cliff

Kovalam & Around

Highlights

❶ Kovalam Beaches
❷ Sri Parasurama Temple, Thiruvallam
❸ Vizhinjam Harbour
❹ Poovar Backwaters
❺ Chowara Beach

An erstwhile pit stop on the hippie trail, Kovalam has been through a metamorphosis since. The serene seaside getaway has emerged as one of the top beach destinations of the country with a good mix of gorgeous palm-fringed beaches and a plethora of cafes, resorts and sightseeing options close by. Apart from its sugar-white beaches, Kovalam also promises an extraordinary Ayurveda-filled holiday. It is the most scenic base to explore Thiruvananthapuram (p51), Varkala (p64) and Kanyakumari (p73).

❶ KOVALAM BEACHES

The stretch of beach is divided by a blurred line between Lighthouse, Hawa, Eve and Grow beaches, of which Lighthouse is the most crowded and action packed. Though there are no organised water sports at Kovalam, surf boards can be rented (₹50–100, depending on the season). Else, you can hire a beach lounger for a few hours (₹100–200). Further down the beach is the lighthouse, a towering landmark at Kovalam. If you want to take in the beauty of the horizon and landscape, climb the lighthouse in the evenings. You might have to jostle for some space on the railing with other visitors, but the sight is worth it. Caution: Kovalam is a busy place and thefts are not uncommon.

Lighthouse Beach; adult/child/camera/video ₹10/3/20/25; 3–5pm

📷 Snapshot: Of myths and legends

The myth behind Kerala's creation is based on the story of Parasurama (Rama with the axe), the sixth incarnation of Vishnu. He is believed to have freed the region from the oppressive Kshatriyas. After killing all the male Kshatriyas, Parasurama meditated near Gokarna, and then Kanyakumari, to repent for his sins. From here, he threw his axe towards the ocean, forming the landmass that is now Kerala.

❷ SRI PARASURAMA TEMPLE, THIRUVALLAM

The Sri Parasurama Temple lies about 6km from Kovalam towards Thiruvananthapuram, on the banks of the Karamana River. A small dusty compound next to the main Thiruvallam junction is the site of this 2000-year-old temple, the only one in Kerala dedicated to the legendary creator of the state.
Thiruvallam; 4–11am, and 5–8pm

✓ *Top Tip: Dangers & annoyances*

• There are strong rips at both ends of Lighthouse Beach that carry away several swimmers every year. Swim only between the flags in the area patrolled by lifeguards – green flags show the area is safe, red flags warn of danger zones.

• Kovalam has frequent blackouts and the footpaths behind Lighthouse Beach are unlit, so carry a torch (flashlight) after dark.

---

❸ VIZHINJAM HARBOUR

Vizhinjam harbour comes to life as early as 7am as the fishing boats arrive with the late night catch. The place is bustling with the frenzied activity of selecting and sorting fish and makes for a great photo opportunity. Across the harbour lies an imposing long pier that juts into the sea.

❹ POOVAR BACKWATERS

Though Kovalam is not on the typical backwater sector of Kerala, a handful of operators provide the leisurely

The picturesque fishing harbour at Vizhinjam

Exploring the Poovar backwaters

✅ *Top Tip: Forbidden fruit*

When cruising in the backwaters, do not grab a low hanging mango look-alike fruit. The poisonous othalanga is lethal and was once dreaded as the suicide snack for many fishermen.

experience at the Neyyar River close to the Poovar junction (17km). Hop onto a small country/speed boat for a cruise through the mangroves down the narrow water canals that eventually open out into the sea. The backwaters and the Arabian Sea are bifurcated by a small stretch of sand, the **Golden Beach.** You can stop at any of the floating restaurants, which bob up at the cusp of the Arabian Sea and the backwaters for a meal. Hiring a boat for a small group is the most economical way to do this laid-back ride.

Leela Backwater Craze; ☎093497 56521; Bridge Road, cruise per person 1hr/2hr ₹1500/2000

⑤ CHOWARA BEACH

If you are not a fan of the umbrella-crammed beaches of Kovalam, head to Chowara (6km from Kovalam) for a comparatively secluded experience. If you are not a guest at one of the resorts here, you may have to carry your own paraphernalia like umbrella, towels and snacks. It's worth the trouble as you can find a quiet spot for yourself and not be part of the mass experience.

Detour: To the southernmost tip of India

Kanyakumari (Cape Comorin) is just 82km from Kovalam and makes for a short and informative detour. Sightseeing in Kanyakumari will not take longer than a day but you may want to spend a night to catch both a sunset and a sunrise. Here are a few key highlights:

• Take a ferry to **Vivekananda Memorial** (ferry/entry ₹30/10; 8am–5pm) to see the spiritual guru's meditation hall.

• A sandy patch at the **Triveni Sangam** where Bay of Bengal, Arabian Sea and the Indian Ocean meet.

• The **Gandhi Memorial** (7am–7pm), where some of his ashes are still kept, resembles an Orissan temple.

India's southernmost tip, the Vivekananda Rock Memorial

• The best sunset view is from the **Beach View Park** and the **Viewing Tower** which can be climbed by paying an entry fee of ₹5.

• The **Devi Kanyakumari Temple** (Kumari Amman Temple, 4.30am–12.30pm, 3.30–8.30pm) is dedicated to kanya (virgin) goddess Kumari. The temple is visited by hundreds of pilgrims each day.

• East Car Road is packed with hotels of which the **Sea Shore Hotel** (☎04652 246704) is the best option with well-furnished rooms that overlook the sea. There are plenty of fruit stalls and basic veg restaurants in the bazaar area. **Sebaa Restaurant** (7.30am–10.30pm) and **Geetha Bhavan** (6am–10pm) on East Car Road are simple joints offering good north Indian meals.

OTHER STOPS EN ROUTE

If you are travelling by car, consider stopping at the **Padmanabhapuram Palace** located 60km southeast of Kovalam (adult/child/camera/video ₹25/10/25/1500; 9.30am–1pm, 2–4.50pm). Constructed of teak and granite, the exquisite interiors include carved rosewood ceilings, Chinese-style screens, and floors finished to a high black polish. This is Asia's largest wooden palace complex and the best example of traditional Kerala architecture. Parts of it date back to 1550; it is a conglomeration of 14 palaces. It was once the seat of the rulers of Travancore.

Another worthwhile stop is **Suchindram Temple** (4am–1pm, 4–8.30pm), 11km before Kanyakumari. There's a white mesh of godly figures on the gopuram and a large statue of Hanuman in black granite. The temple is famous for its Sthanumalayan deity (Brahma, Vishnu and Mahesh in one sanctum).

🛏 Accommodation

Kovalam is chock-a-block with hotels, though budget places here cost more than usual and are difficult to find. Beachfront properties are the most expensive, but they do offer great sea views. Look out for smaller places tucked away in the labyrinth of paths behind the beach among the palm groves and rice paddies; they're much better value. Those looking for some isolation and peace should head towards Poovar and Chowara, the other two hubs to stay in. The resorts here are more atmospheric and they also have good access to the sea.

Vivanta by Taj   **Hotel** ₹₹₹
📞 0471 6613000; www.vivantabytaj. com; GV Raja Vattappara Road; d ₹8500 Prettily placed on a quiet

The Leela lobby designed by Charles Correa

extension of Kovalam, this Taj property has 59 stone and wood cottages placed at different levels in a tropical garden. All have balconies and sit-outs, and the better placed ones look on to the ocean. The all-day dining space overlooks the newly renovated pool. There is also an Indian restaurant and seafood beachside restaurant (Bait) where you can while away the evening. This is the kind of place families and couples can check into for a self-contained holiday at Kovalam.

TOP CHOICE **The Leela**   **Hotel** ₹₹₹
📞 0471 3051234; www.theleela. com/locations/kovalam; d ₹12,500–18,500 One of India's first five-star hotels and designed by Charles Correa, the Leela is a gracious and sprawling property perched on a cliff with breathtaking views of the ocean. Retaining its classic Correa touches (especially its stunning reception

area), it has now added a swank and modernistic section called The Club. The beach-view and garden-view rooms are the older ones, the latter being a good bargain. The three pools and landscaped greenery are the property's plus points, and the cuisine is top class (especially the authentic Malayali fare).

Turtle On The Beach   Resort ₹₹₹
☎0471 2514000; www.
turtleonthebeach.com; VPI/439
ITDC Road; d ₹10,000–11,000, ste
₹13,000–27,000 (incl of breakfast)
Turtle on the Beach lies at the bend of Lighthouse Beach with large artistic wooden sculptures strewn across the resort. It has a lovely sunny wooden deck overlooking the sea, an exotic garden, sea-view rooms, a pool and free yoga classes (5.30–6.30pm). The resort also provides wi-fi. The rates change weekly as per occupancy or season; this flexi tariff policy could land you a good deal in the low season.

Marina Guest House   Guesthouse ₹
☎0471 2488220; Lighthouse
Beach; d ₹1600–2800 Situated just behind Beatles (p78) restaurant, the 10 sparkling clean rooms of Marina Guest House are real value for money. Its welcoming atmosphere and it's proximity to the beach are pluses too.

Varma Cottages, Kovalam Cottages ₹
☎09847498007; www.
calangutebeach.com; Hawah Beach;
d ₹2500–3000 The charming picket fenced cottages at the edge of the

Great sea-views make Turtle on The Beach a good choice

beach offer comfortable rooms. Though it's tempting to take the rooms which are right beside the sea, we recommend that you go for those that are a little behind the grassy patch for better privacy; many people on the beach seem to enjoy peeking inside from the pavement.

Adam Beach Resort   Guesthouse ₹
☎09387813908; www.
adambeachresort.com; Near
Lighthouse Beach; d ₹2200 The real luxury in Kovalam is if you're close to the sand or have a sea view. These standards are unquestionably met by Adam Beach Resort right on Lighthouse Beach, even though the interiors are rather austere. Ask for the ocean-facing upper-floor room, which is spacious enough for at least four people and has a personal

balcony. The place is a real steal and Mr Vijayan's (the owner) enthusiastic hospitality is an added bonus.

Manaltheeram, Chowara Resort ₹₹₹
📞0471 2268610; www.
manaltheeram.com; Near Chowara
PO Vizhinjam Poovar Road; d
₹6329–15,173 (incl of breakfast and
taxes) Location-wise, Manaltheeram
is a dream! This Ayurveda-specific
resort (sister concern of the Ayurveda

The cottages of Somatheeram are set amidst lush greenery

stalwart, Somatheeram) sits on the edge of the cliff with steps leading down to the beach below. The garden cottages, with a small personal grassy patch in front, are the most economical. It's a good place to have an Ayurvedic treatment. The outdoor restaurant is the most popular haunt here.

For a similar experience by the same chain, stay at Soma Palm Shore at Lighthouse Beach or Somatheeram Ayurvedic Resort in Chowara (central booking: 📞0471 2266111).

✓ *Top Tip: Somatheeram branches*

Somatheeram (📞0471 2268101; www.somatheeram.in; Chowara P.O) is one of the most credible names for Ayurveda treatment in the Kovalam region, and has only three branches; Palmshore, Somatheeram and Manaltheeram. With its growing popularity, many smaller resorts have used similar logos to lure travellers.

Niraamaya Retreats, Chowara

TOP CHOICE   Resort ₹₹₹

📞 0471 2267333; www.niraamaya.in; Pulinkudi, Mullur Post; d ₹18,000–35,000 (incl of breakfast) One of the finest resorts in the area, Niraamaya (earlier Surya Samudra) is draped with an air of extravagance. Built in the shadow of large banyan trees, it has two restaurants, an infinity pool, Kerala-style cottages, yoga pavilions, a gym, wi-fi facility and a spa.

Karrikathi Beach House

Guesthouse ₹₹₹

📞 0471 2720238; www.karikkathibeachhouse.com; via Nagar Bhagavathi Temple, Mullur, Vizhinjam; d ₹9665 (incl of breakfast) Escape from the ubiquitous resorts and predictable guesthouses to this double-bedroom unit off Chowara Beach in Mullur.

The cottages at Manaltheeram overlook the sea

Enter through a red door and drift into the lazy cliff-top beach house with only the sound of the waves to keep you company. You are unlikely to bump into other guests at this isolated spot.

Isola Di Cocco, Poovar

Resort ₹₹₹

📞 0471 2210800; Poovar; d ₹6000–10,000 (incl of breakfast) The Island of Coconuts is a terrific option for the family despite its faraway feel. Sandwiched between swampy coconut plantations and the Arabian Sea, it has multiple categories of accommodation (the Kerala-style lake-view one being the best). There's also a pool, wi-fi facility, children's play area, Ayurveda clinic, free transfer to the Golden Beach in front of it and a courteous staff, that you will love.

Eating

Each evening, dozens of open-air restaurants line the beach promenade displaying the catch of the day – just pick a fish and decide how you want it prepared. Menus and prices are largely indistinguishable – it's more about which ambience takes your fancy. Settle for a spot on the first floor to soak in the view of the sea. This also ensures no intrusion from the hawkers.

Try different varieties of fresh fried fish at the restaurants on the beach

Mini House
(Sea Pearl Cafe)   Multi-Cuisine ₹₹
☏09947480969; www.minihousekovalam.com; Lighthouse Beach; mains ₹250–500; 10am–11pm
A short walk away from the restaurant hub, Mini House is just behind the Lighthouse right at the edge of the sea. The decor and menu might be frugal, but the ambience is brilliant. Visit this place for a light snack while you gorge on the view.

Santana   Multi-Cuisine ₹₹
☏0471 2481599; Lighthouse Beach; mains ₹500–750; 7.30am–11pm
Plastic chairs covered with towels (if you have just emerged from the sea) are perfect to settle in for an ocean-view meal at Santana. Order from the fresh catch of the day or staples from the long menu.

Jeevan   Multi-Cuisine ₹₹
☏0471 2483062; www.jeevanresort.net; Lighthouse Beach; mains ₹500–750; 10.30am–11pm
If you are hoping to hear the latest Bollywood tunes and enjoy fresh grills, visit Jeevan – one of the few to actually have an alcohol licence amongst the beachside cafes.

Rock Cafe   Seafood ₹₹
☏0471 2480411; Bend at Lighthouse Beach; mains ₹250–500; 10.30am–11pm Visit Rock Cafe for the real thing – a view of the fishermen folk bringing the catch home and packing up for the day while you fork in utterly delicious fresh fried and grilled seafood.

Beatles   Multi-Cuisine ₹₹₹
☏09387801942; Lighthouse Beach; mains ₹500–750; 9.30am–11pm A relief from the identical cafes which line Lighthouse Beach, Beatles provides an exclusive atmosphere, well thought-out menu and a first-floor view of the sea from its wooden-floored and thatched-roof deck. Familiar rock music will put you in a good mood; sometimes it can veer off into 90s Hindi pop, which you can request them to change.

 Shopping

Anugraha Galleria   Souvenirs
📞 0471 2485968; I/1483, near Orion Hotel, Lighthouse; 9.30am–8pm
Though a little pricey, it's a good stop to indulge in some non-essential bric-a-brac – there are some unusual antiques and handmade paper diaries at Anugraha.

Tibetan Handicraft Shop   Souvenirs
📞 0471 2483540; Near Lighthouse; 10am–10pm Earthy Tibetan scrolls, silver jewellery and brass figures are laid out temptingly at Sangmo's handicrafts shop. Women are likely to spend more time here as the silver is quite irresistible.

Hastkala   Souvenirs
📞 0471 2487694; Kovalam Beach Road; 9am–9pm Before you enter the barrage of smaller Kashmiri shops at the beach, this place may be worthwhile with its larger collection of artefacts, paintings, rugs, shawls and a spattering of Kerala wooden curios. They also have some astronomically priced framed photographs of the original Ravi Varma paintings.

Cottage Industries Exposition Ltd   Souvenirs
📞 0471 2485840; Beach Road; 9am–9pm The CIE showroom on Beach Road has a greater air of credibility than the numerous shops by the beach. Its vast collection of carpets, brass items, candles, wood-crafted souvenirs can keep you engaged for long.

Chowara Lanes   Lifestyle
Chowara Beach Road; 10am–10pm
Chowara's narrow lanes have tailoring establishments and curio shops springing up at breakneck speed. Shops that are very much like the ones at Lighthouse Beach sell similar bohemian clothes and jewellery here.

Ancy's Book Store   Bookstore
Lighthouse Beach; 9am–9pm
Exchange, or get your hands on some excellent though pricey second-hand books at Ancy's. The owner, Joy, is unyielding to bargainers as he knows that he has a superb collection.

Chandrakantha Arts   Handicrafts
📞 09633609801; Lighthouse Beach; 9am–10.30pm A sanctuary for painted copies of Dali, Kovalam's heroes, Hendrix and Marley and the Joker are worth a look at Chandrakantha Arts. You can also get customised T-shirts here with similar themes.

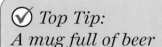 Top Tip: A mug full of beer

Like Varkala, few restaurants (such as Jeevan) have licence to serve alcohol, but beer is available at every eating joint served clandestinely in coffee mugs or newspaper-wrapped beer bottles. Only 650ml bottles are available: there is no sign of pints anywhere in Kovalam.

Alappuzha & the Backwaters

Why Go?

The quintessential Kerala experience lies in the green backwaters of Alappuzha (Alleppey), Kumarakom and Kollam (Quilon). While the channels of Alappuzha and Kumarakom open out into the massive Vembanad Lake, the Kollam water bodies congregate at Ashtamudi Lake. As you float past palm-fringed canals, you can glimpse vignettes of village life along the banks from a houseboat. The region is one of the most treaded travel hubs, and it offers you a perfect mix of local culture and a laid-back holiday.

Getting There & Away

Air: The closest airport from Alappuzha is Kochi (84km). Kochi is well connected to all the important cities of the country. If you want to arrive in Kollam first, Thiruvananthapuram (69km), with regular flights from across the country, is a better option. Taxi fare to Alappuzha/Kollam from the nearest airport is ₹2500–3000.

Bus: Connectivity from key south Indian cities (especially Bengaluru and Chennai) is particularly good to Alappuzha and around. Both Karnataka State Road Transportation Corporation (KSRTC) and private overnight buses ply for ₹1000–1500 per seat and take 12 hours for this trip.

Train: There are over 20 trains heading south towards Kanyakumari along the west coast which stop at Alappuzha, Kottayam (14km from Kumarakom) and Kollam. The Bangalore-Kanyakumari (Island) Express (16526) and Trivandrum Express (12695) are good options that connect to these destinations.

Ferry: Government ferries connect Alappuzha and Kollam. The journey takes 8 hours (usually starting at 10.30am) and costs ₹300 per person.

Kettuvallams (houseboats) and coconut trees are commonly identified with Kerala

Top Highlights

1 Houseboat Cruises in Vembanad Lake

Houseboats (p102) are the best way to experience the lusciously green landscape of the backwaters of Vembanad Lake (p88). The longest lake of the country, Vembanad accommodates over a thousand of these floating structures that glide lethargically past the equally laid-back countryside. With a cook on-board dishing out delicious local fare, a TV and cosy well-furnished rooms (depending on the size of the boat), you are equipped to cruise for as many days as you wish.

2 Sri Krishna Temple, Ambalappuzha

Replete with history and folklore, the Sri Krishna Temple (p89) at Ambalappuzha represents the characteristic architecture of the state – massive walls, large temple grounds, a kalyani (temple pond) in the front and a golden pillar before the sanctum. The temple prasadam consists of payasam that is lovingly made every day for hundreds of devotees. Locals in the area strongly suggest you taste this delicious sweet milk dessert, even if you have to stand in a long queue.

4 Kumarakom Bird Sanctuary

The 14-acre bird sanctuary (p98) on the edge of the Kumarakom group of islands is a treat for birdwatchers. If you are a serious birder, arrive between June and August, during the breeding season of wetland species like the Indian darter, little cormorant, heron, ibis and kingfisher. The thick copse of the sanctuary can also be visited in the cooler months of January and February.

5 Thazhathangadi Houses

Traditional Kerala architecture lives on in the houses of Thazhathangadi (p101), 2km from Kottayam, on the banks of the Meenachil River. One can see intricately carved wooden doors, tiled roofs and unique architectural features in the row of houses that stand testimony to the rich cultural history of the region. The streets of Thazhathangadi once bustled with traders from far away China, Central Asia and Egypt. This was the spot where canal transportation from the sea ended and roads gave access for inland journeys.

6 Ashtamudi Lake

Ashtamudi Lake (p106) in Kollam district is known for its distinct wetland ecosystem as well as the pristine village atmosphere on the edges. Eight water channels spring from the lake, giving it the name 'Ashtamudi' or 'eight coned'. Compared to the rest of the backwater circuit, the houseboat cruise experience of Ashtamudi is unscathed by excessive tourism. The lake and its fringes are dotted with Chinese fishing nets and boat-building yards that give you an insight into local life.

Local Knowledge
Off-beat retreats

Kence Georgey, owner of Eco Trails Kerala, suggests some off-the-beaten-track destinations in the backwater region.

• **Aymanam:** Eulogised as the scenic setting of Arundhati Roy's Booker winning classic, *God of Small Things,* the village of Aymanam, 8km from Kumarakom, remains as unassuming as portrayed in the book. It boasts a ludicrously green rural setting with mornings of toddy tapping, fishing and coir making.

• **Akkaara House** (✆09447716951; www.akkara.in; Mariyathuruth; d ₹3750 incl of breakfast): The 198-year-old house by the river is perfect to soak in some Syrian Christian hospitality with lip-smacking non-veg food. The traditional house has been kept intact with a few modern infusions to make your stay comfortable. What you will love most here is the garden that opens out into the Meenachil River.

• **Maya Heritage** (✆09847086099; Aymanam; d ₹12,509 incl of breakfast): Flanked by 3-acres of fruit trees, this 110-year-old river-facing heritage homestay has retained its period look. Newly furbished, the house is a perfect getaway for those who shun the tourist buzz. Despite its elusive location, it is just 11km from the houseboat hub.

Alappuzha & the Backwaters

Best Trips

❶ **Alappuzha**
❷ **Kumarakom**
❸ **Kottayam**
❹ **Kollam**

A maze of canals, rivers, lagoons and islands constitutes the enchanting backwater landscape of Kerala. To experience these alluring vistas, kick off your journey at **Alappuzha** – a green town set around a grid of canals – followed by the **Kumarakom islands.** Though much smaller than Alappuzha, Kumarakom offers a host of luxury resorts at the edge of Vembanad Lake. Further down the coast, **Kollam** is relatively unexplored and offers a glimpse of local life at close quarters from the banks of Ashtamudi Lake. While the languid backwaters of this area are its highlight, the drenched green paddy fields (called kuttanad) are unique as they lie 2m below sea level.

❚ Endless backwaters
❚ of Alappuzha

GETTING AROUND

Alappuzha, Kumarakom and Kollam are relatively small and the attractions are within walking distance. However, if you wish, you can hire autorickshaws that are easily available and minimum charges are ₹20.

Alappuzha

Alappuzha is the gateway to Kerala's famed backwater region, which largely spreads across three districts. The magical green topography of the town derives from an endless carpet of water hyacinths that flourish in its network of narrow canals. As you manoeuvre your way past watery highways, which eventually meet the Vembanad Lake on one side of the town, you realise why Alappuzha is also called 'Venice of the East'. Towering palms with thick undergrowth, and its proximity to the Arabian Sea, add to its enchantment.

Highlights

❶ Backwaters Cruise
❷ RKK Memorial Museum
❸ Sri Krishna Temple, Ambalappuzha
❹ Pathiramanal Island
❺ Beach Area & Vijay Park
❻ Sea View Park
❼ Jain Temple

❶ BACKWATERS CRUISE

The presence of over 1000 houseboats in Alappuzha alone bears testimony to the popularity of the cruise experience. Even though you are going to be inundated with house boat offers, once you have decided on your cruise, it is difficult to have your fill of gliding in the placid waters. Besides, with all the comforts close at hand, it's the ultimate form of relaxation. An overnight stay (22-hour cruise) is the best way

📷 *Snapshot: Eco-friendly cruises*

It's not all perfect in paradise. Pollution and land reclamation threaten the habitat of the waterways and the communities on their banks. It's estimated that the water levels have dropped by two-thirds since the mid-19th century, and many migratory birds no longer visit the area. The sheer number of houseboats mean that pollution is a major problem, and although outboard motors are not permitted, some operators use them on smaller boats. To ensure that your cruise is eco-friendly, ask to see operators' certification: houseboat owners who have a 'Green Palm Certificate' are the ones to go for, which means they have installed solar panels and sanitary tanks. It's also better for the environment to avoid using AC as this requires a great deal more power. Best of all are the few remaining punting, rather than motorised, boats.

📷 *Snapshot: Vembanad Lake*

Vembanad Lake is where all the water channels of the town converge. Spread over 2033sq km, it covers a large part of Kerala, flanked by the three districts of Alappuzha, Kottayam and Ernakulam. The longest lake in India, it is known for its impressive variety of fish and migratory waterfowl. Shrimps and clams thrive here, providing a productive environment for fisheries. Vembanad's wetland system also supports other water-centric traditions like lime shell collection, coir retting and fishing, apart from inland transportation and, of course, tourism.

to enjoy delicious home-cooked meals, Kerala hospitality and picturesque waterways. Day cruises last 4–6 hours. For detailed information on houseboat operators, see p102.

② RKK MEMORIAL MUSEUM

Embark on an international odyssey of artefacts, murals and paintings: porcelain from China, a 1948 Buick, sculptures from Africa, curios from Belgium, South America, Japan, Italy and Turkey, among other places. The RKK Museum is the private collection of Mrs Betty, wife of deceased coir magnate, Revi Karuna Karan. Her worldwide acquisitions consist of the largest private collection of ivory and Swarovskis in the world. The museum is remarkably organised and well kept.

📞0477 2242923; www.rkkmuseum.com; Shree Karunakaran

Houseboats can be booked for overnight cruises

Charitable Trust, Shanthi Bhavan; Indian/foreigner ₹100/250; 9am–5pm, Mon closed

❸ SRI KRISHNA TEMPLE, AMBALAPPUZHA

One of the most revered temple in Kerala, this temple lies only 14km south of Alappuzha in a small town called Ambalappuzha. Visit as early as 5am for a spiritual start to your day. Built in AD 790, the temple is famous for its prasadam (payasam), which is prepared every day for hundreds of devotees.

You can walk around the beautiful lamp-lined walls of the sanctum, where a black granite idol of Krishna sits in a unique pose, holding a whip and a conch. A large weighing scale is placed outside the sanctum – it's a common practice to match the weight of rice or oil to the person making offerings to the deity.

Ambalappuzha; 3am–noon, 5–8pm

❹ PATHIRAMANAL ISLAND

Eloquently translated to 'midnight sands' this pastoral island in the middle of the Vembanad Lake is only accessible by boat. Migratory birds are partial to this location, given its green surroundings of 10-acres. You can spot many avian species such as egrets, Indian pond herons, gulls, terns,

 Snapshot: The legend of paal payasam

It is said that Lord Krishna himself appeared in front of the ruler in the disguise of a sage and challenged him to a game of chess. An astute player himself, the king accepted and bid the sage to choose his prize if he won. The sage simply asked for grains of rice on the chessboard in a manner that each square has double the grains of its predecessor, starting from one point. If he won, he should be paid equal to the sum of grains on the board. Little did the king realise that it was a mathematical trick. When the sage won, the number of grains had grown to an astronomical figure of 18,446,744,073,709,551,615 grains. Of course, this amount was not present in the granary and the king was then requested to offer rice payasam to devotees till the debt was paid off. The tradition lives on till this date.

jacanas and cormorants. Visitors can walk around a 2km path inside. Even the hour-and-a-half motor boat ride (speed boats take only 30min) offers spectacular sights of cormorants diving for fish from their secret hideaways in water hyacinths, as fishermen set up their nets.

☏0474 22244599; boats ply only until 6pm; motor boat/speed boat ₹600 (10 persons)/1500 (4 persons)

❺ BEACH AREA & VIJAY PARK

You can enjoy a breezy evening admiring the view of the setting sun on the busy Alappuzha Beach. It's a local hot spot where impromptu football games are held while vendors sell balloons and hot bhaji. There is no entry into the old lighthouse across, though a section of the beach has been converted into a children's park with a few rides and swings.

Vijay Park; Beach Roadd; ₹5; 3–8pm

❻ SEA VIEW PARK

Another way to enjoy the seafront is the Sea View Park across Alappuzha Beach, which has a few options for boat rides in an adjoining backwater canal.

Beach Road; row boat/pedal boat/photography/video ₹20/25/10/50

↻ *Detour: Aranmula*

A 53km detour, south of Alappuzha, lands you in the modest town of Aranmula at the edge of the Pampa River. Apart from the colossal Sree Parthasarathy Temple here, the town is famous for unique mirrors made from polishing an alloy of copper and tin. You can get a glimpse of this art at a modest workshop in the town centre. Call TK Sundaram Achary (☏0468 2319173; www.aranmulakannadionline.com; Thikkinampallil Building, Thekkenada, Aranmula) to fix an appointment.

❼ JAIN TEMPLE

A fair number of traders from the western state of Gujarat settled here many years ago. A narrow street named after them houses a white marble temple built by the community, which is open to visitors. Enter through the small blue gate of the ashram on the left and a dark passage full of paintings will lead you into the temple.

Gujarati Street; 7am–5pm

📷 *Snapshot: Snake boat races*

Kerala's snake boat races are a marvellous display of sinew and sportsmanship on the otherwise serene backwaters of the region. The honour of an entire village hinges on the annual 'Vallam Kalli'.

Such races are held between July 15 and September 15, Four most popular ones are: Nehru Boat Race in Punnamada Lake, Champakkulam Moolam, Payippad Jalotsavam on Payippad Lake and the Aranmula race. Historically, it is believed that the kings of the surrounding areas manoeuvred the canals on these vehicles to conduct wars. Even 400 years later, the tradition continues in a battle of vigour and strength. The 100-seater narrow boats are about 80–100ft long with oarsmen sitting on either side and 6–7 team members steering it. The team also consists of 2-3 people who clap and sing rhythmically to encourage the rowers and maintain the tempo.

The Nehru Boat Race is held on the second Saturday of August. Bangalore-based Photography Onthemove (📞09980655944; www.photographyonthemove.com) holds a four-day SLR workshop for beginners to capture the event from close quarters and to be allowed to catch behind-the-scenes action.

Vallam Kalli or the snake boat race is a major tourist attraction

🛏 Accommodation

Citrus Retreats   **Resort ₹₹₹**

☎ 0477 2288611; www.citrushotels.
in; 8/504A-504N, Karimba Valavu,
Punnapra North; d ₹7500–18,000
(incl of breakfast) Flanked by the
paddy fields of Kuttanad and the
Pallathuruthy River, Citrus is one of the
latest additions to the smart chain of
hotels across Alappuzha. A refreshing
stay by the river, it has well-equipped
rooms, an in-house restaurant, wi-fi,
pool, choice of an organic menu,
Ayurveda services – all with a touch of
earthy Kerala aesthetics. The water-
facing rooms offer scenic views from
your balcony.

**Vembanad
House**   **Boutique Homestay ₹₹₹**

☎ 0478 2868696; www.
vembanadhouse.com; Puthankayal,
Muhamma; d ₹10,500 (incl of
breakfast) Vembanad House enjoys
one of the most serene locations on
the edge of its namesake lake with
a more than 180-degree view of the

| This 150-year-old house is now known as
Emerald Isle

backwaters. The property, an erstwhile
coconut farm, is just a stone's throw
away from Pathiramanal Island. The
hosts can arrange for a small boat to
take you across to it. The family-run
homestay offers authentic home-
cooked meals and has a garden
which opens out from the main house
towards the water. There is reasonably
good wi-fi connectivity.

Lake Palace   **Resort ₹₹₹**

☎ 0477 2239701; www.
lakepalaceresort.com; d ₹13,000–
25,000 (incl of breakfast) A boat
at the Alappuzha ferry junction
brings you straight to the resort. The
excitement of this special entry via
the backwaters follows right through,
even after you check in at the rooms
overlooking a central manmade lake.
If travelling with family, the water
villas may be a more spacious and
practical option. Though the building
looks slightly dated, Lake Palace has
all the facilities of a resort; there is a
large central pool on an elevation, an
in-house restaurant, wi-fi and a range
of activities to keep you occupied.

Detour: Marari Beach

Since Marari and Alappuzha are only 15km apart, you can get the best of the beach and the backwaters if you stay at Marari Beach (between Fort Kochi and Alappuzha). Private service villas, hotels and homestays are all available:

• **Marari Villa** (☏09947948707; www.mararivillas.com; Marari Beach; d ₹11,500–24,500 incl of breakfast): Olga and Rupert's three villa units are done up aesthetically in warm hues, with private pools and a small team of staff. Just metres off the beach, it is extremely popular with those who want an isolated holiday.

• **CGH Earth** (☏0484 3011711; www.cghearth.com; Marari Beach; d ₹17,900–36,000 incl of breakfast and taxes): Another plush property, skirted by the fishing village of Mararikulam is CGH Earth. Enjoy the lush green expanse of its herb garden from your verandah or relax in the deluxe pool villas. The hotel is famous for its earthy look, Ayurveda and a luxurious experience of Alappuzha.

Lemon Tree Vembanad Lake Resort   Resort ₹₹₹
☏0478 2861970; www.lemontreehotels.com; Jana Sakthi Road, Kayippuram, Muhamma; d ₹9500–14,375, ste ₹16,675–29,325 (incl of breakfast) Lemon Tree has all the trappings of a resort with its list of engaging activities, well-furnished rooms and well-trained staff, making it a good choice for a family vacation. If not interested in the activities planned by the resort, you can simply relax by the pool. All but four rooms face the backwater expanse, so ensure that you book right. There is wi-fi facility.

⬛TOP CHOICE Emerald Isle   Homestay ₹₹
☏0477 2703899; www.emeraldislekerala.com; Kanjooparambil, Manimalathara, Chathurthyakary; d ₹5700–7300 (incl of breakfast) Leading the heritage experience in homestays is the much awarded Emerald Isle, a 150-year-old house owned by Mr Vijo. Portions of the old house, like the granary, have been converted into beautiful rooms. Situated at the edge of the Pampa River and the paddy fields of the Kuttanad region, Emerald presents an enviable access to the best of Alappuzha.

Punnamada Resort   Resort ₹₹
☏0477 2233691; www.punnamada.com; Punnamada Thondankulangara Road; d ₹6500–8600 (incl of breakfast) A small winding road from Alappuzha town surprisingly opens up at this 10.5-acre property at the periphery of Vembanad Lake. Here you can choose between lake-, pool- or garden-facing rooms. The cottages give you a feel of Kerala architecture with materials sourced from traditional houses. Notice the Manichitrathazhu door locks and the verandah seating, also typical of Kerala.

Akkarakalam Memoirs Homestay ₹₹
☎ 0477 2762345; www.
akkarakalammemoirs.com;
Chennamkary; d ₹5000 (incl of
breakfast) The well-preserved 150
year-old Syrian Christian house has
a backyard to die for – the Pampa
River itself. Period furniture, open
showers, an intact ancient granary
and authentic Kerala cuisine are the
highlights here. Akkarakalam Memoirs
also offers a range of activities such as
canoeing, fishing, Ayurveda massages
and cycling around the village.

TOP CHOICE **Raheem Residency Heritage Hotel ₹₹**
☎ 0477 2230767; www.
raheemresidency.com; Beach Road;
d ₹6000–7800 (incl of breakfast)
This lavish heritage property, by the
main Alappuzha beachfront, was built
in 1868 by an Englishman and later
owned by the Raheem family of Kerala
merchants. Its current avatar is the
work of an Indo-European couple who
have catalogued the story of Raheem
Residency in a beautiful picture book
that lies in the lounge area. The rooms
are aesthetically furnished with four-
poster beds and antiques.

Keraleeyam Ayurvedic Resort Resort ₹₹
☎ 0477 2231468; www.keraleeyam.
com; Thathampally; d ₹4156–5289
(incl of breakfast, treatment
costs extra) This 18-year-old
establishment's USP is its Ayurvedic
treatments. Though largely used by
long-stay guests who are looking

for elaborate prolonged treatments,
one can also come here for a quick
rejuvenation package. Keraleeyam
lies at the border of the Punnamada
backwater canal, where the Nehru
Boat Race is held each year.

TOP CHOICE **Taamara Homestay ₹₹**
☎ 09388988811; www.taamara.
in; near Kannankara Church,
Thaneermukkam; d ₹5500 (incl
of breakfast) You wouldn't want to
step out of this one! A fresh green
garden spreads over in front of the
four cottage units, each with personal
wooden decks, right at the edge of
Vembanad Lake. A semi-covered
common area and attached open
kitchen is where most guests spend
time catching up. Opt for the upper
storey rooms for more privacy.

Tharavad Heritage Resort Hotel ₹
☎ 0474 22244599; www.
tharavadheritageresort.com; west of
North Police Station, Sea View Ward;
d ₹1500–2000 (incl of breakfast) Of
the plentiful heritage accommodation
in Alappuzha, Tharavad stands out
with its 100-year-old architecture,
terracotta-tiled roof, teakwood
furniture and old artefacts. Its
proximity to town as well as the beach
is a big advantage. The house has
good wi-fi connectivity.

Arcadia Regency Hotel ₹
☎ 0477 2230414; www.
arcadiaregency.com; near Iron
Bridge; d ₹1800–3300 (incl of
breakfast) Arcadia is a good place

Taamara offers scenic views of
Vembanad Lake

for a quick stopover, with neat, well-
equipped rooms at reasonable prices.
The occasional tardiness of the staff
can easily be overlooked thanks to
their otherwise cheerful disposition.

Bamboo Lagoon   Homestay ₹
09446818893; www.
bamboolagoon.net; near Punnamada
Jetty; d ₹2500 (incl of breakfast)
Cross a small canal on a local boat
to reach Bamboo Lagoon, a new
homestay in the Punnamada area of
Vembanad Lake. Its location on the
edge of the lake and sparkling clean
rooms make it an inviting choice.

Cherukara Nest   Homestay ₹
0477 2251509; www.
cherukaranest.com; IX 774,
Cherukara Buildings, east of KSRTC
Bus Station; d ₹1500 (incl of

breakfast) This 85-year-old homestay
sits on the edge of town, just behind
the bus stand but pleasantly away
from the entire touristy din. The back
of the house opens out into a unique
tomb-like pigeon coop in a sunny
garden, with a long rope swing and
a common eating area. Cherukara
Nest is very reasonably priced for
the facilities it offers, its location and
comfortable rooms.

Eating

Hotel Royale Park   Multi-cuisine ₹₹
0477 2237828; www.
hotelroyalepark.com; YM A Road;
7am–10.30pm; mains ₹200–500
This is your best bet in town for a
lavish spread of 'Kerala meals'. You
will be given a choice of white rice
versus brown. Choose the latter with
a combination of fish curry for an
appetising lunch. Vegetarian food is
also available.

♥ If You Like: Toddy & toddy shops

If you step out at about 6am or later in the evening at 4pm, you will encounter a number of palm tops with agile toddy tappers perched precariously to extract the stuff of local wine. Also known as 'kallu', the white frothy alcoholic beverage is best consumed fresh and is pretty potent. Tapping is no easy feat: hard husk tied to the tree at intervals defines the steps for tappers. Despite these, they have to propel themselves up along the trunk to reach the coconuts. Some of them walk across trees on thick coir ropes, to avoid going down and up again.

A classic black-and-white sign announcing a toddy shop is hard to miss on the side of the roads. Their frequency is visibly more in the backwater regions. Most of these shops are dingy and rarely have anyone (especially women) other than locals taking a swig of the drink. Toddy is usually served with delicious beef fry, meen (fish) and tapioca. To see what this is all about, you can visit **Tharavadu Family Restaurant** (p105), a toddy shop converted into an 'all permitted' restaurant in Kumarakom.

Kream Korner
Restaurant   Multi-cuisine ₹₹
☎ 0477 2252781; www.
kreamkornerartcafe.com; Mullackal;
9am–10pm; mains ₹200–500 Kream
Korner is an art gallery and restaurant
rolled into one bright and spacious art

| Pick up these brightly coloured wooden
| masks as souvenirs or gifts

cafe. The constant buzz of travellers keeps the cafe alive at all times, many coming in to see the paintings based on local Kerala themes.

Sisir Palace   Multi-cuisine ₹₹
☎ 0477 2254100; www.sisirpalace.
com; north of boat jetty; 8.30am–
10pm; mains ₹200–500 The newly

constructed Sisir Palace serves both elaborate meals and snacks. Spacious and brightly lit, the cafe often teems with tourists as it's squeaky clean and has a decent selection on the menu. Stick to Kerala specialities.

Alleppey Prince Hotel   Multi-cuisine ₹₹
📞0477 2243752; www. alleppeyprincehotel.com; AS Road; 6.30am–10.30pm; mains ₹200–500 Grab a beer with your food at the Prince Hotel, just as you enter Alappuzha. This multi-cuisine restaurant has ample choices and a two-section seating arrangement; the one on the left is more conducive to families as it does not have a bar.

Indian Coffee House   Coffee Shop ₹
📞18004251125; www. indiancoffeehouse.com; Mullakkal outlet: 8am–9pm, mains below ₹200; Beachside outlet: noon–8pm, mains below ₹200 The nostalgic air and turbaned waiters of the oldest national coffee establishment has had both locals and visitors filling up its cool blue-walled interiors for the last 52 years. Apart from the near-perfect

coffee, try the rose milk, mutton cutlets and bread-butter-jam combos. The cafe also serves beef fry which can be teamed up with dosa. Don't forget to pick up a sweet milk peda while paying at the counter.

🅰 Shopping

Pulickattil Handicrafts   Souvenirs
📞0477 2264558; www.pulickattil. com; boat jetty; 8am–8.30pm Alappuzha is far from being a shopper's paradise – there are very few options to pick up souvenirs and this one tops the sparse list. Find a plethora of wooden boat replicas, elephant heads, key chains and the much talked about Aranmula mirrors. These can range from ₹800–12,000 and are rarely stocked by shops.

Collections   Souvenirs
📞0477 2261434; Mullakkal; 9.30am–8pm A reasonable collection of brass, wooden and coir bric-a-bracs awaits you at Collections. Since the mementos here are not expensive, much of your time might be spent on deciding and picking up small trinkets for gifting friends and family.

 Snapshot: The umbrella war

The legendary umbrella rivalry between **Popy's** (📞 0477 251425; www.popy.in; PB No 4010, Iron Bridge; 9.30am–7.30pm) and **John's** (📞 0477 2253082; www. johnsindia.com; Iron Bridge PO; 9am–7.30pm) is rampant in the entire state. The two umbrella companies are owned by brothers, who have taken their business rivalry to heightened limits. Almost identical mascots and showrooms loudly claim each one's place on the street, often not too far from each other. For no credible reason, Popy's is regarded better by the locals.

Kumarakom

Sixteen kilometres west of Kottayam (p101), the backwater gem of Kerala, Kumarakom, lies on the shore of the Vembanad Lake. Despite its popularity on the travel map, Kumarakom's peaceful environs make it an extremely relaxing destination. A number of upscale resorts dot the landscape, and the exotic location works like a charm for honeymooners, families and bedazzled tourists who have never seen anything like it.

1 KUMARAKOM BIRD SANCTUARY

This well-maintained KTDC (Kerala Tourism Development Corporation) sanctuary draws a number of birds such as night herons, paradise fly-catchers, golden backed woodpeckers and more. You can spot these during a walk through the 2km trail, which leads up to three watchtowers at the edge of the lake.

Tourists enjoying a ride on the backwaters

Even if you arrive in low sighting season, the lush environs are therapeutic enough. Though most visitors choose to walk, there is a provision of a boat (₹550 per hour) to cruise the fringes of the sanctuary. The best time to visit is from January to June.
www.ktdc.com; Kumarakom North; Indian/foreigner/guides ₹30/100/300; 6am–5pm

❷ BAY ISLAND DRIFTWOOD MUSEUM
Spend some time with the inrepid Raji Punnoose and her collection of driftwood, acquired from the shores of the faraway Andaman Islands. A trip through her meticulously arranged wooden collection requires ample ingenuity to decipher the shapes of various animals. Of course, Raji is constantly close at hand to nudge you in the right direction.
☎09447464296; www.bayislandmuseum.com; Chakranpady; ₹50; 10am–5pm, Sun 11.30am–5pm

❸ BACKWATERS
Veer off the route and take your boat behind Windsor towards the Lighthouse. Most cruise boats tend to take you

Spot a wide variety of water birds at the Kumarakom Bird Sanctuary

straight to the C Block and R Block islands, where, typical of the Kuttanad region, the paddy is grown 2m below sea level. The other route is more scenic and refreshingly secluded.

❹ VAIKOM MAHADEV TEMPLE

Those interested in history and spiritual pursuits will find the 29km trip to the Shiva temple at Vaikom worth their while. In typical south Indian style, the massive walls enclose a spacious ground with the sanctum in the middle. Unusual to Hindu religious practice, this temple attracts both Shaivite and Vaishnavite devotees. If you happen to be in the region in the months of November or December, look out for the annual **Vaikkath Asthami festival**. Caparisoned elephants and grand celebrations are held for the entire day. Arrive in the evening at 7pm to see the evening aarti.

www.vaikomtemple.org; Vaikom; 4am–noon, 4.30–8.30pm

✓ Top Tip: Boat trips

If you are hiring an hourly boat, head to the government jetty point. Boats are available at ₹450 an hour but boatmen are open to bargaining depending on the season. Do not insist on being on the lake after 6pm as it's mandatory for larger boats to anchor on the sides to make way for fishing nets to be thrown in at night.

Detour: Kottayam

Only 14km away from Kumarakom, Kottayam is renowned for being the centre of Kerala's spice and rubber trade. Apart from the rubber plantations, you can also check out the following:

• **Churches:** The weathered white building, **Valiyapally Church** (8.30am–6pm) built in 1550, stands testimony to the historic migration of Syrian Knanaya Christians to India in 345 AD from Jerusalem. The other important church, **Cheriapally** or **St Mary's Orthodox Church** was built in 1579 (9am–6.30pm).

• **Thazhathangadi Houses & Juma Masjid** (5am–6pm): The row of traditional Kerala houses (150 years-old plus), along the Meenachil River is a picturesque stretch. The 1000-year-old Juma Masjid stands at the end of the road. Women are not allowed inside.

• **CVN Kalari** (☎09349501263; District Sports Council; Mon 6am–noon, 4–8pm): The famous CVN Kalari School holds kalaripayattu classes on Mondays at the city's stadium. You can attend the class to see young students learn this exciting martial arts form.

• **Bell Metal Workshop** (☎04822 226737; PP Road, Kuruvikkoodu): Learn about the painstaking craftsmanship of traditional lamps and vessels out of bell metal, a hard alloy made of copper and tin, at the Jayakumar Bell Metal workshop off the Pala–Kottayam road.

• **Alphonso Weaving Centre** (☎09387626216; Naithashala, Erattupetta–Pala Road, Malampara;

8am–8pm): Shopping for the classic Kerala white sari with gold border is even more fun if you get to see the weaving process closely. This is possible just off the Pala–Erattupetta Road where a family of weavers enthusiastically display and explain the weaving process.

• **Eating** For a meal, stop at **Fairmont** (☎0481 2569256; www.hotelfairmont.in; SH Mount PO; 11am–11.30pm; mains ₹500–750): in Kottayam town. There is a choice of buffet or a la carte options for both vegetarians and non-vegetarians. Don't forget to pick up some treats at the famous **Ann's Bakery** (☎0481 2585517; Shastri Road; 9am–8pm).

• **Accommodation** Stay at the **Teekoy Bungalow** (☎09846212438; www.nazaranitharavad.com; Teekoy; d non-AC/AC ₹8000/11,000): to get a feel of the rubber plantation business. This 80-year-old British bungalow is 42km from Kottayam. It's atop a small hill, surrounded by frangipani trees, pineapple bushes and rubber thickets. Hosts Thressi and John are a treasure trove of knowledge.

Thazhathangadi Juma Masjid is one of the oldest mosques in India

If You Like: Backwater tours

Kettuvalams or houseboats are an architectural marvel and one can find basic to ultra-lavish accommodation. Peak season rates can be up to 25–30% higher. Do not hesitate to bargain and book ahead. Here are some of the top operators (incl of full board):

ALAPPUZHA

• **River & Country Tours** (☎0477 2253581; www.riverandcountry.com; No 13, Municipal Library Shopping Centre, opposite boat jetty; d from ₹6000): With a small but reliable fleet of five houseboats, the company is well regarded in the area.

• TOP CHOICE **Pulickattil Tourism Group** (☎0477 2264558; www.pulikattilbackwaters.com; Nehru Trophy Finishing Point; d from ₹6000): One of the top houseboat groups, Pulickattil has a troupe of one- to six-bedroom houseboats. Ask to see their construction boatyard.

• **Rainbow Cruises Backwaterworld** (☎0477 2261375; www.backwaterkerala.com; Green Shore Holidays & Resorts (P) Ltd, VCNB Road, opposite boat jetty; d from ₹9000): Over 12 years of experience,

25 kinds of houseboats plus classy aesthetics makes it a good option.

• **Marvel Cruise** (☎0477 264341; www.keralahotel.com; Mullakkal; d from ₹6000): Marvel has eight comfortable houseboats which promise great eco-friendly features.

• **Evergreen Tours** (☎0477 2763385; www.evergreen-kerala.com; Room No 709, St Thomas Church Building, Pallathuruthy; d ₹7500–13,000): Years of cruising and 14 houseboats makes Evergreen a fitting choice for the backwaters. The interiors are neat and the staff well versed with the region.

• **Lakes & Lagoons** (☎0477 2266842; www.lakeslagoons.com; DTPC Building, Pallathuruthy; d from ₹6000): With a choice of 21 luxury houseboats, choose your own package. They have been honoured with an award by the Kerala State Tourism Department.

• **Tharavad House Boats** (☎0477 2244599; West of North Police Station; Sea View Ward; d from ₹6000): Tharavad organises long as well as short trips. You can use their services to go till Pathiramanal (p89).

KUMARAKOM

• **Eco Trails Kerala** (☎0481 2526201; www.ecotourskerala.com; Tharavadu Heritage Home; d from ₹6000): Eco Trails is definitely off-beat and Kence Georgey (owner) can chalk out a unique experience of the backwaters.

• **St Crispin Heritage Houseboat** (☎0481 2524314; www.kodianthara.com; Kodianthara; d ₹6000–12,000) All three boats in Mr Crispin's fleet are cheerfully furnished and comfortable.

There are houseboat packages for various budgets

Accommodation

Coconut Lagoon   Resort ₹₹₹

0481 2525834; www.cghearth.
com; d ₹16,300–31,000 (incl of
breakfast and taxes) A CGH Earth
initiative, Coconut Lagoon embodies
the true essence of Kerala in a lavish
avatar. Traditionally dressed staff,
authentically styled cottages, a
kalaripayattu (martial art form) rink,
yoga pavilion and a maze of canals in
the lush property makes this a great
choice for those who want to soak in a
luxurious version of local Kerala living.

Vivanta by Taj   Resort ₹₹₹

0481 2525711; www.vivantabytaj.
com; 1/404 Kumarakom; d
₹12,500–24,000 (incl of breakfast)
Replete with history, the 140-year-old
structure has secured a spot as one of
the best hotels at Kumarakom with its
inventive cottages, including one with
a private pool. The 28-room property
overlooking Vembanad Lake offers
warm personalised service, yet has
all the trappings of a five-star hotel,
namely wi-fi, swimming pool, in-house
restaurant and well-planned activities
for the guests.

Philipkutty's Farm   Homestay ₹₹₹

04829 276530; www.
philipkuttysfarm.com; Pallivathukal,
Ambika Market PO, Vechoor; d
regular/peak season ₹12,500/15,000
(incl of full board) Ferry across a
hyacinth-carpeted wide canal to
six independent and artistically
styled Kerala villas at the edge of

Coconut Creek provides
Kerala living in style

Vembanad Lake. Delicious local food,
a lovely coconut plantation and the
backwaters complement charming
frangipani trees in the middle of
an open courtyard in front of each
cottage. Having run the luxury farm
stay for more than 13 years, the hosts
have certainly notched up hospitality
standards with their attention to detail
and lovely company.

Kumarakom Lake Resort   Resort ₹₹₹

0481 2524900; www.thepaul.
in; Kumarakom North; d
₹12,500–17,500, ste ₹48,000 (incl
of breakfast) Kumarakom Lake
Resort offers all premium services
like a swimming pool, wi-fi, stylish
cottages and a well-packaged 'Kerala'
experience with houseboats and
Ayurveda treatments at the Ayurmana
Spa. You can also enjoy local snacks at
Thattukada, the in-house street food
joint, in the evenings (4.30–6pm).

Zuri Resort ₹₹₹

☎ 0481 2527272; www.thezurihotels.
com; V235 A1 to A54, Karottukayal;
d ₹7500–35,000 (incl of breakfast)
Zuri's 72 rooms guarantee a high-
energy ambience with plenty of other
guests on activity-packed itineraries.
To relax, head straight to the pool or
the Maya Spa and get pampered by
traditional Kerala treatments or Thai/
Swedish massages. You can also use
the wi-fi facility.

Cruise 'N Lake Homestay ₹

☎ 0481 2525804; www.
homestaykumarakom.com;
Puthenpura Tourist Enclave; d
non-AC/AC ₹1500/2000 As any
estate agent will tell you, it's all
about location, location, location.
Crowning the tip of a small peninsula
surrounded by backwaters on one side
and a lawn of rice paddies on the other,
this is the ideal affordable getaway.
The rooms are plain, but it's lovely
and secluded out here, surrounded by
bucolic villages where houseboats are
made by hand. To get to it, go several
kilometres past the sanctuary and

| A 143-year-old house is now Tharavad
Heritage Home

take a left, it's then 2km down a dirt
road. Management can arrange pick-
ups from Kottayam, and houseboats
are available from here.

Kodianthara
Heritage Farm House Homestay ₹

☎ 9495333849; www.kodianthara.
com; Kumarakom PO, Vechoor; d
non-AC/AC ₹2000/2500 (incl of
breakfast) The sunny nadumuttam
(central courtyard) encircled by
the cosy refurbished rooms is the
most popular spot of this 160-year-
old house. The carefully preserved
structure, with a granary and old
portraits, is a pleasure for history
lovers. Traditional food, a canal running
inside the house, a backwater cruise
and an idyllic village setting are the
highlights of the property.

Coconut Creek Homestay ₹

☎ 0481 2524203; www.
coconutcreek.co.in; near Nazareth
Church; d non-AC/AC ₹1750/2250
(incl of breakfast) The sprawling
garden, a canal passing through the
house and clean rooms with modern
bathrooms make for a wonderful stay
with a local family. Do chat with your

Traditional Kerala food is served on a banana leaf

hosts for local information. Only three rooms of the heritage house are let out for guests, ensuring that there is privacy. Moreover, the lakefront is less than five minutes away by foot.

Tharavad Heritage Home   Resort ₹
0481 2525230; www. tharavaduheritage.com; near Boat Jetty; d ₹950–2500 (incl of breakfast) The fact that one gets to stay in a house built in 1870 at a moderate price is reason enough to ignore the slightly dowdy but cheerful service. Identified as a landmark in town, it's conveniently located near the government boat jetty. Since the resort gets a steady stream of north Indian guests, the staff is well-versed in preparing an assortment of dishes.

 Eating

KTDC Waterscapes   Multi-cuisine ₹₹₹
0481 2525861; www. waterscapeskumarakom.com;

Kumarakom North; 7.30am–9.30pm; mains ₹500–700 The enthralling view of Vembanad Lake from this glass-and-wood restaurant will make you want to stretch your lunch for many hours here. Built on stilts, the structure overlooks the hyacinth-clad calm waters for miles and miles. Reasonable veg and non-veg multi-cuisine food is served here.

Dubai Hotel   Kerala Meals ₹₹
0481 2525821; Anna Centre; 9am–9pm; mains ₹250–500 You cannot miss the big red signs of Dubai Hotel as you enter Kumarakom town and it is without doubt the best place to grab a local Kerala meal. Vegetarians will not find an exhaustive menu here but can manage.

Tharavadu Family Restaurant   Kerala Meals ₹
Kavanattinkara; 9am–9pm; mains less than ₹250 This local toddy shop optimistically stretched out to become a family restaurant, has few takers for the latter. However, it certainly is an interesting concept where the entrepreneur has tried to elevate the local beverage to a legitimate status for families!

 Shopping

Old Curiosity Shop   Souvenirs
0481 2526160; Tourist Complex, Cheepumkal; 9am–6pm Pick up small bric-a-brac or more elaborate antiques from Liji's shop, just off the main Kumarakom road. You will find old lamps, wooden artefacts, period furniture and spices.

Kollam

Highlights

1. Ashtamudi Backwaters & Munroe Island
2. Kollam Beach & Mahatma Gandhi Park
3. Thangaserry Fishing Village & Lighthouse
4. Neendakara Fishing Harbour
5. Thirumullavaram Beach
6. Oachira Parabrahma Temple
7. Amritapuri
8. Alumkadavu
9. Sasthamkotta Lake and Temple

The calm waterways of Ashtamudi Lake

Of all the spice trade junctions on the southwestern coast, Kollam (Quilon) was exalted by ancient travellers like Marco Polo and Ibn Batuta. The Arabs, Chinese and later Portuguese, Dutch and British made a beeline for this commercial hub to tap on cashew resources. Traces of a bustling seaport can still be seen in the town, with an active industry focused on fishing, coir making and, lately, tourism.

1 ASHTAMUDI BACKWATERS & MUNROE ISLAND

The backwaters of the Ashtamudi Lake are the main highlight of Kollam. Compared to Alappuzha and Kumarakom, these are virtually untouched; there is little houseboat traffic here and you can peacefully enjoy the rural scenery on the banks. The 16km long stretch of the lake has eight channels covering 30% of the town. There are 10 islands in the lake, of which Munroe is the most famous. The district tourism department has convenient day-and night-long tours of the lake, which one can board from the District Tourism Promotion Council (DTPC jetty). Chinese nets sprawl over the lake, fishermen are at work and boat-building yards are bustling as you cruise along. There is a range of trips that one can take, of which the day-long one (with food served on the boat) is most practical and popular. Private boats are a tad better, such as Dream Cruise (☎09048871486).

Top Tip: Backwater circuit

A visit to Kollam completes the backwater circuit, which starts in Alappuzha and makes its way through hundreds of kilometres of lakes, estuaries and canals. In fact, you can also take the eight-hour-long (10.30am–6.30pm; ₹300) cruise to Alappuzha to get your fill of the backwaters.

0474 2745625; www.dtpckollam.com; near KSRTC bus stand; Munroe cruise ₹400 per person; 9am–1.30pm, 2–6.30pm

② KOLLAM BEACH & MAHATMA GANDHI PARK

Kollam Beach is good to drive by or take a walk in the evening to see the sunset, but it's not awfully clean. Swimming here is not recommended as the sea is a little rough. The beach remains alive late into the evening with a children's park on one edge and food stalls along a short stretch. The park is well lit and it has a few easy rides to keep the young ones engaged.

Beach Road; ₹5; 9am–9pm

③ THANGASERRY FISHING VILLAGE & LIGHTHOUSE

Colourful fishing boats line the sandy banks of this village stretch, ending in the Thangaserry Fort, a historical landmark of the trading era with the Portuguese, British and Dutch. The 18th-century fort now stands crumbling at the end of the beach. Slightly further down is the 144ft-high lighthouse, which is surprisingly well kept. A climb up the 193 steps will give you a breathtaking view of the sea and surrounding areas; the sunset vista from here is enchanting.

Thangaserry Point Lighthouse; Indian/foreigner/camera/video ₹10/25/20/25; 3–5pm

④ NEENDAKARA FISHING HARBOUR

Arrive by 7am at the harbour to watch the frantic activity of fishing

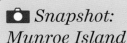 *Snapshot: Munroe Island*

The island is named after the British Resident, Colonel Munroe, who was instrumental in making the canals that branch out from the lake.

boats coming in, fishermen sorting the catch and busy distributors leaving with their fresh stock for sale. It might be an olfactory challenge but you will soon get accustomed to the smell. The harbour makes for great photo opportunities and you can really feel the vibe of a busy port town here.

Neendakara Fishing Harbour; suggested visiting hrs 7–8.30am); parking ₹20

❺ THIRUMULLAVARAM BEACH

A refreshingly quiet but small stretch of beach, perfect to get away from the crowded alternative at Kollam. Thirumullavaram is just 6km from the town and has a kalyani (pool) right behind it, usually full of local children.

❻ OACHIRA PARABRAHMA TEMPLE

Thirty two kilometres from Kollam, Oachira may at first seem like a small dusty town but the unique idol-and-structure-less temple here is sure to amaze you. A large ground ends in two trees around which devotees pray with a small wooden doll in hand (dosh doll), which apparently is said to help you atone for your sins. A small selection of these dolls lies with the officiating priests who mechanically hand them over to devotees before a circumambulation around the tree. Two annual festivals – Ochirakkali (May/June) and Panthrandu Vilakku (Nov/Dec) – have the temple ground teeming with devotees from all over south India.

Oachira village; open 24 hrs

❼ AMRITAPURI

You'll be greeted with a warm therapeutic hug from spiritual guru Mata Amritanandamayi Devi here. Amma, as she is fondly known the world over, is engaged in an impressive amount of charitable work in the areas of healthcare, disaster relief, education and social welfare. If you take a tour of her seaside ashram at Amritapuri (33km from Kollam) you can participate in meditation, chanting and bhajans (from as early as 5am). Queue up before 9am for the famous hug if she is in town. Amma's travel and discourse schedule is displayed on the website of the efficiently run establishment.

📞0476 2897578; www.amritapuri.org; Amritapuri

⑧ ALUMKADAVU

One of the highlights around Kollam is the small village of Alumkadavu, where the main occupations are coir making and boat building. Kishore (📞9497364263) is pleased to show his boat building yard to wandering guests. You can club this destination with the Oachira temple and Mata Amritanandamayi's Ashram.

⑨ SASTHAMKOTTA LAKE AND TEMPLE

This is the largest freshwater lake in Kerala. It lies 29km from Kollam and can be reached by ferry or road. It's the main source of drinking water here, owing to the presence of a unique larva called chaoborus in it that destroys bacteria. At the edge of the lake stands the ancient Sasthamkotta Temple dedicated to Lord Ayyappa.

Sasthamkotta; 4am–8pm

Elevated view of the coast, Kollam

Accommodation

Raviz   **Resort ₹₹₹**

📞0474 2751111; www.theraviz.
com; Thevally, Mathilil PO; d
₹11,000–22,000, ste ₹30,000 (incl of
breakfast) The latest addition to the
handful of 5-star properties in Kollam,
Raviz is a lavish Kerala-themed hotel at
the edge of Ashtamudi Lake. An easy-
to-miss lane leads to the grand facade
of Kathakali statues and a snake boat
replica in the lobby. The plush rooms
overlook the backwaters and are
equipped with all the mod cons. Don't
hesitate to ask for discounts, as the
rates vary according to the season and
you may be lucky enough to get a good
deal if the management wants to fill
the 93 rooms.

Club Mahindra, Backwater
Retreat Ashtamudi   **Resort ₹₹₹**

📞0476 2884000; www.
clubmahindra.com; Chavara South;
d ₹7000–15,000 (incl of breakfast)
Ashtamudi Lake provides a brilliant
backdrop to the Club Mahindra
property at Chavara. In typical
Mahindra style, the Backwater Retreat
experience is chock-a-block with
activities for children, making it an
excellent choice for families. If you
are feeling especially indulgent, book
a floating cottage for your family.
A multitude of cruise, boating and
sightseeing day trips are listed in the
games room and can be arranged by
the management.

The Quilon Beach Hotel   **Hotel ₹₹**

📞0472 2769999; www.
thequilonbeachhotel.com; on
the beach; d ₹6450–7450, ste
₹9450–18,950 (incl breakfast) All

TOP CHOICE *Ayurvedic*
rejuvenation

Santhigiri (📞0474 2763014; www.
santhigiriashram.org; Residency
Road, Kadappakada; treatments
from ₹1000) is one of the most
authentic establishments for
Ayurvedic treatment in Kerala,
both for long-term and short
rejuvenation packages. The facility
is not extravagant, but it is clean
and the masseurs are well trained.

✓ *Top Tip: Bite of nostalgia on Main Street*

There are few stand-alone eateries in Kollam and all the suggested hotels have
decent multi-cuisine restaurants. However, there are a few establishments
on **Main Street,** some hailing from the 1940s, that are the highlight in Kollam
market. Vegetarian establishments **Padma** and **Guruprasad** (📞0474 2741 359,
7am–9.30pm) were set up in the 1960s and still retain the old charm with bright
blue walls and sturdy wooden furniture. **Hotel Azad** (1940), near Guruprasad,
serves both vegetarian and non-vegetarian food. **Indian Coffee House** (1965,
8am–9.30pm), on the opposite side of the street, has its classic nostalgic feel
and is great to relax after a day of sightseeing.

📷 *Snapshot:*
Erstwhile cashew country

| Local women separating the nut from the
| shell in a cashewnut factory

The moniker 'cashew country' seems inappropriate for Kollam in the present day. Cashew plantations and processing units are fast disappearing from the topography, leaving behind a faint memory of what used to be a robust item for trading. With land and labour prices soaring, cashew cultivation is not considered lucrative anymore. Even though it's difficult to see any cultivation close to Kollam you can still buy processed cashew easily at **Vijayalaxmi Cashew Company** (📞0474 2741391) and the Kochupilammoodu area in town.

the rooms at The Quilon Beach Hotel offer a fabulous view of the Arabian Sea. Apart from the musty carpets in the hallway, the rooms, lobby, restaurant and 24-hour coffee shop are decent. The staff is extremely helpful in arranging day trips to nearby sightseeing destinations. There is a swimming pool and wi-fi here.

Nani   **Hotel ₹**
📞**0474 2751141; www.hotelnani. com; opposite Clock Tower,**

Chinnakada; d ₹1850–3250 (incl of breakfast) This boutique business hotel comes as a surprise in Kollam's busy centre, and is of exceptionally good value. Built by a cashew magnate, it is gorgeously designed and mixes traditional Kerala elements and modern lines for an appealing look. Since there aren't many places to eat in town, the in-house restaurant serves a reasonable spread of multi-cuisine food. The hotel also has wi-fi facilities.

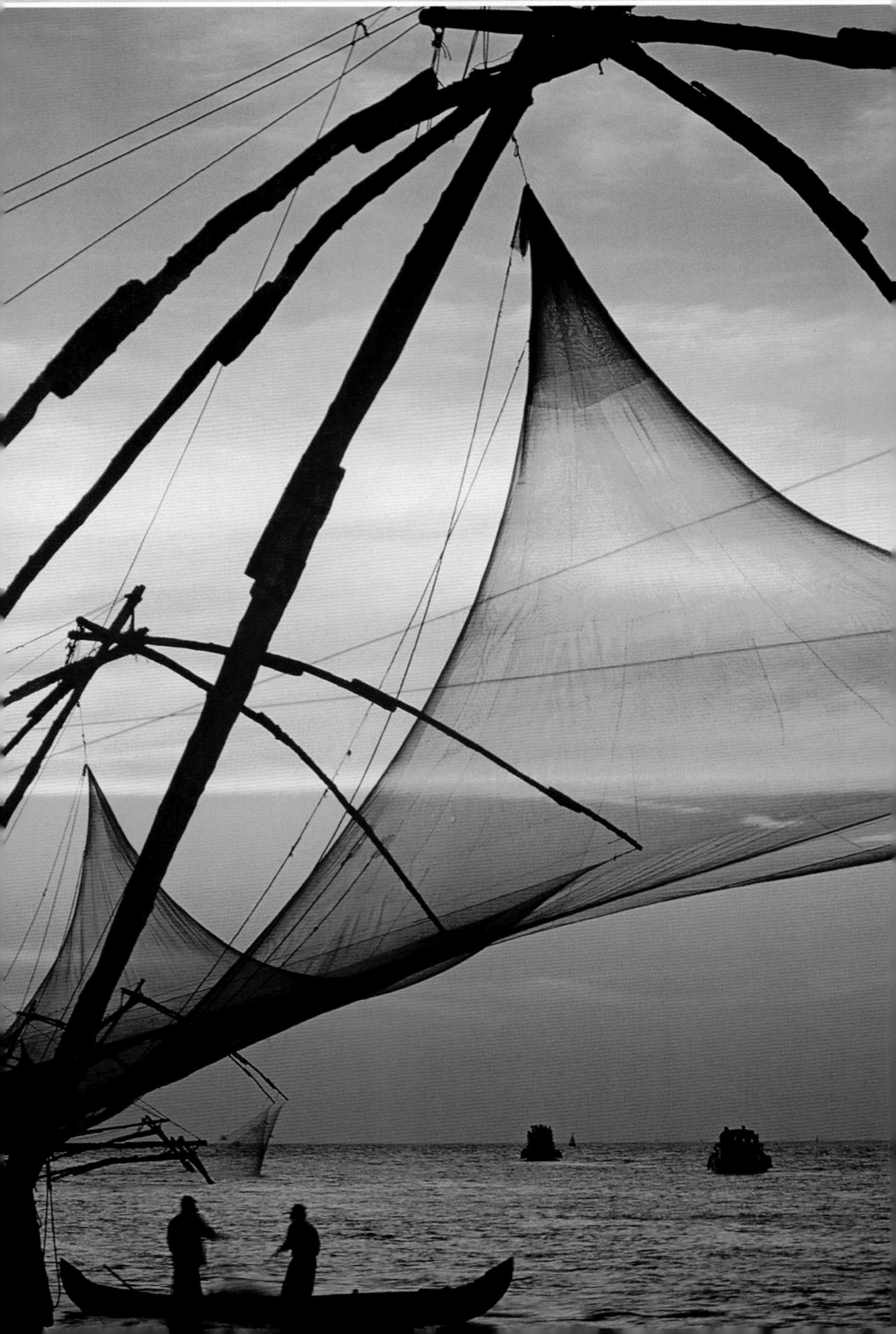

Kochi & Around

Why Go?

Serene Kochi (Ernakulam, Fort Korchi and a knot of tiny islands) has been drawing traders and explorers to its shores for over 600 years. Nowhere in India could you find such a cultural mix. Thrissur is the cultural hub of Kerala where performing arts flourish and Guruvayur is famous its centuries-old Sree Krishna Temple.

Getting There & Away

Air: Cochin International Airport, the most convenient air node for the region, is well connected to all the main cities of the country. Frequent flights are available by major carriers such as Air India, IndiGo, Go Air, Jet Airways and SpiceJet.

Bus: For overnight rides from Bengaluru, Mangalore, and Chennai, book Volvo buses from private operators. They may cost 75% higher than government services but are very comfortable. From Bengaluru, Karnataka State Road Transportation Corporation (KSRTC) services are timely and reasonably priced.

Train: Ernakulam has two stations – Ernakulam Town and the Ernakulam Junction – both linking it to several major cities. The *Kerala Express* (12626) from Delhi, *Kanyakumari Express* (16381) from Mumbai and the *Ernakulam Express* (12677) from Bengaluru run daily. Thrissur and Guruvayur are also well connected through Ernakulam, via multiple trains plying within the region. Check for train timetables and schedules on www.irctc.co.in.

Chinese fishing nets are a unique contraption seen only in Kerala

Top Highlights

1 Dutch Palace, Mattancherry

Though the Portuguese built it for the Raja of Kochi, the palace eventually landed in Dutch hands and was rechristened Dutch Palace (p134). Today, this is a museum hosting galleries and royal artefacts. The star attractions are the beautifully preserved murals depicting scenes from the *Ramayana*, *Mahabharata* and Puranic legends in intricate detail.

2 Pardesi Synagogue, Mattancherry

A graceful clocktower looming over the streets of Mattancherry signals the iconic Pardesi Synagogue (p134). Originally built in 1568, this synagogue was partially destroyed by the Portuguese in 1662, and rebuilt two years later when the Dutch took Kochi. It features an ornate gold pulpit and elaborate hand-painted, willow-pattern floor tiles from Canton, which were added in 1762. It's magnificently illuminated by chandeliers from Belgium and coloured glass lamps.

3 Chinese Fishing Nets, Fort Kochi

Chinese fishing nets (p131) against the orange sky is possibly one of the most picturesque panoramas Fort Kochi has to offer. Vasco Square erupts into a flurry of activity starting at the crack of dawn – teams of four to five fishermen labour over a row of elaborate spiderlike contraptions which descend into the sea every 15 minutes and scoop up kilos of seafood. Sit close by and watch this enigmatic sight for hours.

4 Kerala Kalamandalam, Thrissur

Founded in 1930, the Kerala Kalamandalam (p144), or school of performing arts in Thrissur makes an interesting stopover. The most popular activity here is 'A Day With the Masters' where you get to see famous teachers and their disciples in class. It's a guided tour by the institution's staff and is time well spent as you learn about the various art forms particular to this region. You are likely to see Kathakali, Kootiattam, Thullal and Mohiniyattam classes in progress.

5 Guruvayur Sree Krishna Temple

A remarkable hallmark of Hindu devotion, this Vishnu temple (p142) cannot be missed. It's the fourth largest temple of India and second richest in Kerala, so get ready to join the crawling line of hundreds of devotees to get a glimpse of the deity. The devotional zeal is quite contagious.

Local Knowledge
A nostalgic gastronomic trail

Priyadarshini Sharma, chief sub-editor of *The Hindu* in Cochin, she recommends some of her favourite long-standing joints in Fort Kochi and Ernakulam.

• **Quality Bakery** (☎09995156615; Pattalam; 7am–9.30pm; mains less than ₹100): Keeping years of culinary history alive, the dingy, humble bakery in Pattalam is the only place where one can taste the famous Dutch bruder bread. The sugar plum brown loaves come out of the oven regularly on Saturdays, but have to be ordered Monday to Fridays.

• **Kayees Hotel** (☎0484 2226080; New Road, Mattancherry; 5.15am–9pm; mains ₹100–200): Yet another notable gastronomic stop is this famous biryani joint, also known as Rahmatulla Hotel. Tucked away in the Kutchi Memon area of Mattancherry, it should be visited before 12.30pm, as stocks deplete at breakneck speed. You may have to strain your eyes to find a little memento (a small painting of a horse) by MF Husain on the

cluttered wall, but his classic style is immediately recognisable.

• **Shantilal S Mithaiwala** (☎0484 2229860; opposite Gujarati High School, Gujarati Road; 8.30am–9.30pm; mains less than ₹100): If you are craving for some delicious rich Gujarati snacks, visit the legendary khandvi and gathiya maker of Fort Kochi. The evenings see it packed with other hungry shoppers.

• **Onasadya at Sarovaram, BTH** (☎09946103081; NH 47, Cochin Bypass, Maradu PO; noon–3pm; mains ₹500–750): For an authentic Onam banquet, visit Sarovaram's in-house restaurant in Ernakulam. If you are going at the time of the festival (August), ensure that you book in advance. The food here is worth the wait.

Dutch bruder bread is available at Quality Bakery, Pattalam

Kochi & Around

Kochi is a cluster of islands and mainland **Ernakulam**, the hectic transport and commercial hub. The historical towns of **Fort Kochi** and **Mattancherry** remain redolent with the past. The other major places of interest in this sector are **Thrissur** and **Guruvayur**, 83 and 95km north of Ernakulam, respectively. Thrissur's temple festival, Thrissur Pooram, is unforgettable, while Sree Krishna Temple in Guruvayur, the second richest temple in the state, pulsates with religious intensity.

▌ A tourist admires the old-style chandeliers
▌ in the Pardesi Synagogue

GETTING AROUND THE REGION

• **Bus:** Red non-AC buses, operated by KSRTC (Kerala State Road Transport Corporation), speeding through town, are a common sight. These have great connectivity to destinations within Kerala. The Ernakulam bus stand is just off MG Road and has frequent buses to Thrissur and Guravayur.

• **Taxi:** If you want a more comfy ride, book a taxi to take you around the region. This may cost you between ₹8–12 per km, plus daily driver bata and tolls.

• **Train:** More than 70 trains ply on the Ernakulam-Thrissur route, covering the distance in less than two hours. Four daily trains run between Ernakulam and Guravayur as well, but most travellers take the train till Thrissur and do the Thrissur–Guruvayur stretch of 33km by road.

Kochi

You need some orientation to the cluster of islands that make Kochi (formerly Cochin), before you start the trip. **Ernakulam**, the district, and also the urban centre on the mainland, is chock-a-bloc with residential areas and narrow roads bursting with prosperous businesses. Stop here for the museums and a hearty fill of shopping. Lying close to the mainland, but joined by bridges, are the small islands of Willingdon (mostly government offices), **Fort Kochi** and **Mattancherry** (the tourist hub), **Bolgatty** and **Vypeen**.

Fort Kochi and Mattancherry have an easy, rustic charm about them, with breezy open-air cafes serving top-notch seafood, narrow history-filled streets and a burgeoning art scene.

Highlights
❶ **Ernakulam**
❷ **Fort Kochi & Mattancherry**

GETTING AROUND

• **Bus:** Plenty of local buses connect Ernakulam to Willingdon, Fort Kochi and Mattancherry. A ride will cost less than ₹20.

• **Taxi/Autorickshaw:** Taking a taxi between Ernakulam and Fort Kochi is unnecessary when there are convenient buses and the ferry, but if you must, it will cost you ₹8–12 per km. Autorickshaws take between ₹150–200.

• **Ferry:** All islands of Kochi are connected by ferry but one is likely to use the Ernakulam–Fort Kochi (Customs) and Mattancherry route the most. The service, every 20 minutes, starts at 6.30am and ends at 9.30pm. The cost is a mere ₹2.50 per head.

• **Private Boats:** There are a few private boat operators at the Ernakulam Jetty. These take up to 12–15 people and cost ₹1000 for four hours.

Ernakulam

Ernakulam might as well have been the capital of Kerala with its urban character and commercial significance. Bursting out of its narrow streets is a chaotic mix of unruly traffic, Lego-like residential areas and official buildings. This hectic transport and cosmopolitan hub serves as a good stopover for shopping and a quick dose of culture. For a more heritage-filled holiday atmosphere, head to Fort Kochi, but try and spend some time at Ernakulam to see the **Kerala Folklore Museum** and the **Durbar Hall Art Centre**, and also take in the pleasures of a walk around **Marine Drive** and the shoping centre at MG Road.

Highlights

❶ Kerala Folklore Museum
❷ Hill Palace Museum
❸ Sri Poornathrayeesha Temple
❹ Durbar Hall Art Centre
❺ Ernakulam Shiva Temple (Ernakulathappan Temple)
❻ Marine Drive
❼ Edappally Church
❽ Museum of Kerala History
❾ Wonder La
❿ Cherai Beach
⓫ Ndanju Kadu (Crab Island)
⓬ Kodnad Elephant Camp

❶ KERALA FOLKLORE MUSEUM

Here lies an incredible private collection of traditional masks, theatrical costumes, artefacts, sculptures and art, packed into an absorbing three storeys. Better than many government establishments, the museum has more than 5000 artefacts and covers three architectural styles: Malabar, Kochi and Travancore. A visit here is time well spent. Check for classical dance performances at the beautiful wood-lined theatre; these take place sporadically, depending on daily bookings.

☏ 0484 2665452; www. keralafolkloremuseum.org; Thevara; ₹100; 9.30am–7pm

❷ HILL PALACE MUSEUM

Located 16km southeast of Ernakulam, this museum was formerly the residence of the Kochi royal family, and is an impressive 49-building palace complex. Leave your slippers outside and huddle up with other visitors to hear the guide's discourse on the 14 key exhibits, which are divided into ornaments, sculptures, artefacts, coins, weapons and more.

Avoid Sundays as it's a hot spot for locals and the queues are
rather long.
**Tripunithura; adult/child/camera/video ₹20/10/20/150;
9am–12.30pm and 2–4.30pm**

Marine Drive
is a popular
hangout for
the locals

❸ SRI POORNATHRAYEESHA TEMPLE
Twelve kilometres from the centre of town, the Sri
Poornathrayeesha Temple lies close to the Hill Museum at
Tripunithura.The temple is dedicated to Lord Vishnu and is
popular amongst childless devotees who come here to pray
for an offspring. It is also known for its small school that
teaches young boys the art of playing temple percussions. If
visiting around 4pm, you will hear the synchronised beating
of wooden blocks with sticks during the practice session.
4am–noon, 4–8.30pm

❹ DURBAR HALL ART CENTRE
Art lovers will appreciate local and international exhibitions
showcased at the Durbar Hall. Once owned by the Maharaja
of Kochi, the hall is a highly regarded venue for art shows.
The sprawling field outside also holds local sports and
cultural events.
Durbar Hall Road; ₹50; 10am–6pm

Caparisoned elephants during a festival at the Shiva Temple

❺ ERNAKULAM SHIVA TEMPLE (ERNAKULATHAPPAN TEMPLE)

Do visit the deity that looks after the city of Ernakulam in this temple, conveniently located within the Durbar Hall compound. Dedicated to Shiva, it was built in 1846 and patronised by the royal family. The large complex also accommodates a Hanuman and Murugan Temple, so one can see a daily congregation of devotees here.

Durbar Hall Road; 3–11.30am and 4–8pm

❻ MARINE DRIVE

Running parallel to Shanmugham Road (behind Bay Pride Mall), Marine Drive is perfect for a sunset stroll. As in every seaside town, local food carts, balloon vendors and couples cosying up behind black umbrellas are an integral part of the topography. Having undergone extensive refurbishment, the clean seafront benches now invite you for some harbour gazing – especially in the evenings as vessels become mere twinkling jewels in the distance.

❼ EDAPPALLY CHURCH

It's official name is St George's Syro-Malabar Catholic Forane Church. Built in 594, it is one of the oldest in Kerala. Make a quick stop to see the intricate facade and detailed architecture. The church is famous for a visit by Mother Teresa in 1994. The current church bell was installed to commemorate her visit; it is now a big tourist attraction.

Edappally; 4am–5pm

❽ MUSEUM OF KERALA HISTORY

The dome-shaped stone building at Edappally houses a well-maintained repository of information on Kerala's history, depicted in miniatures that are lit up as one walks around barefoot during a sound-and-light show. The museum also has a small display of dolls, a shop, gallery and,

◈ *Detour: Athirappally & Vazhachal Falls*

The famous Athirappally Waterfalls are a popular weekend tourist spot as they are just 64km from Ernakulam. You can choose to do a day trip here or make it part of a longer loop covering other destinations like Thrissur (p144) and Guruvayur (p142) as well. The falls provide a dramatic entrance to the Sholayar mountain range on the Western Ghats and have acquired the moniker 'The Niagara of India'. Lying 1000ft above the Chalakudy River, they provide a refreshing break from the city. The height of the falls is 80ft and are at their best just after the monsoons. Visitors are allowed to walk down to a bathing spot at a distance below. Needless to say, they have been a backdrop to many Malayalam and Hindi movies.

The **Vazhachal Falls** are 5km ahead on the same road, though not as picturesque. Since they lie within the forest area, it is not uncommon to see stray wildlife on the roads. Bison, deer and sometimes elephants are found crossing into the forest on the road leading to the falls (Forest Checkpost; 8am–5pm; adult/child/foreigner/camera ₹20/2/60/10).

If you are planning on staying a night here, stay at the comfy boutique resort facing the roaring Athirappally Falls. The **Rainforest** (📞09539078888; www.rainforest.in; Kannamkuzhy PO; d ₹10,500–18,500, tree house ₹11,500 incl of breakfast) property undoubtedly offers the best view in town (nine luxurious rooms and a tree house with a 180-degree view of the waterfalls), The in-house restaurant and the swimming pool area are located against the breathtaking backdrop. The hotel arranges a short walk within the property to the falls. If you want to stop here only for a short meal break, call ahead and make a booking.

A scenic snapshot of the Athirappally Waterfalls

most importantly, clean loos. A wonderful effort has been made in the detailed presentation by the Madhavan Nayar Foundation; even the tickets are aesthetically designed in the form of old palm leaves.

📞0484 2558296; www.artandkeralahistory.org; adult/child ₹100/30; 10am–5pm, Mon closed; no photography

9 WONDER LA 😊😊

The kids are going to love this famous amusement park away from the main city, and promising many happy memories. The park has water and dry rides with both high thrills and mild options. Be well prepared for the water park with a dress code of shorts, tees and appropriate swimwear. Avail student discounts with ID cards.

📞0484 2684001; www.wonderla.com; Pallikara, Kumarapuram; adult/child ₹460/360 (weekdays), ₹600/470 (weekends), ₹660/530 (peak season); 11am–6pm (weekdays), 11am–7pm (weekends)

10 CHERAI BEACH

A good 45-minute drive to the northwest of Ernakulam brings you to Cherai Beach at Vypeen Island. It's a long stretch, so you can bypass the line of snack shops and a

Tourists relaxing beneath colourful beach parasols, Cherai Beach

package-tour feel to find an isolated spot. Swimming here is not recommended. Though there are a handful of resorts to stay here, the quality and service is not great. The drive to the beach is marvellous, as the road is flanked by a glistening backwater lagoon.

⑪ NDANJU KADU (CRAB ISLAND)

The winding mangrove-filled backwaters of Poothotta River lie 24km from Ernakulam town. Earlier uninhabited, the island village now has eight fishing families who are happy to give insights into their lives and occupation; such as coir retting, fishing and toddy tapping. An exclusive trip can be arranged by Peter from **Salmon Travels** (☎09847217874; www.salmontours.com; H No 44/2016, Desabhimani Road, Friends Lane 4, Kaloor; ₹2000; 8.30am and 2.30 pm; taxi ₹1400 extra) that ensures a non 'package tour' experience; you should book ahead. This includes as two-and-a-half hour-long country boat ride in narrow canals flanked by ludicrously green surroundings. A local snack and coffee is also included in the price.

⑫ KODNAD ELEPHANT CAMP

The 36km ride from Ernakulam to Kodnad Elephant Camp is worth it if you are travelling with children and not planning on going to the **Guruvayur camp** (p142). Five adult elephants and two babies are part of this establishment that is run by the Forest Department. The highlight here is the morning bath given to the gentle giants at the edge of the Periyar River. You can even give the mahouts a hand and click photographs (you are expected to tip). The elephants then amble back with a trail of visitors to the camp where they are fed. Arrive before 8am to witness the entire spectacle.

☎0484 2649052; 8am–5pm; adult/child/camera/video ₹10/5/50/250

✓ Top Tip: Getting Oriented

The privately run travel helpdesk next to the Ernakulam Ferry Point is of great help if you want specific details of ferries or places to visit. Mr Varghese (☎09847044688) who has been running the place for over 20 years is patient and friendly. Most of all, he is accurate in his advice.

 Accommodation

The Taj Gateway   Hotel ₹₹₹
☎0484 6673300; www.tajhotels. com; Marine Drive; d ₹9500–11,500, ste ₹16,000 (incl of breakfast)
One of the older establishments in Ernakulam, The Taj Gateway offers seaview rooms, impeccable hospitality and comforts like an in-house spa, pool and wi-fi facility. The sightseeing trips organised by the hotel are well researched and efficiently run.

Dream   Hotel ₹₹₹
☎0484 4129999; www. dreamcochin.com; SA Road, Elamkulam Junction; d ₹12,000– 13,000, ste ₹14,000–25,000 (incl of breakfast) The glitzy new hotel in town has garnered quite a reputation with its modern decor, luxurious rooms and friendly staff. With four in-house restaurants and comfortable lounge spaces, you needn't step out for meals. The hotel also has a pool and wi-fi facility.

Bolgatty Palace Heritage   KTDC Hotel ₹₹₹
☎0484 2750500; www. bolgattypalacekochi.com; Bolgatty Island, Mulavukadu; ste ₹13,300 (incl of breakfast) The only reason to make a trip to the Bolgatty Island off Ernakulam is the Kerala Tourism Development Corporation (KTDC) – run heritage hotel. An erstwhile Dutch mansion built in 1744, it has an unmatchable location. Golf enthusiasts will like its proximity to the Golf Club of Cochin.

Grand Hotel   Hotel ₹₹
☎ 0484 2382061; www. grandhotelkerala.com; MG Road; d ₹3000–4200, ste ₹4500 (incl of breakfast) A landmark on MG Road, the Grand Hotel is known for its 1960s classic construction. The in-house restaurant (The Grand Pavilion) serves excellent Kerala food and is the top choice for many travellers. Stay here to be in the central part of the city and enjoy unobtrusive hospitality.

Travancore Court   Hotel ₹₹
☎0484 2351120; www. travancorecourt.com; Warriam Road, opposite Lotus Club; ste ₹5000–6000 (incl of breakfast) The plush Travancore Court promises a comfortable stay in the heart of town, just a parallel lane away from the arterial MG Road. The supposed colonial theme of the hotel is easy

| Travancore Court is at the heart of Ernakulam

Idlis and vadas are common breakfast items across the state

to miss, but one can appreciate the polite staff and the choice of luxurious rooms. There is a pool and wi-fi facility.

Abad Plaza   Hotel ₹₹
☎ 0484 2381122; www.abadhotels.com; MG Road; d ₹3500-3750, ste ₹5000 (incl of breakfast) Conveniently located on the arterial MG Road in Ernakulam, Abad Plaza is just 2km from the railway station and is also close to the town's shopping hub. Other facilities include wi-fi, swimming pool, Ayurveda spa, fitness centre, two in-house restaurants and travel assistance.

Times Square Business   Hotel ₹
☎ 0484 2374488; www.timesquarehotel.in; Club Road, near Collector's Camp Office; d ₹2000–2700 (incl of breakfast) Times Square is a good choice if you are looking for a clean and comfortable stop in the heart of the city. The hotel

is parallel to MG Road, it's peaceful and yet walking distance from the shopping hub.

Hotel Aiswarya   Hotel ₹
☎ 0484 2364454; www.aiswaryahotels.com; Warriam Road, Opposite Lotus Club; d ₹2100–2700 (incl of breakfast) Hotel Aiswarya is a good choice if you're looking for a clean budget stay near MG Road. It's walking distance from the shopping hub and good enough for a night's stay. The restaurant is, however, dingy, so you might want to hop across the road to the busy Sree Krishna Inn (p127) for delicious meals.

Eating

Sree Krishna Inn   South Indian ₹₹
☎ 0484 2366664; Warriam Road; 8am–11pm; mains ₹250–500; No matter what time you arrive, Sree Krishna Inn is likely to be buzzing. The busy scenario is testimony to the quality of food and atmosphere here. Breakfast and tiffin items are a

| Kerala is one of the best places for
| variety in gold jewellery

favourite. A fresh garden frontage, old wooden furniture and brilliant food will keep you wanting for more. Don't miss this one!

Coffee Beanz   Coffee Shop ₹₹
📞0484 3292229; No 40/2964, opp Pioneer Tower Shanmugham Road; 12.30–3.30pm, 7.30–10.30pm; mains ₹250–500 Step in for some delicious appam and stew or beef fry at this cheerfully bright cafe on Shanmugham Road. The cafe is known for its reasonable prices and scrumptious mix of both local and urban cuisines.

Dwaraka Restaurant Multi Cuisine ₹₹
📞0484 2383236; MG Road;

7am–10.30pm; mains ₹250–500 This old run-down joint deserves a visit purely for its nostalgic atmosphere and authentic Kerala food.

Pai Brothers   South Indian ₹
📞0484 2374879; Pai Brothers Line, MG Road; 9am–1.30am; mains ₹100–200 There are 187 types of the south Indian staple – the dosa, of which 36 are supposedly copyrighted by Pai Brothers. The 'thattil kutty' (small) dosa is really popular. This joint is hard to miss because of its bright yellow and red decor, even though it lies in a lane off MG Road.

Shopping
The main MG Road of Ernakulam is packed with gold jewellery and sari shops. If you are visiting during Onam or any shopping festival (Dec–Jan), expect heavy discounts.

Jayalakshmi   Saris
📞484 4299999; www.jayalakshmisilks.com; MG Road, Ernakulam; 9.30am–8.30pm One of the most renowned names for silk saris, the brand is more than 65 years old and promises a large collection of not only saris, but also branded clothing. The place is bustling with busy shoppers.

Kalyan Silks   Saris
📞0484 4081111; www.kalyansilks.com Hospital Road, near Maharaja's College, Ernakulam; 9am–9pm The sprawling six-storey Kalyan Silks store offers a variety of silk saris and

Indian branded garments. Needless to say, there is plenty of choice to suit all pockets.

Seematti   Saris

PB No 3651; MG Road, Ernakulam; 10am–9pm Originally a sari shop, Seematti now offers a range of garments over four floors, with a coffee shop inside the premises. This is a one-stop shop for authentic Kerala saris and dress materials.

Karalkada   Saris

0484 2352911; Opposite TD Temple Gate, MG Road; 9.30am–9pm Mon–Sat, 9.30am–8pm Sun The clean, spacious and minimal decor of this sari and dress material shop is soothing after the visual assault of all the regular sari and gold shops in Ernakulam. Visit here for the typical white with gold border saris, half saris and mundu (lungi).

Kasavu Kada   Saris

0484 2372395; Church Landing Road, Ernakulam; 9am–8pm, Sun closed If the focus of your buying spree is only traditional Kerala saris, then head straight to Kasavu Kada for a decent variety and prices.

Joyalukkas   Gold

0484 2350512; www.joyalukkas. com; Marine Drive; 9.30am–7.30pm A household name in Kerala, Joyalukkas is one of the top destinations for gold shopping. Visit here for a large assortment of contemporary and traditional designs.

Bhima   Gold

0484 2378382; MG Road; 10am–8pm Another name to reckon with for gold shopping is Bhima on MG Road. Locals will suggest this over other newer brands.

Josco   Gold

0484 2353295; www.joscogroup. com; MG Road; 10am–7.30pm Josco is definitely one of the places to visit if you are looking for variety in designs and if the cost of gold jewellery is not a concern.

Kairali   Handicrafts

0484 2354507; www. keralahandicrafts.in; MG Road, Ernakulam; 9am–8pm, Sun closed Do not be disappointed with the dowdy exterior of the government-run Kairali showroom – this is actually the best place for handicrafts and souvenirs. You can pick from an assortment of Ravi Varma miniature paintings (copies of course), brass bric-a-brac and souvenirs made from coconut husk.

Lulu Mall   Mall

0484 2727777; www.lulumall.in; 34/1000, N.H 47, Edapally; 10am-10pm Whet your appetite for shopping at the recently opened Lulu Mall. It is India's largest mall which is spread over 2.5 million sq ft of space. The mall consists of more than 300 outlets including restaurants, entertainment zones, a nine-screen multiplex as well as a large ice skating rink and a 12 lane bowling alley. It has all the top international brands that are in vogue.

Fort Kochi & Mattancherry

The most captivating of Kochi's pack of islands, Fort Kochi and Mattancherry are a heady mix of well-preserved colonial history, a lively art scene, boutique hotels, exceptional seafood and elements that are still reminiscent of Kerala's indigenous culture. An influx of Western travellers over the years has moulded the harbour town into a haven of English-speaking, perfect-pasta-serving inhabitants, and antiques oozing from every shop. But this has served well for Indian tourists as well; it's safe, clean, and language is not a problem at all. Equip yourself with comfortable walking shoes and a map and discover the narrow streets.

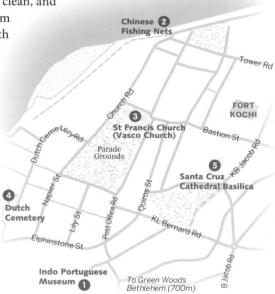

Highlights

1. Indo Portuguese Museum
2. Chinese Fishing Nets
3. St Francis Church (Vasco Church)
4. Dutch Cemetery
5. Santa Cruz Cathedral Basilica
6. Southern Naval Command Maritime Museum (off map)
7. Dhobi Ghat (off map)
8. Thirumala Devaswom Temple (off map)
9. Dutch Palace & Temple
10. Pardesi Synagogue

❶ INDO PORTUGUESE MUSEUM

This museum in the garden of Bishop's House preserves the heritage of one of India's earliest Catholic communities. Artefacts from different churches of the Catholic diocese from the region are displayed here. The wheelchair-friendly museum is spread over different storeys, each denoted by a different theme: Altar, Treasures, Procession, Civil Life and Cathedral. The artistic Portuguese-influenced collection of altars, crosses, chasubles and more, dating as far back as the 16th century, are a rare and marvellous sight.

📞0484 2215400; Bishop's House; 9am–1pm, 2–6pm, Mon & public holidays closed; adult/child/foreigners ₹10/5/25

❷ CHINESE FISHING NETS

At the tip of Fort Kochi sits the unofficial emblem of Kerala's backwaters: cantilevered Chinese fishing nets. The enormous ladle-like nets are permanently positioned here and it takes teams of four to five fishermen to heave the heavy nets out of the water with a pulley system and make a dash for the fish. There is stiff competition from a brigade of crows close at hand. The frenetic activity here starts as early as 6am and you are allowed to help the fishermen and can also take pictures for a small tip.

Vasco Square

❸ ST FRANCIS CHURCH (VASCO CHURCH)

Believed to be India's oldest European-built church, it was originally constructed in 1503 by Portuguese Franciscan friars. The edifice that stands here today was built in the mid-16th century to replace the original wooden structure. The highlight of the church is the dusty tombstone of explorer Vasco da Gama, who died in Kochi in 1524. He was buried here for 14 years before his remains were taken to Lisbon.

River Road; 8.30am–5pm

❹ DUTCH CEMETERY

Another landmark colonial presence in the harbour town is the Dutch Cemetery at the end of River Road. It contains the dilapidated graves of Dutch traders and soldiers. Now locked to keep curious intruders at bay, you can just about peep over the gate and have a glimpse of the over 200-year-old graves. **River Road.**

✅ *Top Tip: Exploring Fort Kochi*

The walk- and cycle-friendly Fort Kochi allows you to visit all the sightseeing places at your own pace, especially as they are not too far apart. If you have less time at hand, the Tuk-Tuk Odyssey is your best bet.

Hire a Bike: Hop on to a cycle or a motorbike to explore the town. Contact Arafath of **Rent a Bike** (☏9947478328; ₹300 motorbike/₹100 cycle) at the corner of Quiero's Street.

Tuk-Tuk Odyssey (☏09995205828) :Travel Graham Hughes style in a tuk-tuk, employed brilliantly for sightseeing. A handful of rickshaw drivers are part of this scheme where they take you for a 2-3 hour sightseeing tour, with the driver doubling as a guide.

📷 *Snapshot: Muziris*

When in Fort Kochi, you will encounter this word often. This was the name of an ancient port in the 1st century on the western edge of Kerala, not too far from the current region of Fort Kochi and around. Though the exact location of the area could not be documented after a flood, it is conjectured to be either present-day Kodungallur (p135) or Pattanam (43km from Fort Kochi). Many hotels and restaurants have nostalgically acquired the name 'Muziris' as a reminder of the thriving trade of that era.

❺ SANTA CRUZ CATHEDRAL BASILICA

The imposing Catholic basilica was originally built on this site in 1506, though the current building dates to 1902. Inside you'll find artefacts from the different eras in Kochi and a striking pastel-coloured interior.

📞**0484 2215799; www.santacruzcathedralbasilica.org; KB Jacob Road; 9am–6pm**

❻ SOUTHERN NAVAL COMMAND MARITIME MUSEUM

If you are remotely interested in sailing the seas, the spic and span Maritime Museum will keep you engrossed with exhibits on steering wheels, maps, replicas of battleships and more. It is especially enjoyable, as the upkeep of the place is excellent.

Beach Road; 9.30am–12.30pm, 2.30–5.30pm, Mon closed; Indians/foreigners/children/photography ₹25/75/15/100

❼ DHOBI GHAT (VANNARSANGHAM)

If you haven't seen an active dhobi ghat for some time, stop over to see the pre-washing machine era come alive in a sea of white sheets. More than anything, the insistent thrashing of clothes at the washing stone makes for excellent photo opportunities. Posters of Rajnikanth, instead of the famous Malayalam actor Mohanlal, are an instant giveaway to the Tamil community that manages this ghat.

Cemetery Road, Veli; 6am–6pm

❽ THIRUMALA DEVASWOM TEMPLE

Mattancherry's vivid history begins with the Vishnu temple at Cherlai. The enormous, Hindus-only temple has a large

The portrait gallery at the Dutch Palace

kalayani (pond) in front of it and a huge bell that is constantly rung by someone sitting at one end of the rope. The spiritual fervour is kept alive with the temple ensemble playing the panchavadyam (traditional temple instruments) during the day. Situated in the heart of the Hindu area, the spacious compound also contains numerous cowsheds.

RG Pai Road, Cherlai; 5.30am–noon, 6–9pm

⑨ DUTCH PALACE & TEMPLE

Mattancherry Palace was a gift presented to the Raja of Kochi, Veera Kerala Varma (1537–61), as a gesture of goodwill by the Portuguese in 1555. The Dutch renovated the palace in 1663, and hence it was renamed the Dutch Palace. The Kerala-style wood-floored mansion is now a museum with coins, murals, paintings and objects reminiscent of the lives of the rajas of the 16th century. The complex is also home to the Pazhayannur Bhagvathi Temple, dedicated to the deity who was the royal guardian.

Palace Road, Mattancherry; 9–5pm, Fri closed; ₹5

⑩ PARDESI SYNAGOGUE

At the end of a narrow lane in Jew Town, the synagogue is a symbol of religious tolerance under the Kochi kings. This is the oldest active synagogue in the Commonwealth countries. Silently observe the ornate central chandelier, Hebrew calendars and scrolls, a central pulpit and a narrow passage with paintings recording the Jew influx in Kochi. The synagogue was built in 1568. There is an upstairs balcony for women, who worshipped separately according to Orthodox rites. Shorts or sleeveless tops are not allowed inside.

Jew Town; 10am–1pm, 3–5pm, Fri & Sat closed; ₹5

Detour: Kodungallur

Fifty kilometres from Fort Kochi, the historical port town of Kodungallur is a less travelled destination. You need a sprightly imagination to visualise the erstwhile Cranganore, beyond the busy traffic-clogged streets of its modern-day avatar. Once the most significant maritime junction of south India, today it comprises a handful of monuments showcasing the cultural diversity of the region between 100 BC–AD 1341. The two crumbling **Jewish synagogues, St Thomas Church, Cheraman Mosque** and the **Bhagvathi Temple** draw few visitors to this part but history buffs would definitely consider the trip worthwhile.

The two synagogues (one of them the oldest in Kerala) were possibly built around the same time as the Pardesi Synagogue (p134) in Mattancherry. The town is also famous for a mosque (5am–9pm, women are not allowed inside the sanctum; museum 7am–7pm; ₹5) that marked the arrival of Malik bin Dinar, the Islamic missionary who was responsible for propagating the religion in Kerala. Built in 630, the mosque's original construction was done in traditional Hindu style and later renovated in the 11th century. The highlight here is the single-roomed museum that borders the mosque.

The first church in India, St Thomas was founded by the revered apostle when he arrived in Kerala in AD 52. Jacob Joseph (☏09744423124; north Paravur; 7am–5pm) is the in-house guide who can tell you more about the relics of the deceased saint which lie in the church. A tip is expected.

The most interesting stop here is the Bhagvathi Temple (6am–12.30pm, 4pm–8pm). Also known as the Kurumba Devi Temple, this is an interesting addition to your day's itinerary for several reasons. If you arrive at about 4pm, you will hear the sound of crude gun powder bombs piercing the air. This tradition of waking the Goddess after her afternoon siesta has been followed for ages. If you are visiting in March, witness the Bharani festival in which, curiously, lewd comments and gestures are 'offered' to the deity.

| Bhagvathi Temple is dedicated to
| Kurumba Devi

📖 Accommodation

Fort Kochi, like the rest of Kerala, follows a season-dependent pricing pattern. October to February tariffs can shoot up by 30–40%. Despite this, there is a good mix of budget and luxury places – something for every pocket.

Brunton Boatyard — Hotel ₹₹₹
📞 0484 3011711; www.cghearth. com; Fort Kochi; d ₹25,600–34,000 **(incl of breakfast and taxes)** Brunton Boatyard has a historical Dutch ambience, complete with high ceilings, aged artefacts and decor themed after the shipping culture of Fort Kochi. All of the rooms look out over the harbour, and have bathtubs and balconies with a refreshing sea breeze that beats AC any day. You can also use the wi-fi facility and swimming pool.

Tea Bungalow — Heritage Hotel ₹₹₹
📞 09388719679; www.teabungalow. in; 1/1901, Kunumpuram; d ₹10,500 **(incl of breakfast)** The decor of the rooms in this heritage boutique hotel is themed on important ports of the Indian Ocean. Take your pick from rooms that are variously called Zanzibar, Goa, Galle and seven other ports. The classy furnishings, bright paintings and open-roofed bathrooms offer a rare luxury. You can take a relaxing dip in the swimming pool. The staff here is exceptionally warm.

Old Harbour Hotel — Hotel ₹₹₹
📞 0484 2218006; www. oldharbourhotel.com; 1/328,
Tower Road; d ₹9250–15,950 **(incl of breakfast)** Overlooking the picturesque Chinese fishing nets, Old Harbour Hotel has an intimate coterie of 13 rooms. Its sprawling garden restaurant behind the white walls is a pleasant surprise and the most exquisite part of the heritage hotel on Tower Road.

Koder House — Hotel ₹₹
📞 0484 2218485; www.koderhouse. com; Tower Road; d ₹3500 **(incl of breakfast)** It's difficult to miss the prominent red building overlooking the Children's Park at Vasco Square. Koder House, the erstwhile home of a Jewish family, is now a six-room luxury boutique hotel with spacious suites and a wooden-floored vintage aura. Its highlight is the in-house restaurant, Menorah, where you can order Jewish delicacies – try the pudding. Wi-fi facility is available.

The Malabar House — Hotel ₹₹
📞 0484 2216666; www. malabarescapes.com; Parade Road; d ₹4000–6000 **(incl of breakfast)** One of the most awarded hotels in

Tom's Old Mansion is a 100-year-old structure converted into a heritage hotel

town, Malabar House draws you into its charmed world, replete with touches of history and designer decor and an open courtyard cafe which serves delicious food. You can treat yourself to an Ayurvedic massage, laze around the poolside. All this comes with impeccable hospitality.

Elphinstone Residency   Hotel ₹₹
📞0484 2218222; www. elphinstoneresidency.com; Beach Road; d ₹2800–4000 (incl of breakfast) If you're looking for a personalised stay with the standard facilities of a hotel, you will love the cheerful hosts, gleaming new rooms and sprawling garden with an old well of Elphinstone. A relatively new hotel, it has a combination of five rooms attached to the main house and two cottages that overlook the garden. Choose the cottages for more privacy.

Old Courtyard   Hotel ₹₹
📞0484 2216302; www.oldcourtyard. com; Princess Street; d ₹3500– 5000, ste ₹5500 (incl of breakfast) Though located on the central Princess Street, the large atmospheric garden and eight vintage rooms of Old Courtyard miraculously cut out any of the disturbing buzz. The 200-year-old restored building houses a multi-cuisine restaurant which hosts Indian classical musical evenings during season. The hotel offers wi-fi facilities.

TOP CHOICE Fort House   Hotel ₹₹
📞0484 2217103; www. hotelforthouse.com; 2/6A Calvathy Road; d ₹4945 (incl of breakfast and taxes) Another inviting option, Fort House has a waterfront backyard, 16 chic rooms in soft earth and ochre colours and warm personalised service. There's a relaxing central space filled with shady trees, behind which sits the excellent restaurant with a view. The hotel offers wi-fi facilities.

Fort Muzuris   Hotel ₹
📞0484 2215057; www.fortmuziris. com; 1/415 Burgar Street; d ₹1000– 1500 (incl of breakfast) If a tariff that's easy on the pocket and a central location are prime considerations, then head straight to Fort Muzuris at the end of Burgar Street. The six AC rooms are complemented by friendly service, efficient wi-fi facilities and a hearty breakfast. The place is a little rough around the edges but great value for money.

Noah's Ark Homestay   Homestay ₹
📞0484 2215481; www. noahsarkcochin.com; 1/508 Fort Kochi Hospital Road; d ₹2800–3100 (incl of breakfast) Noah's Ark truly represents the homestay culture of Kerala. Tap into the vast knowledge of your hosts, Diana and Jerry, who have let out only three rooms of their house. You will enjoy your stay in the modern well-furnished rooms with wi-fi facility as well.

Eden Garden Heritage Homestay   Homestay ₹
📞09847930003; www. edengardenhomestay.com; Fort

Kochi Police Quarters, Amaravathy; d ₹2500 (incl of breakfast) Mel and Judith's 250-year-old traditional Cyprian home is a pleasant change from the tourist-heavy area at Fort Kochi. They have three simple rooms overlooking a small lotus pond and a lush garden, creating a veritable Eden in Kochi. Besides the peaceful atmosphere, the food is scrumptious.

Tom's Old Mansion   **Hotel ₹**
☏ 0484 2215605; www.tomsoldmansionkochi.com; Princess Street; d ₹1500–3000 (incl of breakfast) A creaking wooden floor, soaring ceilings and a central courtyard testify to the age of this heritage hotel. A hundred years old, most of its 15 rooms are spacious and aesthetically pleasing. The central location, period feel and a rational tariff makes this a good choice. You can use the in-house wi-fi facility too.

Ann's Residency   **Homestay ₹**
☏ 0484 2216424; www.annsresidency.com; 1/307 A, Bishop Joseph Kureethara (Rose) Street; d ₹2500–3000, ste ₹4000 (incl of breakfast) A bright white-and-gold sign at the corner of Rose Street ushers you through a traditional Kerala entrance and into a comfortable, modern, nine-room homestay. Ann and Leslie are warm and informative hosts (and the fifth generation in this originally Portuguese house). All rooms look over refreshing green patches around the house.

Silver Weed Homestay   **Homestay ₹**
☏ 09645450703 ; www.silverweedhomestay.com; 11/88 near ESI Junction; d ₹1500 (incl of breakfast) Only a few months old on the homestay circuit, Silver Weed has outdone itself in cleanliness, hospitality and a refreshing ambience. The family's love for plants has the spacious common balcony of the two rooms inundated in fresh potted foliage. The two guest rooms are sparkling clean and have a separate entrance, giving you plenty of privacy. The home-made food is delicious.

 Eating

Oceanos   **Restaurant ₹₹₹**
☏ 0484 2218222; www.oceanosfortkochi.com; Elphinstone Road; 12.30–3.30pm, 7–10.30pm; mains ₹500–750 Candle-lit outdoor seating in the evenings provides the perfect atmosphere for a delicious meal of seafood specials. The absence of a needlessly long menu is welcome. And if you're looking for a safe option, the Kerala combos are flawless.

Kashi Art Cafe   **Art Gallery & Coffee Shop ₹₹**
☏ 0484 2215769; www.kashiartgallery.com; Burgher Street; 8.30am–7.30pm; mains ₹250–500 Kashi is Fort Kochi's foremost art gallery-cum-cafe, setting the tone for most of the others that are now springing up by the dozen. Kashi Cafe is one of the most popular joints in town, it serves delicious chocolate cake and other confectionary. The

interior is a maze of small seating areas with wooden furniture and lots of green vines that are prettily draped on the walls.

Dosas and Pancakes   Cafe ₹₹
09387542000; www.dosasandpancakes.com; 10am–10pm; mains ₹250–500 An all-day menu of delights like puttu, appams, stew, fish curry, and even waffles can keep you hanging here for hours. Try the Sunday Kerala special brunch if you are looking to dig into local specialities over a lazy long morning. The cafe is attached to Greenix Village (p140); keep in mind that it can get crowded before the shows.

Loafers Corner   Cafe ₹₹
Princess Street; 11am–9.30pm; mains ₹250–500 The name of the cafe recalls a time when the spot was a local haunt for boys (loafers) hanging around on the street corner. Wooden floors and an austere setting are a refreshing break from the usual vintage decor of other cafes. The menu is tiny so you can make a super

quick choice and ring the small bell on your table for the waiter's attention.

Tea Pot Cafe   Cafe ₹₹
0484 2218035; Peter Celli Street; 9am–9pm; mains ₹250–500 A large teapot collection and other tea-themed paraphernalia unfolds in this yellow-walled cafe as you enter past a small modest sign on the street. It has a definite character of its own, making it an interesting place to spend a relaxed evening.

Ginger House Restaurant   Restaurant ₹₹
0484 2211145; Jew Town Road; 9am–6.30pm; mains ₹250–500 A 100-ft-long traditional snake boat lies in the centre of the Heritage Arts antique shop, which eventually opens out to a sunny cafe overlooking the Willingdon Island shipyard. Multi-cuisine options are quickly served out of an open kitchen, quite contrary to the laid-back atmosphere of the place.

Dal Roti   North Indian ₹₹
Lilly Street; noon–3.15pm, 6.30–

♥ *If You Like: Vintage Bars*

Apart from the high-end restaurants, try what the locals have to recommend. The harbour-facing Seagull and XL bar are often suggested for their vintage value.

• **Seagull** (Kalvatty Road; 9am–10.30pm): The service here may be abysmal but the view of the harbour makes up for it after a few drinks. You can laze around on the sunny deck for hours over a couple of beers and enjoy the view.

• **XL** (Rose Street; 9am–10.30pm): This old bar must be the hottest hangout – judging from the stream of visitors, babble of voices and constantly squeaking wooden floors. XL has different sections for visitors and local regulars.

10.15pm; mains ₹250–500 Arrive no later than 12.30pm to grab a place at the hugely popular Dal Roti. Though the interiors are nothing to write home about, the north Indian food will surely impress you.

⭐ Entertainment

Cultural shows are abridged and easy to understand. These versions of Kerala's performing arts can be seen under one roof in less than two hours. You should definitely try to catch an evening of kalaripayattu, classical dance and music here.

Greenix Village   **Cultural Program**
☎0484 2217000; www.greenix.in; Kalvathy Road; 5.30–7.30pm; ₹450
This is the most organised and well-maintained establishment offering abridged folk performances of Kerala. Arrive at 5.30pm to see the Kathakali dancers painting their faces for the show. An hour later, you are ushered into different theatres for a dance-martial arts-music package which lasts for an hour. Greenix also has a museum, cafe and book shop.

Kerala
Kathakali Centre   **Cultural Program**
☎0484 2217552; www. kathakalicentre.com; near Santa Cruz Basilica, KB Jacob Road; ₹250; 6–7.30pm The Kerala Kathakali Centre is another place where you can get your fix of culture. A narrow path takes you to the wooden-floored auditorium on the first floor, where a hour-and-half long shows pack in Kathakali, Bharatnatyam, Kuchipudi and Carnatic vocal music performances.

🤸 Activities

Village Rubble   **Cycling**
☎09645411433; www.glhindia.com; 10/1252 KB Jacob Road; ₹8000 for two; 14 hours For a countryside experience, hop onto the well-maintained bicycles of Village Rubble and explore the rural set-up and local activities around Fort Kochi with a trip leader. You can join an existing group or customise your own trip. Get acquainted with fishing techniques, coir making, crab cultivation, prawn farming, toddy tapping, and also meet village women empowerment groups.

Kumbalangi   **Cycling**
The nearby village of Kumbalangi offers fascinating insights into the workings of prawn/crab farms, toddy tappers, coir making and local fishing methods. All this can be organised by the 70 year-old **Gramam Homestay** (☎0484 2240278; www. keralagramam.com; Neduveli House, Kumbalangi; d Rs3000, ste Rs6000, rates incl of breakfast), which is located just 13km from Fort Kochi. A refreshing break to enjoy the tranquil backdrop of backwaters.

🔒 Shopping

Spices, antiques, boho cotton clothes and indigenous art will greet you at every corner. Your bargaining prowess might come handy, especially in Jew Town in the Mattancherry area.

Jew Street and
Mattancherry   Market

Antique masks, wooden chests, traditional doors and an ocean of antique artefacts are jammed together in rows of shops around the Jew Town area. The **Isidore Art Palace** (☎9447054369; Synagogue Lane, Jew Town; 9am–6pm) at the end of the Jew Street (just before the synagogue) is less overwhelming than the others and has a decent collection. However, price-wise, most items tend to fall on the higher-end of the spectrum but it's not impossible to find something that suits your budget. And that may take a couple of hours. Most shops can ship your purchase.

Spices in Mattancherry   Market

The atmospheric Mattancherry area is certainly *the* centre of spice shops in town. The pungent aroma of an amazing variety of spices is hard to miss, even if you have your nostrils are jammed. You should try for a fair deal at one of the wholesale dealers (**Kaycee Corporation**; ☎0484 2225255; PB No 240, Bazaar Road;

9am–6pm). Walk through the drying yard and inspect a large collection at massive godowns. You will be able to pay slightly less than what you might shell out in retail shops.

Ecoutree Boutique   Clothing
& Jewellery

☎09961375553; Bastin Street; 11am–9.30pm Ecoutree Boutique has an innovative collection of semi-precious jewellery, comfy cottons and smart bags.

Indian Industries   Handicrafts

☎0484 2216448; Indian Industries; Princess Street; 9am–8pm Closer to where you are likely to stay (if opting for a central location), Indian Industries on Princess Street has a fair collection of old artefacts that you can pick as souvenirs.

Idiom Book Sellers   Bookstore

☎0484 2217075; 1/348, Bastion Street; 10am–9pm If you have run out of your travel-read supply, head to Idiom Book Sellers for a substantial collection of titles.

 Snapshot: Art at Fort Kochi

Fort Kochi's vivacious art scene truly exhibits the sentiments of the entire state. Influenced by its rich traditional heritage and colonial infusion, it's easy to find a mix of poignant, dramatic and contemporary work here. The **OED Gallery** in Mattancherry (☎944710811; 6/500 Bazaar Road, Mattancherry; 11am–7pm, Sun closed) often showcases creations of Kerala-based artists. In fact, if you walk down Bazaar Road from Mattancherry all the way to the ferry point of Fort Kochi, you will find a number of bright contemporary murals on the walls, which have spilled onto the blocks near Princess Street.

Guruvayur

Highlights

1. Guruvayur Sree Krishna Temple
2. Guruvayur Anna Kotta
3. Guruvayur Devaswom Institute of Mural Paintings

At Guruvayur, expect to be awed by the most revered **Krishna Temple** and the sight of thousands that visit here each day. This, and a camp that is run for the resident elephants, are its highlights.

1 GURUVAYUR SREE KRISHNA TEMPLE

Visit the fourth largest temple in India to see its grand gopuram, ancient pillars and sculptures that are said to date back to 5000 years. Visiting the temple requires a patient meandering through congested lines for hours to catch a glimpse of the deity. In fact, the fervour of devotees is visible in bizarre ways; for instance, people rolling around the premises. Only Hindus are allowed inside. Men should be bare-chested and women have to wear saris.

3am–12.30pm and 4.30–9.15pm

2 GURUVAYUR ANNA KOTTA

This sanctuary for 63 elephants is worth a visit, especially if you're travelling with children. You can easily spend a few

A couple seeks blessings at the Guruvayur Temple

📷 Snapshot: Weddings at Guruvayur

Three huge wedding mandapas have been created just outside the temple for low-cost weddings. Hundreds line up here to be blessed by busy priests. With such a dash for the weddings, matrimonial errors are not uncommon – there have been times when the wrong couples have gotten hitched. Watch the razzmatazz with the temple as the backdrop if you visit in the mornings before 8am.

✓ *Top Tip: Culture & nature circuit*

The Kodungallur (p135), Guruvayur, Thrissur (p144) and Athirappally (p123) loop can be done in a day if you start early from Fort Kochi. Leave at about 6am to reach the historic town of Kodungallur (44km) as all the points of interest open early. You can then go past the pristine beaches of Nattika and reach Guruvayur (51km) in time before the temple closes for the afternoon, and then head on to Thrissur's (33km) Kerala Kalamandalam. If the day is turning out to be hectic, stop for the night at Rainforest (p123) at the Athirappally waterfalls. Ensure that you reach before 5pm as the town lies in a forested region.

entertaining hours amidst the pachyderms, who lazily spend the day eating, bathing in a stony pool and swishing their tails below shady trees.

8am–6pm; adult/child/camera/video ₹5/1/25/1000

Chinese fishing nets at the Cape of Kodungallur

❸ GURUVAYUR DEVASWOM INSTITUTE OF MURAL PAINTINGS

This institute hones the skills of young artists to create compositions on religious themes, in an attempt to revive the ancient art of mural painting. Narrow steps near the left of the temple lead up to this small two-room institute. You can stop by to see artists at work and view some of their pieces exhibited outside.

☎ **098470 17044; 10am–4pm, Sat closed**

Thrissur

Highlights

❶ Kerala Kalamandalam
❷ Kerala Lalithakala
  Akademi
❸ Thrissur Vadakkunnathan
  Temple

The presence of some of the most important cultural institutions of the state has earned Thrissur the sobriquet of 'Cultural Capital of Kerala'. It is also the venue of one of the most stunning temple festivals of south India, **Thrissur Pooram**. Here, gold-caparisoned elephants stand in a line, parading their finery as they nonchalantly pose before wide-eyed photographers.

❶ KERALA KALAMANDALAM

The bastion of performing arts, Kerala Kalamandalam was founded in 1930 by the well-known poet, Padma Bhushan Vallathol Narayana Menon. It is still the best performing arts school in the state. 30km northeast of Thrissur, the institution should be visited for an introduction to the lives of young aspiring artistes. The 'Day with the Masters' programme is the best way to get a close-up account of how

Uthralikavu
Pooram
festival, Shri
Rudhiramahakalikav
Temple

artistes are trained by their gurus, but one can tour the school unaccompanied.

☎ 04884 262418; www.kalamandalam.org; Cheruthuruthy; entry without guide/with guide ₹10/1000; 9am–1pm, Sat & Sun closed

❷ KERALA LALITHAKALA AKADEMI

The most respected art centre of the state, the Akademi should be visited by those interested in the visual arts. The gallery is open to visitors. Works of many famous artistes are regularly displayed in this building, designed by world-renowned architect Laurie Baker.

☎ 0487 2333773; www.lalithkala.org; Chembukkavu; 10am–5pm

❸ THRISSUR VADAKKUNNATHAN TEMPLE

This Shiva temple stands in the centre of a large field (Thekkinkadu Maidan) atop a small hill. This is the venue for the world-famous Thrissur Pooram festival, held in April–May each year. The 36-hour-long festivities involve two other major temples (Paramekkavu Bhagavathy and Thiruvambadi Bhagavathy) which have processions too. A parade of richly caparisoned elephants are the main attraction here. The central field holds throngs of locals and visitors, and the energy of the place is palpable as temple instruments play in unison, leading up to the dramatic fireworks show. This goes on for the whole night.

4–10am, 5–8pm

 ## *Snapshot: Uthralikavu Pooram*

Adding to Thrissur's vibrant cultural spirit is the **Uthralikavu Pooram** festival that is celebrated in the Shri Rudhiramahakalikav Temple in Wadakanchery (16km from Thrissur town) in veneration of Goddess Kali. In February/March, the otherwise sleepy setting of paddy fields and low-lying hills undergoes a metamorphosis. Wadakanchery along with the neighbouring village temples of Enkakkad and Kumaranellur come together to celebrate the festival. The festivities include elephants circling the shrine, musicians and fireworks that go on late into the night.

Accommodation

The small towns of Guruvayur and Thrissur are 33km apart from each other and you can opt to stay at either of the towns to explore this interesting region.

GURUVAYUR

Nattika Beach Resort, Guruvayur   Ayurveda Resort ₹₹₹

0487 2396770; www. thenattikabeach.com; Nattika Beach; d ₹7700–12,390 (incl of breakfast and taxes) Though Nattika Beach Resort lies 26km away from Guruvayur, you can choose to stay here for an atmospheric, beachside experience. The yoga and Ayurveda-focused resort promises a salubrious holiday with an ideal setting to relax in. All the villas are garden facing and have a rustic charm about them; the breezy verandah is the best spot to catch up on a good book. You can use Nattika

Mayura Residency is just a short drive from the Sree Krishna Temple

Beach Resort as your base, and explore both Guruvayur and Thrissur.

Mayura Residency, Guruvayur   Hotel ₹₹

0487 2557174; www. hotelmayuraguruvayur.com; West Nada; d ₹2000–3000, ste ₹4500 (incl of breakfast) One of the few good options in town, Mayura Residency is good for an overnight stay if you want to visit the temple. It lies on the West Nada (gate) of the temple, but the entry is on the east (it's a short drive away). The hotel has sparkling clean interiors and the furnishings are decent.

Sreekrishna Residency, Guruvayur   Hotel ₹

0487 2556505; www. sreekrishnaresidency.com; West Nada; d ₹995–1250 (incl of breakfast) A good budget option in town is the Sreekrishna Residency. A far better option than the packed guesthouses near the temple entrance, it lies behind the main gate, a short distance away. The rooms are basic but well maintained and clean. You can opt for a family room for eight, if travelling with a group.

THRISSUR

Hotel Pooram International, Thrissur   Hotel ₹₹

0487 2225555; www.hotelpooram. com; Kuruppam Road; d ₹2200–4000, ste ₹5000 (incl of breakfast) Overlooking the festival grounds, this hotel must be booked well in advance

| Nattika Beach Resort has a focus on yoga and Ayurveda

if you are arriving during the Thrissur Pooram. The rooms are spacious and comfortable but cost 10 times more than usual if you book during the festival. The USP of the hotel is its vantage viewpoint of the festival.

Lulu Garden, Thrissur   Hotel ₹₹
📞0487 301111; www.luluicc.in; Puzhakkal, Ayyanthole; d ₹4000, ste ₹6000–7000 (incl of breakfast) Pleasantly away from the bustle of the town, Lulu Garden is a little too opulent in decor but very comfortable. The restaurant serves great multi-cuisine food. The hotel has a helipad.

Hotel Luciya Palace, Thrissur Hotel ₹
📞2424731; www.hotelluciyapalace. com; d ₹2700 Set in a cream, colonial-themed building, this is one of the few places in town that has some character. Sitting in a quiet cul-de-sac, this grand looking hotel has comfortable and spacious rooms.

Eating

For both Thrissur and Guruvayur, the in-house restaurants of the above hotels are the best option for meals. However, you could try the option below in Thrissur.

Navaratna Restaurant   North Indian
Round West; lunch & dinner; mains ₹57–96 Cool, dark and intimate, this is the classiest dining joint in town, with seating on raised platforms, and soothing piped music. Expect lots of veg and non-veg dishes from north India, plus a few Keralite specialities, served in AC surrounds.

Malabar & Wayanad

Why Go?

The northern coastal stretch of Kerala (the Malabar region) and lush coffee-clad Wayanad, further inland, encompass a travelling experience unblemished by cliches. It is a rich mix of Wayanad's verdant forests and the virgin coastline from Kozhikode to Kasaragod, the northernmost tip of Kerala. There is plenty of diversity here, from architecture and traditional arts, to pristine beaches and coffee plantations.

Getting There & Away

Air: Kozhikode Airport is most convenient for the Malabar region, with the exception of Kasaragod and Bekal, which are better accessed by Mangalore Airport (55km/68km). SpiceJet, Air India, Jet Airways have daily flights from Delhi, Mumbai and Bengaluru to both Kozhikode and Mangalore.

Bus: Overnight buses (private operators and KSRTC) are available from Bengaluru to Kozhikode, Kannur and Wayanad. A few of them also run right along the coastline till Kasaragod and stop in Wayanad, Mahe and Thalassery as well. Local buses ply in abundance between these towns.

Train: There are direct trains to Kozhikode – Trivandrum Rajdhani (12432) and Mangala Lakshadweep Express (12618) from Delhi and Yesvantpur-Kannur Express (16527) from Bengaluru. Major and local trains through the day connect the coastal cities well. The Malabar Express (16629) is your best option; else choose between any of the other 31 trains that cover this stretch. Wayanad does not fall under any of the rail routes.

▌▐ Elephants playing at the Tholpetty Wildlife Sanctuary

Top Highlights

1 Mappila Cuisine

The Arab-influenced cuisine of the Mappila community (p158) offers some of the most flavourful dishes in Kerala. The use of fragrant spices, especially pepper, cardamom and cloves, is the highlight. The Mappila biriyani is a must-have, and so are the layered parottas that go wonderfully with chicken curries. Outstanding dishes are muttamaala (egg garland), kadukkanira chathu (stuffed mussels) and kozhinira chathu (stuffed chicken).

2 Muthanga & Tholpetty Wildlife Sanctuaries

Both Muthanga (p177) and Tholpetty (p172) Wildlife sanctuaries in Wayanad give visitors a chance to be dazzled by the many shades of green in its thick forested regions. One cannot be assured of tiger sightings but that shouldn't be a deterrent especially since one get's a chance to spot a

variety of fascinating creatures such as Indian bison, elephants, deer and birds. A safari in the jeep amidst the wild undergrowth and sounds of the jungle can be quite therapeutic.

3 Edakkal Caves, Wayanad

Pictorial writings from 5000 BC in the Edakkal Caves (p176) are testimony to the presence of a prehistoric civilisation in the region. Ever since these writings were discovered in the deep fissures of the massive rockscape, the area has been regarded as a sight of great importance. Hundreds visit the caves that are perched on a steep hill to witness the remains of this extraordinary civilisation.

4 Bekal Fort

The presence of a number of forts on the coastal edge of Kerala recalls the active spice trade that existed here with the Arab, Chinese and European world. Of these, Bekal Fort (p167) is one of the most famous, and offers scenic views. You can climb its ancient water tank to get a bird's eye view of the waves lashing onto the shores.

5 Sri Ananthapadmanabha Swamy Temple, Kasaragod

Travel to the northern tip of Kerala, to see this tranquil water-surrounded temple in Kasaragod (p166), dedicated to Lord Maha Vishnu. It is a soothing oasis in the middle of a vast dry, rocky and dramatic landscape. Typical Kerala architecture, ancient murals and a permanent inhabitant, a crocodile called Babiya, are the highlights here.

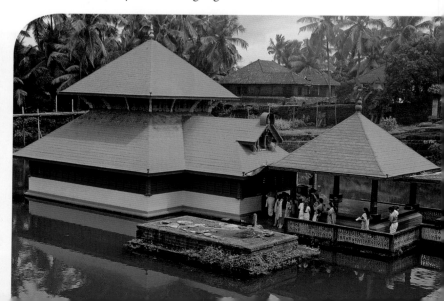

Local Knowledge
Theyyam Rituals

Jagannath Chirakkara Nair, an ardent propagator of the rich heritage of Kerala and owner of heritage homestay, Gitanjali, analyses the complex rituals around Theyyam.

• **History of Theyyam:** Theyyam is a ritualistic Hindu form of worship, which goes back several thousand years in time. It is a religious dance-drama performed by a certain section of society (mostly scheduled castes and tribes) to commemorate innumerable local deities. The worship of spirits, ancestors and even nature are included in this cult worship; the reasons for organising it differ for every village or family.

There is a modern perspective to this strong community event, as it is also a good way to pass on social messages or for annual family get togethers. The custom is deeply venerated amongst local communities and has fortunately not been corrupted or commercialised over the years.

• **Types of Theyyams:** There are more than 450 types of Theyyams, each with its unique aspects, some even involving trance-like performances. They are largely divided into four types: Bhagavathy, Saiva Vaishnava, Manushika and Purana.

• **Dresses and Rituals:** Elaborate dressing in very heavy red costumes and headdresses, with face painting, precede a Theyyam performance. Some performers resort to blood offering in the form of cock sacrifice. The major performances go on for complete days and nights, so it is permissible and a social norm to serve alcohol to the performers – in order to keep the energy levels up.

• **Best months:** The months of October to April are when Theyyam performances usually take place. Some have specific annual dates, while others depend on local calendars. Though Theyyam is a seasonal ritual, daily enactments are held in a few temples like Parassinikadavu and Kannadipara in the region.

| An exquisitely dressed Theyyam
| performer

Malabar & Wayanad

With the erstwhile ports of **Kannur** and **Kozhikode**, the enchanting wilderness of **Wayanad**, the quaint town of **Thalassery** and the charming beaches of **Bekal** and **Kasaragod**, this is definitely a part of Kerala that should not be missed. While here, catch an incredible **Theyyam** performance – an art form developed from harvest folk dances and believed to be older than Hinduism.

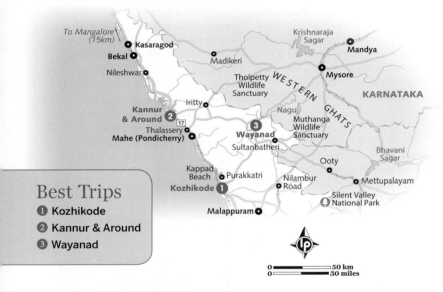

Best Trips

1. **Kozhikode**
2. **Kannur & Around**
3. **Wayanad**

GETTING AROUND THE REGION

• **Taxi:** You can hire a car to get around in the region at ₹8–12 per km (depending on the car and AC usage), plus daily driver bata and tolls. Ensure that you fix rates beforehand to avoid later hassles.

• **Train:** Kannur and Kozhikode are the two main rail junctions for this cluster of destinations. Kannur Express (16517) is one of the most popular trains from Bengaluru. Malabar Express (16629) runs from Thiruvananthapuram to Mangalore, connecting many coastal cities including Kozhikode, Mahe, Thalassery, Kannur and Kasaragod.

• **Bus:** The Kerala State Tourism Corporation buses are good budget options to cover the region. The Kozhikode bus stand on Mavoor Road has regular buses plying to both Wayanad and the coastal stretch.

Kozhikode

After Portuguese explorer Vasco da Gama landed at this port city in 1498, Kozhikode (Calicut) gained prominence as one of the busiest spice trade junctions in the world. The city still has a hectic pace with the commotion of traffic and commercial activity concentrated in the Mananchira Square. Verdant undergrowth and palm stands peeping between flashy new buildings are reminders of Kozhikode's original charm. Explore the famous **boat-building yards in Beypore** and have your fill of the famous **Kozhikode halwa** and banana chips here.

Highlights
❶ **Boat-Building Yards of Beypore**
❷ **Regional Science Centre & Planetarium** (off map)
❸ **Tali Temple**
❹ **Pazhassi Raja & Krishna Menon Museums** (off map)
❺ **Kozhikode Beaches**

❶ BOAT-BUILDING YARDS OF BEYPORE
Come prepared to be greeted by the deafening sound of a drill whirring into a wooden block in this estuarine port just 11km from Kozhikode town. Beypore's glorious history is speckled with exalted names dating back to the 1st century AD: vessels for Cleopatra, Lord Horatio Nelson and many others were built in these yards at the edge of the Chaliyar River. Today, only two big yards craft massive dhows or urus (vessels) for merchants in Middle Eastern countries.
Beypore Village

❷ REGIONAL SCIENCE CENTRE & PLANETARIUM

Graphic models of dinosaurs, mammoths and other prehistoric animals, as well as educational exhibits, will greet you as you enter the Regional Science Centre and Planetarium. A trip here is a sure-fire hit with kids. Other than the 3D and planetarium shows, the science section is particularly popular. Another fun room both for kids and adults is the Mirror Magic Room with its fun optics: you can float in the air, see yourself vanish, become stick-thin or wide enough to cover the entire mirror.

☏ 0495 2770571; www.rscpcalicut.org; Planetarium Road, Jafferkhan Colony; entry Science Centre/Planetarium/3D show ₹10/25/35; 10.30am–6pm, Onam & Diwali closed; Planetarium shows noon, 2pm, 4pm, 6pm; 3D shows 11am, 1pm, 3pm, 5pm

❸ TALI TEMPLE

The 1500-year-old Tali Temple dedicated to Lord Shiva has elements of typical Malabar architecture. A wide path surrounds the tiled-roof inner sanctum. You can witness an elaborate ritual here at 9.30am as the door opens to a loud chorus of traditional instruments. Prayers for a child hang

The scenic Kaapad Beach ▮

in the form of small wooden toy cribs on a tree, while intricate murals decorate the temple walls.

☏ 0495 2703610; www. calicuttalimahakshetra.com; Chalappuram; 4.30–11am, 5–8.30pm

❹ PAZHASSI RAJA &
KRISHNA MENON MUSEUMS

The East Hill area of Kozhikode is famous for the **Pazhassi Raja Museum** and the **Krishna Menon Museum** with an **art gallery**. The first, with its wooden floor, is a 200-year-old building built in 1812. Later converted into a museum to commemorate the local ruler, it now exhibits some rusty coins, models of temples and ancient bronze and stone sculptures. Vimal (☏ 9847003743), the resident guide can throw more light on details of these interesting exhibits.

Tali Temple has elements of typical Malabar architecture

The Krishna Menon Museum lies behind this building, with exhibits that focus on the erstwhile defence minister of India, VK Krishna Menon. His personal belongings, awards and medals are displayed on the ground floor. On the first floor of this museum lies a gallery with works of Raja Ravi Varma, one of the greatest and most revered painters of Kerala.

East Hill; Pazhassi Raja Museum: adult/child/camera/video ₹10/5/25/250 (videos can be taken only outside); 9am–1pm, 2–4.30pm, Mon closed; Krishna Menon Museum and Art Gallery: ₹2, 10am–5pm, Wed 1–5pm

❺ KOZHIKODE BEACHES

Closer to the city, the Kozhikode Beach is a breezy stretch along Beach Road. It has been developed with modern sculptures and benches for people to rest on. The more scenic Kappad Beach lies 19km from the town. You can also see an inconspicuous weathered monument that is a reminder of Vasco da Gama's entry into the city.

Accommodation

 Harivihar Heritage   Heritage
Homestead   Hotel ₹₹₹

📞 0495 2765865; www.harivihar.
com; Bilathikulam; d ₹7500 (incl
of full board and taxes) Harivihar
Heritage is a pleasant change from
Kozhikode's many business hotels.
The 160-year-old house has an
atmospheric ambience with its large
courtyard, a sprawling green garden
with a traditional kalyani (pond)
and spacious rooms filled with old
furniture and artefacts. Yoga- and
Ayurveda-driven, the property offers
programmes with qualified doctors
and instructors. A traditional massage
table sits invitingly in the well-kept
Ayurveda room.

The Gateway Hotel   Hotel ₹₹₹

📞 0495 6613000; www.the
gatewayhotels.com; PT Usha Road;
d ₹6750–8000, ste ₹11,000 (incl of
breakfast) One of the oldest hotels
of Kozhikode, the Gateway looks a
little weathered but is still one of the
better options in town. Service is
impeccable and the hotel has facilities

like Ayurveda, gym, swimming pool and
wi-fi. An all-day multi-cuisine restaurant
offers a special menu for guests on
an Ayurveda programme, along with
continental, Indian and Chinese cuisine.

**Kadavu Resort and
Ayurveda Center**   Resort ₹₹₹

📞 0483 2830023; www.
kadavuresorts.com; NH 17, Calicut
Bypass Road, Azhinjilam; d
₹6750–9750, ste ₹15,000–20,000,
houseboat ₹13,000–16,000 (incl of
breakfast) Located in one of the most
scenic spots of the city, the plush
Kadavu Resort is set amidst a 10-acre
coconut grove next to the Chaliyar
River outside the city. Cottages that
face the waterfront are a better choice
as the view from here is splendid.
Ayurvedic massages and swimming
pool apart, a houseboat experience
here is worth your while. The hotel also
has wi-fi facilities.

Hotel Paramount Tower   Hotel ₹₹

📞 0495 3015581; www.
paramounttower.in; Town Hall Road;
d ₹3000–4000, ste ₹6000–8000

📷 *Snapshot: Mappila Culture*

You are likely to hear the word
'Mappila' on several occasions on this
trip. References to unique Mappila
clothing or excellent Mappila food
will be thrown around in local banter
and on menus. As a result of Arabic
influence on the Malabar region, a new
Muslim community known as Mappila
emerged here. The community was
a result of Arab merchants marrying
into Hindu families of Malabar and
thus perpetuating a unique tradition of
language, literature, art and music. For
travellers, the rich Mappila food is a
popular attraction. Try the chemmeen
biryani, kozhinirachathu and meen
biryani at the local joints.

(incl of breakfast) Located in the heart of the city, this business hotel has clean, spacious and comfortable rooms along with features such as swimming pool, wi-fi, an in-house restaurant and 24-hour coffee shop. The service is consistently good, enhanced by the cheerful hospitality of the staff.

Westway Hotel   Hotel ₹₹

0495 2768888; www. westwayhotel.com; Kannur Road; d ₹4200–4700, ste ₹5500 (incl of breakfast) The eight-year-old Westway Hotel has reasonably clean and comfortable rooms and two in-house restaurants. Guests can also use the swimming pool and wi-fi facilities. Though the hotel is slightly rough around the edges, it is better than many other smaller options.

Harivihar Heritage Homestead is decorated with antique furniture

Renai Kappad Beach Resort   Resort ₹₹

0496 2688777; www. kappadbeachresort.in; Chemancheri PO, Thoovapara; d ₹4500–5000 (incl of breakfast) This resort is the only option to stay at the edge of the Kappad Beach. It appears a little sleepy and inefficient, although the rooms are surprisingly well furnished. Ensure that you ask for a first floor room, as the view is much better. The resort also has a small pool and wi-fi facilities.

Marina Residency   Business Hotel ₹

0495 4062222; www. marinaresidency.com; YMCA Cross Road; d ₹1500–3000 (incl of breakfast) The comparatively quiet location, an in-house restaurant, wi-fi and basic but clean rooms make Marina a perfectly decent place for an overnight stay.

Eating

Most hotels in Kozhikode have multi-cuisine restaurants that serve reasonable food, but what you must search for are the local joints famous for Malabar delicacies.

TOP CHOICE **Paragon** **Mappila Cuisine**

📞 0495 2767020; Near CH Flyover, Kannur Road; ; 6am–11.45pm; mains ₹200–500 If you arrive here at lunch time, you might need to jostle for space and eventually share the table with other visitors for a hearty fill of a Kerala meal or Malabar specialties like beef ularthiyath, mutton biryani and kadukka varuval. You can choose between three different sections to sit in, mostly bifurcated by how brightly each is lit and the use of AC. This historic establishment sits at an inconspicuous corner on Kannur Road, but has branches as far as Sharjah and Dubai.

The very sweet and sticky Kozhikode halwa

📷 *Snapshot: Kozhikode halwa*

The famous Kozhikodan halwa has been going through a metamorphosis with changing times. Earlier, the popular flour-sugar-coconut oil-based sweet used to be prepared in four variations: black, white, red and green. The colour infusion was introduced naturally, with almonds for red and pistachio for green. Today, with the growing demand for more choice, the halwa makers have started using jackfruit, mango, grapes, strawberries and even chocolate. Little souvenir packs with mixed flavours are available widely in the range of ₹160–250.

Zain's Hotel **Mappila Cuisine**

📞 0495 2761482; Convent Cross Road; 1–11pm; mains ₹200–500 Famous for its typical Malabar biryani,

Zain's should be reached early in the afternoon as this highly popular restaurant gets packed very quickly.

Bombay Hotel   **Mappila Cuisine**
📞0495 2366730; Court Road; 6am–noon; mains less than ₹200
The Bombay Hotel has been serving delicious Malabar food since 1949. Even now, the small restaurant on Silk Road near the Kozhikode beach is packed in the afternoons.

🅐 Shopping
Kozhikodan Halwa and Banana Chips

Though the entire state of Kerala is famous for its fried savouries and snacks, the banana chips of Kozhikode top the list. The extraordinary sticky halwa of Kozhikode is also something you may want to carry back. Both can be found in small bakeries all over town, but the concentration of

❚ The famous banana chips of Kozhikode are a popular take-away from Kerala

shops on SM (Sweet Meat) Street is maximum, and worth the thrill of surveying before buying.
Head to Calicut Bakery (📞9446428055) on Eranhipalam Road where you can also see fresh chips being fried.

Tasara Centre for Creative Weaving
📞0495 2414832; www.tasaraindia.com; Beypore; 10am–5pm To pick up original and exclusive hand-woven and dyed designs on fabric, head to Tasara in Beypore. Tasara has added a contemporary twist to the age-old art of hand weaving, block printing, batik and other design methods. There are no other outlets other than this. Call them for directions, as there are no signs to reach here. Annual International workshops for students are held twice a year.

Kannur & Around

Best Trips
❶ Kannur
❷ Bekal & Kasaragod
❸ Thalassery

Kannur, **Bekal** and **Kasaragod** are heritage-rich destinations of the Malabar region. Arab traders settled in the small port town of Kannur (previously known as Cannanore) and soon, the Mappila community (p158) came into being. Kannur and the places around are deeply steeped in local tradition. Bekal and Kasaragod in Kerala's far north offer stunning beaches, a gorgeous fort, an important temple and much more. Smaller towns like Mahe (p169) and Thalassery (p168) add to the variety of experiences here.

Highlights
❶ St Angelo Fort
❷ Payyambalam Beach
❸ Lighthouse & Walkway
❹ Arakkal Ketu Museum
❺ Parassinikadavu Temple
❻ Vismaya Water Theme Park
❼ Kerala Folklore Academy
❽ Loknath Weavers' Cooperative
❾ Dinesh Beedi Cooperative

Kannur

The erstwhile port town of Kannur rose to importance with thriving trade and later colonial occupation by the Portuguese, Dutch and the British. Today it is known mostly for its weaving industry and some off-the-beaten-track forts, temples and beaches. It is also the best place to catch the Theyyam ritual, held on most nights of the year.

❶ ST ANGELO FORT
The Portuguese built the St Angelo Fort in 1505 from brilliantly red laterite stone on a promontory a few kilometres south of town. At the edge of Mappila Beach, it

GETTING AROUND
Frequent trains from different parts of south India arrive daily in Kannur. Buses are also a convenient way to get here with many overnight options from Bengaluru, Chennai and Mangalore. Within the region, one can hire a taxi (₹9–12 per km) or even take local trains that run along the coastline.

now overlooks a small fishing harbour full of colourful boats. What is most striking is the impeccable maintenance of this historical fort especially since there is no entry fee.
8am–6pm

St Angelo Fort is one of the best maintained monuments in Kerala

❷ PAYYAMBALAM BEACH

Palm-fringed sands stretch along the edge of Kannur town on Payyambalam Beach. Busy with camel- and horse-rides and plenty of ice-cream carts, this is a vibrant place to spend an evening. A small park sits at the edge of the beach where, apart from some nationalistic memorials, there is nothing much to see. Avoid swimming in the crowded section; instead, look for a quieter spot towards the south.

❸ LIGHTHOUSE & WALKWAY

Enjoy a blissful stroll on the seaside walkway along the PWD guesthouse. The well-paved clean path runs below the lighthouse and has plenty of benches lined up for you to enjoy the view at leisure.
Seaside Pathway; adult/child/photography ₹5/3/25; 2–7pm & 10am–7pm (holidays), Lighthouse 4.30am–6pm

④ ARAKKAL KETU MUSEUM

Showcasing centuries-old furniture, artefacts, coins and memorabilia of the former Arakkal Ali rajas, the wooden-floored museum is one of the few reminders of the Muslim dynasty's stronghold in the region. You can also peek into the family mosque that stands in the same complex. Additionally, there is an art gallery, which displays the work of local artists.

Opp Ayikkara Mappila Bay; adult/child/ foreigner/camera ₹10/5/50/25; 10am–6pm, Mon closed

⑤ PARASSINIKADAVU TEMPLE

Be prepared for the large crowd milling about the modern building constructed around this ancient riverside temple. Though the crowd is overwhelming at first, you will quickly realise that it's because of the daily and enthralling-ritual of Theyyam for Lord Muthappan. The deity is an intriguing fusion of Lord Vishnu and Shiva (a rare depiction). Fish, toddy and other kinds of meat are offered here.

5am–10pm; Theyyam 5.40–8.20am & post sunset daily

A view of the Payyambalam Beach

❻ VISMAYA WATER THEME PARK

If this trip is becoming too history heavy, spend a day at the Vismaya Water Park. Reasonably clean, it has a decent array of rides. Carry a change of clothes and appropriate swimwear (shorts and t-shirts will do). Down the road from Vismaya, one can also make a quick stop at the **Parassinikadavu Snake Park** (☏04972-780738; adult/child ₹10/5). A few but fascinating varieties of snakes are kept in glass cages.
☏**0497-2782850; Parassinikadavu; 11am–6pm Mon– Fri, 10.30am–6pm Sat, Sun & holidays; adult/child ₹350/300 weekdays, ₹400/300 weekends**

❼ KERALA FOLKLORE ACADEMY

The Kerala Folklore Academy announces cultural shows and events on its website each month. The establishment also has a small museum and a picture gallery, but the information here is in Malayalam.
☏**0497-2778090; www.keralafolkloreacademy.com; Chirrakal; 10am–5pm, Sat, Sun & public holidays closed; ₹10**

❽ LOKNATH WEAVERS' COOPERATIVE

Established in 1955, this is one of the oldest cooperatives in Kannur and occupies a large building that is filled with the sound of busily clicking looms. You can see the colourful spools of cotton threads being woven into a variety of fabrics. The small shop here displays the fruits of the loom, which include comfy bathing towels, mats, dresses, bedclothes and bags.
☏**0497-2726330; www.lokfab.com; No LL 99, PO Chovva; 8.30am–5.30pm, Sun closed**

❾ DINESH BEEDI COOPERATIVE

Beedis have been a crucial part of Kerala's economy for long. This small workshop produces the native Indian cigarette. Located in Payyambalam, you can watch how beedis are delicately rolled and packed in small bundles.
Payyambalam; 8.30am–6pm

Bekal & Kasaragod

Highlights

1. Sri Ananthapadmanabha Swamy Temple, Kumbla
2. Srimad Anantheshwara Siddhi Vinayaka Temple, Madhur
3. Bekal Fort
4. Chandragiri Fort
5. Valiyaparamba Backwaters
6. Folkland, Trikaripur

Pleasantly undiscovered compared to the southern parts of the state, Bekal and Kasaragod (barely 13km apart) are slowly scrambling up the tourism ladder with their pristine beaches and a handful of historical gems. Come here for a peaceful, laid-back holiday, knowing that the itinerary will never get too packed.

1 SRI ANANTHAPADMANABHA SWAMY TEMPLE, KUMBLA

This Vishnu temple is situated 13km north of Kasaragod. The sanctum stands in the middle of a placid green lake and is believed to be connected by a narrow cave passage to the Sree Padmanabhaswamy Temple (p54) in Thiruvananthapuram. This stunning temple has another intriguing highlight, a 70-year-old crocodile that seems to have arrived out of nowhere. Babiya, the divine reptile lives in an adjoining pond.

📞04998 214360; www.ananthapuratemple.com; Kumbla; 5.30am–1pm & 5.30–8pm

2 SRIMAD ANANTHESHWARA SIDDHI VINAYAKA TEMPLE, MADHUR

A circular wooden enclosure encases the sanctum of the famous Madhur temple, 8km from Kasaragod. According to legend, this was originally a Shiva Temple, but came to be known as a Ganapathy shrine when a priest's son found a Ganesha statue that started growing in size as the days went by. Another famous legend says that Tipu Sultan's invasion of the temple was averted when he took a sip of water from the temple well. To pacify the Muslim soldiers, he merely made a cut in the temple wall, which can be seen even today. Only Hindus are allowed and photography is prohibited.

Madhur; 5.30–8.30am and 2–5.30pm

❸ BEKAL FORT

Immortalised by Bollywood as the famous seaside location of the movie *Bombay*, Bekal Fort continues to fascinate visitors. The laterite stone structure was built in 1650 to protect the palace of the Shivappa Nayaks of Badnore. The observation tower is the most striking feature here. You can get a fair view of the surroundings after taking a steep flight of steps.

Bekal; 8am–6pm; Indian/foreigner/camera ₹5/100/25

❹ CHANDRAGIRI FORT

Though not as well-kept as the Bekal Fort, the view from this one is incomparable. You can see the Kerala–Konkan railway line passing over the cusp of the sea and the Chandragiri River from the edge of the 17th-century fort.

9am–6m

❺ VALIYAPARAMBA BACKWATERS

Unsullied by excessive tourism, the Valiyaparamba backwaters of northern Kerala provide an exotic addition to your itinerary. A full-day or 22-hour-long luxury houseboat trip (☎0467 2282633; www.bekalboatstay.com; Kottapuram PO, Nileshwar; ₹6000–9000) is best experienced in the Nileshwar region. The small town is also famous for Theyyam performances.

A trip to the Chandragiri Fort is worth your while for the view

❻ FOLKLAND, TRIKARIPUR

For a glimpse of Kerala's folk performances and martial arts, visit Folkland, the brainchild of Dr V Jayarajan. A small institution with a large repertoire of informative presentations, this one is for travellers with a taste for the arts. You can always call ahead and find out if there are any workshops, exhibitions or performances that you may want to attend as listed in their calendar.

☎0467 2210699; www.folkland.org; Elambachi PO, Trikaripur

Thalassery

When talking of the erstwhile spice trading port, Thalassery, you are likely to hear fervent discussion on the three Cs – cakes, cricket and circus. Unfortunately, of the three, cakes are the only item that has not got lost in time. However, it's interesting to know that India owes its cricket fanaticism to this small town, as Indians first played the sport here. Also, Keeleri Kunhikannan, the famous gymnast, was born here and later trained many circus performers.

1 THALASSERY FORT
Built by the British East India Company to safeguard its stronghold in this important trade junction, Thalassery Fort is full of its share of glory, mystery and history, with secret tunnels, strong laterite walls and a towering lighthouse on one end.
8am–6pm

2 MUZHAPPILANGAD DRIVE-IN BEACH
The northern border of Thalassery stretches into a unique flat 4km beach, on which you can even drive. Needless to say, the sandy coast is tyre-marked (but clean) as people successfully attempt to cruise their vehicles on its even stretches. From this spot, you can also see the Dharamadam Island, just off the coast.

The massive Thalassery Fort was built by the British

3 OVERBURY'S FOLLY
Named after a judge who wanted to build a recreational haunt here in the late 19th century, the small, clean picnic spot overlooking the sea is packed in the evenings. The hillside area is well paved and manicured, with a snack shop on the premises.
8.30am–8.30pm; adult/child ₹5/2

⟳ *Detour: Mahe*

This slice of Puducherry on the western edge of the country is no more than 9 sq km in size. The town boasts a vast colonial history and a substantial connect to France (till date). An unassuming fishing village colonised from the early 18th century right up to 1954, Mahe makes for a superb stop in the Malabar region.

Start with **St Theresa's** (6.15am–6pm) shrine, one of the oldest Christian shrines in the region. Note the French inscriptions below the statues; Jeanne d' Arc is one of the names that you may recognise easily. For Hindus, the 1000-year-old **Puthalam Temple** holds special significance. Built in typical Malabar style, it has three sections and a thick unmanicured copse alongside. A marble plaque on the gate recalls Mahatma Gandhi's visit.

The town is also a great showpiece of the arts. You can see mural painters and sculptors at work at the **Malayala Kala Gramam** (☏0490-2332961; www.malayalakalagramam.com; Cochin House, New Mahe; 9am–5pm, Thur closed) in Mahe. Visitors are allowed to take a walk around and look at the classes in progress. For those who like martial arts, head 5km south of Mahe, to **Chombala** (☏09446642954; Chombala; 6am–8am & 4.30–10pm), one of the most authentic kalari rinks run by Guru Devaraj. If visiting, do stop over for an evening of athletic brilliance. Donations are recommended.

Accommodation: French Avenue (☏0490 2334330; www.mahehotelfrenchavenue.com; near St Theresa Church; d ₹1800–2200) is decidedly the best place to stay here. It has bright, spacious rooms, a travel desk and a small restaurant. Though a budget option, **Mahe Residency** (☏0490 2336838; near Sports Ground; d ₹1200) is delightfully clean and spacious .

Of the paltry choice of places to eat in Mahe, **SAS** (☏0490 2371444; near Checkpost, New Mahe; mains ₹200–500) serves decent south Indian meals .

If you need help getting around, ask Mr Tayil Sadanand (tayilsadan@yahoo.co.in or ☏09846787890), a translator of French books, educationalist and a local historian of Mahe. He is especially fond of taking visitors to the only French medium school (Ecole Centrale et Cours Complementaires) in the region.

| A fishing village in the Malabar region, Mahe is actually a part of Puducherry

Accommodation

KANNUR

Neeleshwar Hermitage   Resort ₹₹₹

0467 2287510; www.
neeleshwarhermitage.com;
Neeleshwar; d ₹12,600–17,300
(incl of breakfast) Sixty kilometres
from Kannur towards Kasaragod,
Neeleshwar Hermitage has wonderful
Kerala-themed cottages by the sea. It
sits on the edge of a secluded stretch
of coastline. The Ayurvedic spa makes
this a great option.

Central Avenue   Hotel ₹

0497 2766500; www.
hotelcentralavenue.com; near
subway, Thavakkara; d ₹2750–3550
(incl of breakfast) Central Avenue
has great hospitality and even better
rooms, but is away from the sea. The
in-house restaurant could improve the
quality of food. It is conveniently close
to most of the sightseeing places.

Blue Nile   Hotel ₹

0497 2760077; www.hotelbluenile.
com; S N Park Road; d ₹2700–3800,

> Neeleshwar Hermitage is a good choice for
> the Ayurveda lover

ste ₹7000–9000 (incl of breakfast)
How about staying in a room which
was occupied by football legend
Maradona? The museum-like suite
has glass-encased wall-displays of all
possible objects used by the sports
star. The hotel is close to the beach and
is reasonably clean and well furnished
with wi-fi facility and a pool.

Mascot Beach Resort   Hotel ₹

0497 2708445; www.
mascotresort.com; near Baby Beach,
Burnasseri; d ₹1600–3000, ste
₹4000 (incl of breakfast) One of
the oldest hotels in the city, the only
charm in staying here is its sea-facing
rooms. The decor and ambience is a
little worn out, but the lovely view from
your room makes up for it. The hotel
offers wi-fi facility for guests.

Asokam Beach Resort   Hotel ₹

9446070373; www.
ayurvedaresort.co.in; Beach Road; d
₹2250–3250 (incl of breakfast) Head
to a quieter spot along Kannur Beach
to stay at the Asokam Beach Resort.
The good thing is that there are only a
few rooms here, so you can be ensured
privacy and a great view of the sea
(choose the 1st floor rooms). Ayurveda
massages are also offered.

BEKAL & KASARAGOD

TOP CHOICE Taj Vivanta, Bekal   Resort ₹₹₹

0467 6616612; www.vivantabytaj.
com; Kappil Beach; d ₹7500–16500,
ste ₹20,000 (incl of breakfast) The
serenely white decor of Taj Bekal is

what strikes you first about the hotel. Savour the beachside ambience and great spa.

The Lalit, Bekal   Resort ₹₹₹

📞0467 2237777; www.thelalit. com; Bevoori Udma; d ₹15,000–17,000 (incl of breakfast) Brilliantly landscaped in green and white, The Lalit promises some serious indulgence. The 26-acre property has internal manmade lagoons and sits on the edge of an unfrequented beach. Both its facilities and ambience make it a good choice.

Gitanjali Heritage,   Heritage
Kasaragod   Homestay ₹₹

📞0467 2234159; www. gitanjaliheritage.com; Panayal PO; d ₹5000 (incl of full board and taxes) If you want an authentic experience of northern Kerala, with a good mix of culture and food, try Gitanjali Heritage. Old artefacts and furniture provide an inviting decor to the house.

THALASSERY

Ayisha Manzil   Heritage
Homestay ₹₹₹

📞09847002340; Court Road; d ₹16,500 (incl of full board and taxes) Englishman Murdoch Brown's mansion along the sea was christened Ayisha Manzil in 1900. It was acquired by the local Moosa family, who are fabulous hosts and ensure that you get the freshest of seafood. The old-world charm, wooden floors, high ceilings, four poster beds and a pool make this place a great choice.

Soubhagya Residency   Hotel ₹

📞0490 2341203; www. soubhagyaresidency.com; Mayfair Plaza, Logans Road; d ₹1800-2800, ste ₹3300 (incl of breakfast) Situated in the city centre, Soubhagya is a practical and clean budget option. It is a good enough place to rest your head and spend a night in the small coastal town.

Eating

Kannur and the surrounding towns do not have great eating options; the restaurants in the hotels enlisted are a safe bet. You can, however, try the following places in Thalassery.

Mambally Bakery   Bakery ₹

📞09895012578; Harbour City, near Govt Hospital; 10.15am–8.45pm; mains less than ₹200 This place claims to be Kerala's first bakery. Mr Prakash (owner) tells the story of an Englishman, Murdoch Brown, asking his great-grand uncle to bake the first cake in 1880. Though the bakery has been refurbished to a new avatar in a flashy mall, without any indication of its vintage status, you must go here for the plum cake.

Modern Hotel   South Indian ₹

📞08247-2320860; MG Road; mains ₹25 For a taste of some authentic, spicy Malabar food, do look out for this little vintage-looking coop on busy MG Road. Meals are served only between noon and 3.30pm. Try the fish/mutton/egg combos with rice served during lunch hours.

Wayanad

Highlights

1. **Tholpetty Wildlife Sanctuary**
2. **Thirunelli Temple**
3. **Pakshipathalam**
4. **Kuruva Island (Kuruvadweep)**
5. **Banasura Sagar Dam**
6. **Pookot Lake**
7. **Edakkal Caves**
8. **Jain Temple**
9. **Muthanga Wildlife Sanctuary**
10. **Waterfalls of Wayanad** (off map)

Wayanad invites you to explore the great outdoors with its intensely green cover. Here, all you need is a sturdy umbrella and a taste for wildlife.

The district of Wayanad is spread around three main towns –**Mananthavady** in the northwest, **Kalpetta** in the south and **Sultan Bathery** in the east. It's impossible to cover all in a short time, so depending on your interests, plan your holiday around one of these. Sultan Bathery and Kalpetta are better equipped with hotels, but Mananthavady has its own charm, being slightly further away and isolated.

While the wildlife experience is best near Mananthavady, Sultan Bathery is for those who want to indulge in comfortable resorts. The famous **Pookot Lake** and **Banasura Sagar Dam** are closer to Kalpetta. For a spiritual trip, **Thirunelli**

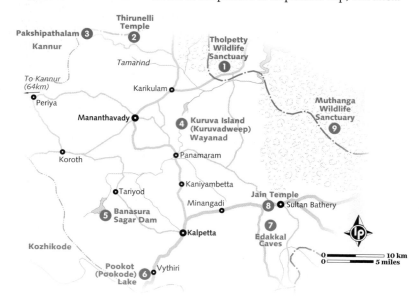

Temple can be accessed best from Mananthavady. Wherever you are planning to stay, you will cross the **Muthanga Wildlife Sanctuary** while entering from Bengaluru, and can make a quick stop here.

❶ THOLPETTY WILDLIFE SANCTUARY

The flip side of Tholpetty is that the picnickers and noisy groups create an atmosphere not befitting of a sanctuary. Your only chance is to hope for a silent jeep ride (one hour) through the forest. If you have received the proper clearance, you can also take your own vehicle (only SUVs) into the forest. This sanctuary is doable only if you stay in Mananthavady (24km). It remains closed during the monsoon months.

📞04936 250853; ₹60; jeep ₹400; camera/video camera ₹25/150; 7am–10am, 3pm–5pm

❷ THIRUNELLI TEMPLE

The scenic drive to the Thirunelli Temple adds to the spiritual experience. A barefoot walk to the Papanasini River

Spotted deer at the Tholpetty Wildlife Sanctuary

The breathtaking Banasura Sagar Dam

behind the temple is an effort, though essential if you are participating in a religious ceremony. Non-Hindus are not allowed in the innermost sanctum area, but it is worth a visit for the otherworldly view of the temple's exterior with its pillars and stone carvings, set against a backdrop of mist-covered peaks.

PO Thirunelli Temple; dawn to dusk; 36km from Mananthavady

❸ PAKSHIPATHALAM

A formation of large boulders deep in the forest makes for an adventurous trek, best done between October and February when the rains have subsided. The lush deciduous forest is particularly good for birdwatching. Permits are necessary and can be arranged at forest offices in south or north Wayanad. Reach the Thirunelli Temple, off Mananthavady at about 8am to start the 7km trek (after obtaining permission). The DTPC office in Kalpetta organises trekking guides (₹600 per day), camping equipment (₹250 per person) and transport.

☎04935 210377; Forest Station, Appapara, Thirunelli; ₹1000 (per 5 people); 8am–5pm; 32km from Mananthavady

❹ KURUVA ISLAND (KURUVADWEEP)

A raft or fibre-glass boat plies across the water for a 10-minute ride to reach this dense rainforest island, which has some unusual species of birds and plants (including rare orchids and herbs). A potentially exotic experience can turn slightly disappointing because of the large crowds, even in off-season. Passes from the Forest Department are necessary to visit this protected island; these are available at the counter.

☎04936-245180; ₹50; camera/video camera ₹25/₹100; 9.30am–3.30pm; 17km from Mananthavady

❺ BANASURA SAGAR DAM

A visit to the largest earthen dam in India – and the second largest in Asia – is worth the time and the climb. Ignore the paltry food stalls and the children's park, and focus instead on the view of the massive reservoir, which is the most striking part of the Banasura Sagar Dam. The sprawling expanse of water has small islands covered in thick foliage and home to a number of elephants, which can be spotted from the top of the Banasura Hill. The speed-boat facility here is erratic.

☎04936 273562; adult/child ₹15/10; camera/video ₹25/100; 9am–6pm; 25km from Kalpetta

❻ POOKOT (POOKOD) LAKE

A bumpy, untarred road leads you to this natural freshwater lake. The lake is reasonably well kept, with options for boating. One can also pack in a snack at the restaurant or

⊘ *Top Tip: Plan judiciously*

Wayanad is very big and you must plan ahead to optimise time, especially if you are only going for a short break. Choose the places you'd like to see, and the activities that you want to engage in, and then decide on a stay in one of the three towns (Mananthavady, Kalpetta, Sultan Bathery). Handy maps are available on the Kerala Tourism website. (www.keralatourism.org/wayanad.php)

Ancient pictorial writings can be seen at the Edakkal Caves

buy souvenirs from the shops in the same enclosure. It gets packed on the weekends, though feels quite peaceful during the week.

☎ 04936 255207; 15km from Kalpetta; adult/child ₹15/5 (boating extra); camera/video camera ₹20/150; 9am–6pm (boating till 5pm)

❼ EDAKKAL CAVES

Make your way, amongst a swarm of tourists, to the steep site of the Edakkal Caves. The trek is worthwhile for two reasons: prehistoric pictorial carvings and jaw-dropping views of Wayanad district. The etchings on the walls of the two natural caves, 25km from Kalpetta, were discovered by Fred Fawcett in 1890. More than 8000 years old, Edakkal's ancient wall art continues to wow visitors.

☎ 09446052134; 12km from Sultan Bathery; adult/child ₹15/5; camera/video camera ₹20/75; 9am–4pm, Mon closed

❽ JAIN TEMPLE

The 13th-century Jain temple in Sultan Bathery has splendid stone carvings and it is a marker of the region's strong

historical Jain presence. You can find a board at the entrance, which gives some information on the monument's history.
Sultan Bathery; 8am–12pm, 2pm–6pm

⑨ MUTHANGA WILDLIFE SANCTUARY
Here, you'll see elephants and deer (among other wildlife) and a lot of avian life, besides the lush flora of the region. The sanctuary is closest to Sultan Bathery (15km). Jeeps can be hired with drivers who double as guides. Personal heavy vehicles are allowed inside, but at extra cost.
04936 271010; ₹60; jeep ₹400; camera/video ₹25/150; 7am–10am, 3pm–5pm

⑩ WATERFALLS OF WAYANAD
Plan a monsoon-aligned trip in Wayanad to see the many spectacular waterfalls. Most of these involve some amount of trekking (check with guides). Among those worth seeing are **Meenmutty, Karalad** and **Soochipara**.
04936 202134; www.dtpcwayanad.com; District Tourism Promotion Council (DTPC), Kalpetta

The Wayanad waterfalls during monsoon

Accommodation

Kerala has been a pioneer in developing the homestay culture. Wayanad is a great destination to experience this kind of lodging. In this sprawling region, a steady supply of warm coffee – and pertinent travel suggestions – are best sourced from local families.

Tranquil   **Plantation Homestay** ₹₹₹
☏ 0947588507; www.tranquilresort.com; Aswati Plantations Ltd, Kuppamundi Coffee Estate, Kolagapaa PO, Sultan Bathery; d ₹7500 (incl of full board) This luxury homestay in a 400-acre coffee estate is a big departure from the regular lodging options here. The eco-conscious Tranquil has walking trails (with a list of birds) that have been interestingly mapped. There is also the option of a massage and a swimming pool to rejuvenate yourself.

| Tranquil, an eco-conscious homestay, has many walking trails

The Windflower
Resorts & Spa   **Resort** ₹₹₹
☏ 09895226611; www.thewindflower.com; VI/108 A, Ammarao, Achooranam Village, Pozhuthana PO, Vythiri Taluk; d ₹14,400, ste 9900 (all rates incl full board) It's difficult to go wrong with the Windflower's luxury rooms, well-equipped spa and the beautiful backdrop of tea estates. Battery-run vehicles take you from one spot to the other efficiently. With an in-house restaurant, and many activities slated for the day, you will hardly ever have to step out.

Silver Woods   **Resort** ₹₹₹
☏ 04936-273310; www.wayanadsilverwoods.com; Manjoora (PO), Pozhuthana; d ₹10,994–24,185 (incl full board) This distant resort, recently opened, would be an apt pick for those looking for complete isolation in luxury. A monsoon view of the Banasura Dam catchment area can be enjoyed from a Jacuzzi in the sit-out of your lavish suite.

Vythiri Resort   Resort ₹₹₹

📞 04936-256800; www.
vythiriresort.com; Lakkidi; d
7500–14,000 (incl of full board)
Nineteen years on and still going
strong, Vythiri is a busy resort which
offers a complete experience for the
family. Book well ahead if you want to
enjoy the spa and Ayurveda facilities.
With its popularity, you can expect
consistent service but don't expect an
exclusive experience.

TOP CHOICE Fringe Ford   Jungle Lodge ₹₹₹

📞 09880086411; www.fringeford.
com; Cherrakarra PO, Talapoya
Post, Mananthavady; d ₹7000 (incl
full board, special off season and
Christmas rates) An apt tag line, 'Get
Lost', follows this faraway jungle resort
(closest to Mananthavady). Present
yourself with a 'middle of nowhere'
holiday, with only birdsong and wildlife
for company. The 520-acre forest
houses four well-furnished rooms;
the knowledgeable staff here will
regale you with wonderful stories from
the jungle. Spot the regular herd of
elephants (and a lone bison) from the
lounge area.

Ente Veedu   Homestay ₹₹

📞 04935-220008; www.enteveedu.
co.in; PO Kayakkunnu, Pananmara;
d ₹3300–4300 (incl of full board)
Boasting comfortable, multi-levelled
rooms with private balconies and
a splendid view of paddy fields
and plantations, Ente Veedu is the
perfect holiday setting. And after
sampling the delicious home-made

✓ Top Tip:
Watch out for leeches

The downside to Wayanad's verdant
surroundings is the leeches. It's a
way of life with the locals, so you may
not be given extra warnings. Leeches
can be quite a menace during the
monsoons if you are on nature trails.
Carry small packs of salt to put on
a leech if you see one on your skin;
once in contact with the salt, it will
fall off immediately. Try not to yank
it out as it tends to dig its teeth into
the skin.

Kerala fare here, you won't feel like
leaving. The homestay is central to
all three locations, Kalpetta (19km),
Mananthavady (15km) and Sultan
Bathery (23km).

Kliff's View   Homestay ₹₹

📞 04936 218452; Vattathuvayal,
Vatuvanchal PO; d ₹6700 (incl of
full board) Get a great view of the
sunset behind the Nilgiris from a
hammock, in the well-manicured
lawn of Kliff's View, a relatively new
establishment. You can be assured
of an enjoyable experience here, and
a holiday that combines luxury and
privacy. The common lounge area
offers a gorgeous vista of plantations.
Ideal for a small group looking for an
understated holiday.

Rain Country   Resort ₹₹

📞 04936-329798; www.
raincountryresort.com; Lakkidi; d
5600–8150 (incl of full board) The

Kerala-style cottages at this resort, which sits on the Kozhikode–Wayanad border, are set apart for privacy but can get musty. The open-roofed bathrooms are a charming addition. Take a dip in the natural pool, with fish for company. A short drive from Rain Country is a spot with a great view of the Ghats.

 # Eating

Mint Flower Family Restaurant   South indian ₹

📞04936 227179; www. hotelmintflower.com; Chungam, Mysore Road, Sultan Bathery; mains ₹250–500; 8am–9.30pm Even though Mint Flower looks better from the outside, the simple setting inside will not disappoint you. The reasonable Kerala fare here is sufficient for a quick lunch. Opt for the filling thaali' which has a large variety of preparations.

Jubilee   South indian ₹

📞04936 220937; Sultan Bathery Market Road; mains ₹100–250; 7am–10pm Only if you are absolutely famished should you step inside this buzzing restaurant. Lunchtime is particularly packed as the food is tasty, and time taken to grab a quick combo is short.

Century Restaurant   South Indian ₹

📞04935 246166; Kozhikode Road, Mananthavady; mains ₹100–200; 7am–11pm This eatery entertains a large number of locals and tourists. It is high on taste but low on experience. Stick to the standard Kerala dishes.

Green Gates   Multi-Cuisine ₹

📞04936 202001; www. greengateshotel.com; TB Road, Kalpetta North; mains ₹100–250; 6am–11pm The slow service at this Kalpetta restaurant is more than compensated for by a delicious and hearty meal. One of the better places in Wayanad for lunch.

The Woodlands   South Indian ₹

📞04936-202547; www. thewoodlandshotel.com; Main Road, Kalpetta; mains ₹100–₹250; 7am–10pm The bright, cheerful interior of Woodlands is inviting for a good local meal or a small snack. It's best to stick to the south Indian preparations here.

 # Shopping

Uravu   Souvenirs

📞04936-231400; www.uravu.net; Thrikkaipetta PO; 11am–5pm; Mon–Sat The bamboo by-products sold by this non-profit establishment (the name of which translates as 'spring') are the most wonderful souvenirs you can carry back. The workshop is tucked away in Thrikkaipetta village, but a visit here is worth the effort – you can see the products being made by the locals. Uravu also provides opportunities for skills training, marketing and eco-tourism. The bamboo blinds, lampshades, paintings and earrings (among other items) are tasteful and value for money. But watch out for the many shops in town that make false claims of stocking Uravu products.

If You Like: Treks

Trekking in Wayanad is extremely dependant on the season, with no expeditions during the monsoons. Chembra Peak is often spoken of with awe, as it's the highest in the region (6890ft), but try the ascent only if you are extremely fit. For beginners, many of the estates have thrilling trails where one can encounter plenty of flora and fauna.

 Activities

While many resorts have spas and massage centres, only a few allow non-guests to book.

Windflower   **Ayurvedic Centre**
☏09895226611; www.thewindflower. com; VI/108 A, Ammarao, Achooranam Village, Pozhuthana PO, Vythiri Taluk; 9am–6pm One of the few resorts that allows outside guests. They have a host of luxury facilities, with an award-winning choice of Ayurveda services. Guests are pampered by the courteous staff.

| Trekkers on top of the misty Chembra Peak,
| Wayanad

Upvan   **Ayurvedic Centre**
☏04936-255272; www.upvanresort. com; Lakkidi; 8.30am–5.30pm A small but clean facility with a in-house doctor. Suitable for short duration treatments. However, they are also equipped for long-duration therapies..

Santhigiri Ayurveda   **Ayurvedic**
& Siddha Hospital   **Centre**
☏04936-347775; www. santhigiriashram.org; 18/213, near Collectorate Bungalow, Madiyoorkuni, Main Road Kalpetta; 8am–5pm An authentic Kerala Ayurvedic centre, run by doctors, in association with an extensive ashram of the same name.

Munnar & Around

Why Go?

The eastern edge of Kerala is a landscape of rolling hills covered with acres of tea and cardamom plantations. A refreshing break from the clammy coastal weather, Munnar and Kumily (entry point to Periyar Tiger Reserve) provide a great hill station experience in south India. Palakkad gives the most convenient access to other forested regions like Parambikulam and Silent Valley National Park. Visit the region to soak in the ethereal sights of plantation estates and to observe the rich biodiversity in some of the most important nature spots of India.

Getting There & Away

Air: Cochin International Airport is the closest airport to both Munnar and Kumily. The 105km distance from Kochi to Munnar, can be covered in 4–5 hours in a bus or car. Kumily lies at a distance of 155km from Kochi and also takes 4–5hours to reach. To reach Palakkad, the closest airport is in Coimbatore (62km); IndiGo, SpiceJet and Jet Airways have frequent flights.

Bus: Regular KSRTC buses from major south Indian cities like Madurai, Coimbatore, Bengaluru and Kochi are available for Munnar, Kumily and Palakkad. Comfortable overnight options by private operators cost between ₹600–1000.

Train: Aluva or Ernakulam (13km apart) are the closest railheads to Munnar and Kumily at a distance of 110km. These are connected to different important cities by major trains like the Kerala Express (12626) from Delhi, Kanyakumari Express (16381) from Mumbai and the Ernakulam Express (12677) from Bengaluru. From Aluva/Ernakulam, you can take a local bus or taxi to reach Munnar. Palakkad is a major rail junction in itself and has regular connectivity with major cities of south India.

■| A tea plantation at Munnar

Top Highlights

1 Periyar Tiger Reserve

One of the best-managed wildlife experiences for travellers in India, Periyar Tiger Reserve (p200) gives you your wildlife fix in south India. The sanctuary houses a scenic manmade lake by the same name, around which the forest spreads to 925sq km. Cruising along the Periyar Lake is a unique way of seeing the jungle, as deer, elephants and packs of wild hogs roam the edges for a drink. And if you are lucky, you may even spot the elusive tiger. You can also opt for jeep safaris to explore this biodiversity hot spot, which is teeming with birdlife and fascinating creatures like the lion-tailed macaque and even otters.

2 Parambikulam Tiger Reserve

Parambikulam Tiger Reserve (p210) has a diverse population of flora and fauna spread across 644sq km. The bamboo stands and shady forests of the reserve create a rich landscape in the Nelliyampathy–Annamalai region in the Palakkad district of Kerala. Well chalked-out jeep and walking trails, nature camps and comfortable accommodation in the heart of the jungle are the highlights here.

3 Living the Plantation Life

Stay in a luxurious plantation accommodation (p194) and enjoy the endless vistas of tea-covered valleys and winding hill paths. The British converted this region into an area for tea and cardamom cultivation in the late 1800s. Needless to say, it's hard to miss the colonial charm which is still deeply rooted in the plantation aesthetic. Apart from charming old bungalows with fireplaces and libraries, a plantation is also the perfect place to test your four-wheel driving skills.

4 Silent Valley National Park

Experienced trekkers and wildlife enthusiasts will love the surroundings of this intensely green rainforest. Silent Valley (p211) provides an incomparable experience under the canopy of tropical forests, rich with mammals, reptiles, insects and birds. In fact, Silent Valley is known for its minimal human intrusion, which has led to the preservation of some astounding species of flora and fauna.

5 Kanan Devan Tea Museum

The Kanan Devan Tea Museum (p189) in Munnar encapsulates the tea history of Munnar and surrounding areas into an affable, tourist-friendly version, which is easy to understand. It introduces you to the trajectory of events that has made Munnar the tea stalwart of India. You can also see the workings of a tea factory and sample the product.

Expert Recommendation
The best of Periyar

Vivek Menon is the founder of Wildlife Trust of India and author of eight books on wildlife, including the best-selling *Field Guide to Mammals of India.*

• **Walk or raft, don't boat:** Most people share a boat (with 60–120 people) to view wildlife from the serene 26sq km waterway. Instead, choose either the rafting trip or the several treks offered by the ecotourism program of the Forest Department. Periyar is one of the very few tiger reserves that permits tourists to walk, so don't miss the opportunity.

• **Stay at Edapalayam or in an eco-friendly place:** You can opt to stay at the Bamboo Grove run as an eco-development measure for local communities or at Spice Village (p203), the only eco-friendly resort. Or book into the jungle camping through the Forest Department. But if you can afford it, stay at the Lake Palace (p92) at Edapalayam.

• **Look out for birds not tigers:** People often overlook Periyar's rich bird life. It is the best place to see several Western Ghats endemics in one spot. In the forests look for the Malabar grey hornbills, the white-bellied treepie, the Malabar parakeet and the Wayanad laughing thrush. On the grasslands look for the Nilgiri pipit and the black eagle, and in the sholas for the White-bellied short-wing.

• **Look for endemics and rarities among mammals:** If you have to stick to animals go for the endemics and the local specialities. See the ubiquitous Nilgiri langur and the Nilgiri tahr, both Western Ghats endemics. Search for the jungle striped squirrel, Nilgiri marten or the spiny dormouse if you trek. If not, go to the river and the Periyar Lake to see large congregations of sambar and pods of smooth coated otters.

The Nilgiri Tahr is endemic to the Western Ghats

Munnar & Around

The relaxing hilly atmosphere of **Munnar** with plenty of sightseeing options attracts tourists from all over India. For those who want to visit the region for a dose of wildlife, the notable **Periyar Tiger Reserve** near **Kumily** awaits them. Once you've explored the bordering destinations of eastern Kerala, you should swerve along the edge of Tamil Nadu into the **Parambikulam Tiger Reserve** and **Silent Valley National Park** via **Palakkad**.

Best Trips
1. **Munnar**
2. **Periyar Tiger Reserve**
3. **Palakkad**

The lake is the centrepiece of the Periyar Tiger Reserve

Munnar

All the features of a classic hill station are here: cool weather, verdant valleys and, of course, tea as far as the eye can see. Munnar's resounding popularity amongst honeymoon couples has ensured that the main bazaar is cluttered with guesthouses, hotels and resorts of all budgets. And, for those yearning for tranquility, there are some wonderful remote places to stay, just a few kilometres away from the main town.

Highlights

1. Kanan Devan Tea Museum
2. Eravikulam National Park
3. Top Station
4. Floriculture Centre
5. Attukal Waterfalls
6. Mattupetty Dam
7. Marayur Sandal Forest
8. Muniyara Dolmens
9. Chinnar Wildlife Sanctuary

1 KANAN DEVAN TEA MUSEUM

The Kanan Devan Tea Museum transports you through the trajectory of events that made Munnar a treasured tea plantation junction since the late 1800s. The small six-room museum documents history through various artefacts and supplements the exhibits with a half-hour audio-visual show. The trip includes a guided tour of the tea factory behind the museum and free tea tasting.
adult/child/camera ₹75/35/20; 10am–4pm, Mon closed

2 ERAVIKULAM NATIONAL PARK

The Kanan Devan Hills of Munnar are home to the Eravikulam National Park, aimed at conservation of the endangered Nilgiri tahr (a type of mountain goat). These elusive creatures, native to the Western Ghats, are adept at traversing the steep hillsides of the Nilgiris. Just 16km from Munnar, Eravikulam is 97sq km and comprises large

GETTING AROUND

Due to the hilly terrain and number of sightseeing options, it is best to hire a four-wheeler in Munnar. The rates range from ₹1500–3000 per day depending on the car.

stretches of grassland with sporadic clusters of Shola forests. The Rajmala section (southern zone) of the park is open to visitors, except during the February–April breeding season of the tahrs. Personal vehicles are allowed on this route. A few guided walking trails have also been chalked out in the forest. The highest peak of the Nilgiri hills, Anamudi (2690m), also lies inside the park.

The rare Neelakurinji flowers bloom once in 12 years

📞04865 231587; www.eravikulam.org; adult/child/ camera/heavy vehicle/light vehicle/park bus ₹15/5/25 100/30/200/50/55; 8am–5pm; 31 Jan–31 Mar closed (this may change from year to year)

📷 *Snapshot: Neelakurinji blooms*

It's still a long way to go but if you do decide to visit Munnar in 2018, chances are you will see one of the most fascinating floral phenomena of the Nilgiris. Neelakurinji flowers are said to bloom every 12 years in the region, when complete hillsides turn a bright purplish-blue. Valleys of Shola grasslands come alive all over the Nilgiri range.

❸ TOP STATION

Kerala's border with Tamil Nadu affords spectacular views over the Western Ghats. Peer down the plummeting valley from a high windy point at Top Station while the misty blue mountains straddling the border keep you company on all sides. Unfortunately the upkeep of the place is a slight disappointment, though nothing diminishes the beauty of the panoramic view. En route to Top Station you should stop at Echo Point where you can shout your lungs out (or preferably watch others) at a lakeside.

❹ FLORICULTURE CENTRE

The meticulously managed Floriculture Centre makes for a short stop on the way to Top Station. A neatly paved, narrow one-way pathway ensures that you see the entire collection of flowers. Needless to say, that this is one of the most photo-friendly places with visitors clicking away against the backdrop of dazzling colours.

Top Station Road; entry/camera/video ₹10/20/50

⑤ ATTUKAL WATERFALLS

Pack some snacks and head 9km out of Munnar towards Pallivasal to the Attukal Waterfalls cascading across the tea plantations. They are especially spectacular after the rains (Jun–Sep) and make a great setting for a lazy picnic. However, at the height of summer, the waterfall is barely a trickle.

⑥ MATTUPETTY DAM

The tranquil green waters of the Mattupetty Dam meet you as you wend your way to Top Station. They warrant a quick picture or snack stop, with a fantastic view from the bridge that runs across it.

⑦ MARAYUR SANDAL FOREST

If you head north of Munnar towards Chinnar Wildlife Sanctuary, a vast copse of natural sandalwood trees at Marayur meets you 42km from the

Mattupetty Dam makes for good photo ops

✅ *Top Tip: Optimise sightseeing time*

The Floriculture Centre, Mattupetty Dam, Echo Point and Top Station can be done in one trip. In the same way, you can optimise your time if you do Eravikulam, Marayur Sandal Forest, Muniyara Dolmens and the Chinnar Wildlife Sanctuary in one loop.

town. Though you can't enter the forest, you can see the beautifully maintained thicket of trees by the Forest Department from outside.

⑧ MUNIYARA DOLMENS

On the Chinnar route, yet another wonder lies off Marayur: the ancient burial grounds or dolmens. Locally known as 'muniyaras', these Neolithic stone formations lie on a vast rocky platform and unfold interesting aspects of prehistoric life. There is no tourism infrastructure here except for a single board leading you to the location.

⑨ CHINNAR WILDLIFE SANCTUARY

The lesser known Chinnar Wildlife Sanctuary ▮

Sixty kilometres from Munnar, the Chinnar Wildlife Sanctuary is relatively unexplored. The vast expanse of semi-deciduous forests is home to an impressive number of wildlife species like the grizzled giant squirrel, the Nilgiri

tahr, leopards, gaur, sambar, spotted deer and a variety of birds. The only way to see the forest is on foot, with a guide. This is organised by **Tribal Trackers Eco Development Committee** (office at the check post). Book for a trek upfront at the Munnar office. And if you are feeling especially adventurous, you can also stay overnight in one of the three types of accommodation available; Tree House, Log House and Hut. This is truly for the adventurous as there is no electricity at night and no toilets in the tree house. You need to walk anywhere between 3–7km to reach the latter.

04865 231587; trek ₹100 per head for 3 hr; Tree House ₹1000 per head (extra person ₹250), Log House ₹1500 per head (extra person ₹300), Hut ₹2500 per head (extra person ₹500), (rates incl of meals and a guard); 7am–3pm

Detour: *Valparai*

Located 153km from Munnar, the non-touristy tea plantations of Valparai in Tamil Nadu make for a fantastic detour. The distinct 40-hairpin bend drive from the Anamalai Tiger Reserve in Tamil Nadu takes you to the top of a misty green expanse of splendid tea plantations. A drive past the semi-deciduous Anamalai forests will lead you to the lush plantations. From here there are the views of the blue waters of the Aliyar Reservoir below.

Valparai is replete with wildlife and spotting a leopard is not rare for the locals. These hills are also famous for the black lion-tailed macaque and other mammals, making it a top spot for wildlife photographers.

Immerse yourself in a planter's life by staying at the luxury plantation stay, **Sinna Dorai's Bungalow**, (04253 222362; www.sinnadorai. com; d incl of full board ₹6500)

in the Parry Agro plantations. The vintage ambience of this hilltop British property blends in perfectly with the modern facilities and furnishings of its six cottages. There is sumptuous food, a fireplace on chilly evenings and comfortable lounging areas like the front porch and the benches overlooking the plantations. You can go on accompanied hikes planned by the manager (45min–5 hours). This holiday spells complete indulgence.

Another great staying option is one of the three cottages of **Waterfall Plantations** (09443337022; Waterfall Estate Post): Indraprastha (₹2800), Valley View (₹1800) and Tennis Court (₹1800). Of these, Indraprastha is the most comfortable, with scenic views of the plantations from the front verandah. Easy chairs, antique furniture and superb hospitality are all part of the deal.

Accommodation

Ambady Estate Plantation Homestay ₹₹₹

☎ 09447662193; www.
ambadyestate.com; 3rd Mile,
Pallivasal, PO Chithirapuram; d
₹8000 (incl of breakfast) Ambady
Estate embodies the warm homestay
culture of Kerala, with Dr Rajesh
Madenan and his wife ensuring that
guests have a stimulating experience
of Munnar. Their 75-acre estate
sprawls behind the century-old
smoking house, which is still used to
dry and process the cardamom from
the plantations. Eight cottages sit
amidst aged trees. The rooms have
high ceilings and large French windows
– some even come with a yoga
pavilion. Expect authentic Kerala food
and plenty of tips on sightseeing. This
is a haven for naturo-therapy, yoga and
conservation enthusiasts.

The sprawling Ambady Estate has eight
pretty cottages

Windermere Plantation Estate Homestay ₹₹₹

TOP CHOICE

☎ 04865 230512; www.
windermeremunnar.com; PO Box
21, Pothamedu; d ₹7000–15,500
(incl of breakfast) Experience
an English-style farmstay at the
Windmere plantation cottages nestled
amidst cardamom thickets. The three
categories of spacious cottages are
stylishly furbished. This is the place
to put up your feet. You can choose to
stay in and read at the library, or take a
guided plantation stroll. The in-house
cafe is rather dhaba-like in decor and
ambience, being perhaps the only non-
English element at Windermere.

Spice Tree Boutique Hotel ₹₹₹

☎ 08606332011; Bison Valley PO,
Muttukad Nadukurissu; d ₹9500–
11,500 (incl of breakfast) This newly-
built boutique resort, 25km from
Munnar, sits at the edge of Muttukad
with incredible views of the valley
below. The serenity in the ambience

is ideal for Yoga and Ayurveda enthusiasts. Both the classic and spa suites have rooms with balconies overlooking the hills, but the latter has an additional touch of luxury with a copper bathtub and massage tables. Enjoy a quiet meal at the in-house restaurant. Spice Tree also has a pool and wi-fi.

Nature Zone   Resort ₹₹
☏ 0484 6493301; www. naturezoneresort.com; Pulippara, Pallivasal, d tent ₹6000, tree house ₹7700 (incl of all meals, trek, bonfire) Rumble along a bumpy forest road along tea plantations to reach Nature Zone, a camping and tree-house facility on top of a hill. Nature Zone arranges pick-up from the KSRTC bus stand. It has 10 well-furnished African-style tents and plush tree houses. The property sits on a ridge with breathtaking views of the Pothamedu Valley below. Nature Zone also has an in-house restaurant and offers guided

Spice Tree is one of the latest additions to Munnar's stay offerings

activities like rappelling, birding, trekking and nature walks.

Devonshire Greens   Resort ₹₹
☏ 04865 230011; www. devonshiregreens.com; Attukad Waterfall Road, Pallivasal PO; d ₹6000–8000, ste ₹12,000 Only a few months old, Devonshire Greens commands brilliant views of the Attukad Valley, just 4.5km away from Munnar town. The rooms are chic, minimally furnished, with balconies overlooking acres of plantations speckled with small villages. The Valley View rooms are the best. There is a restaurant, health club, coffee shop and wi-fi.

The Tall Trees   Resort ₹₹
☏ 09447111726; www.ttr.in; PB No 40, Munnar; d ₹6400–11,600 (incl of breakfast) The name comes as no surprise as this 66-acre property has

700 towering trees (of 80 varieties). Pretty ivy-clad cottages overlook the valley below. Each room has a large balcony. You are bound to have a busy holiday with treks, day trips and spa treatments. The hotel has wi-fi.

Casa Del Fauno
Boutique Homestay ₹₹

📞 0484 3048769; www. casadelfauno.in; Peak Gardens, Chinnakanal PO, Muttukadu; d ₹5500–6000 (incl of breakfast) This stone cottage with wooden flooring and fireplace sits in a hidden spot in the Muttukadu region. The house has seven rooms. Ask for the one with a garden and valley view; sunsets here are breathtaking. Three rooms are attached to the main house, while two twin-roomed cottages, slightly away, offers more privacy.

Green Spaces
Guesthouse ₹₹

📞 09844731099; www. greenspacesmunnar.com; Ottamaram, near Oak Fields Resort, Pothamedu Via, Bison Valley Road; d ₹3500–3900 (incl of breakfast)

Finding your way to Green Spaces may get a little confusing but you're likely to forget it all once you see the wooden deck outside the two spacious rooms. This cottage with the feel of a homestay fits perfectly into the hill station set-up. Think sinuous creepers, wooden floors, benches on the deck and cardamom plantations for a backyard. There is a caretaker to organise meals.

Swiss County
Hotel ₹₹

📞 04865 263300; www.swisscounty. com; Chitirapuram PO, Pallivasal; d ₹6500–8500 (incl of breakfast and taxes) Though Swiss County is a service villa, the property operates with all the comforts of a hotel, including an in-house restaurant, room service and wi-fi. It lies 9km from Munnar town and sits at the bottom of a valley; the views from the balconies of the rooms are just lovely. The bright interiors with chic furniture in cheerful colours is sure to perk you up.

❘ Nature Zone has a mix of African-style tents ❙ and tree-houses

Bracknell Forest Hotel ₹₹
04865 231555; www.
bracknellforestmunnar.com; Bison
Valley Road, Ottamaram; d ₹5000–
6000 (incl of breakfast and taxes)
At the far end of the quiet Bison Valley
Road, Bracknell's cluster of deluxe and
superior rooms snuggle together into
two sections – the deluxe section has
a sunny courtyard and a restaurant
with large glass windows up a wooden
flight of steps. The superior rooms
are in a separate unit with larger
balconies and better furnishings. All
the rooms and the restaurant overlook
cardamom plantations below. There is
a games room, wi-fi and lounge area
with books. The service is exemplary.

Violet Woods Hotel ₹₹
09495881276; www.violetwoods.
com; Byson Valley Road, Ottamaram;
d ₹5000 (incl of breakfast) All seven
rooms of Violet Woods are spacious,
with airy sit-outs that overlook the
valley below. With modern facilities
in each room, your stay will be
comfortable, yet pleasantly away from
the market hub of Munnar. There is
also one family room that can be taken
up as a single unit.

Eating

Hotel Saravana Bhavan South Indian ₹₹
04865 231129; MG Road; mains
₹250–500 Tried and tested across
Tamil Nadu (and abroad), Saravana
Bhavan is the safest option if you are
looking at quickly served delicious
south Indian vegetarian meals. The

small restaurant in the main bazaar
area of Munnar is forever lively with
visitors and waiters milling about,
balancing plates precariously.

Maya Bazar Multi-Cuisine ₹₹
04865 230238; The Silver Tips;
mains ₹250–500; 7.30am–10.30pm
Largely focusing on north Indian
cuisine, Maya Bazar's cinema theme
is not out of place. Enjoy a multitude
of veg and non-veg dishes with the
background score of old Hindi songs.

Sree Krishna Gujarati Marwari Restaurant Vegetarian ₹₹
09656251694; Adimali Road;
mains ₹250–500; 8am–10pm Given
the number of north and west Indian
holidaymakers, this restaurant is an
absolute hit. Go here for a speedy
service of delectable north Indian
dishes. The thali is value for money.

Surya Soma Multi-Cuisine ₹₹
09446327777; mains ₹250–500;
9am–9.30pm Surya Soma is perfectly
located for aching legs after a bout
of shopping. Here you can settle
down and dig into multi-cuisine veg
and non-veg dishes. The food is not
extraordinary but decent enough for
one meal on your trip.

Entertainment

Thirumeny Cultural Centre
09447827696; Temple Road;
Kathakali (5–6.30pm), kalaripayattu
(7–8pm), ₹200 each Thirumeny
organises hour-long shows of
kalaripayattu and Kathakali every day

in a cosy hall that has a muddy kalari rink and a stage, with theatre-like seating. You can also see Kathakali artists painting their faces from 5–5.30pm prior to the show.

Activities

Fun Forest
📞 08943355440; www. munnarfunforest.com; Second Mile; packages ₹300–500 Tyre walking, spider web, Burma bridge and a zip-line are amongst the many attractions for adventure lovers at Fun Forest. Eight kilometres from Munnar town, the establishment is spread over 12-acres and is great for an adrenalin-filled day. There are reasonable packages to cover a group of instructor-led activities, and if you are more than 15, you can even ask for an attractive discount. Safety ropes and helmets are available for each activity, strewn across the jungle surrounds. Though slightly unkempt, visitors nevertheless have a good time here. Unfortunately, there is no restaurant or coffee shop for those awaiting their turn .

Carmelgiri Elephant Park
📞 09446291042; Korandakkadu; elephant ride₹350 per head for 30 min If you fancy riding an elephant or washing it, the Carmelgiri Elephant Park is home to six pachyderms who provide constant entertainment.

Art of Bicycle Trips
📞 09538973506/www. artofbicycletrips.com Bangalore-based cycling expeditions group Art of Bicycle Trips organises 10–12 day cycling tours in Kerala. One of their favourites, 'Classic Kerala', covers the rolling hills of Munnar, along with some other significant destinations of the state. Led by accomplished trip leaders, the cycling tour is well equipped with a back-up van, medical aid and hand-picked stay options. Give this a try to get the adrenalin pumping and see Munnar from a different travel perspective.

 Shopping

KDHP Co (P) Ltd   Tea
📞 04365 230761; KDHP House; 8.30am–9pm You cannot leave Munnar without a packet of tea. To choose from a large array, there is no better place than the KDHP (Kanan Devan Hills Plantations) outlet. A multitude of varieties are available at different prices and the staff is more than happy to help you select according to your requirement.

Greenland Spice House   Spices
📞 09446130135; Main Road; 9am–9pm; Mon closed Apart from tea, the Munnar region is famous for its aromatic spices, especially cardamom. You will find plenty of shops at the market junction, among which Greenland has a reasonably large variety.

Sweet Land   Home-made Chocolates
📞 04865 230759; Main Road; 9am–9pm Mon closed Choose from an array of home-made chocolates in

flavours such as milk, orange and dark chocolate arranged in piles of irregular blocks. Some of them come in smarter packing for sale.

Spices Park and Handicrafts   Handicrafts
📞**09495651433; The Highrange Service Co-op Society Ltd No I 153; 9am–9pm** A collection of wooden bric-a-brac, from elephants to Kerala vallams (boats), jewellery and more, fills every inch of the shop. You have a lot to choose from for gifts.

K Krishna   Spices and Handicrafts
📞**04865 231069; Chelackal Complex, Krishna Nagar; 9am–8pm** This small complex houses a vast collection of spices and handicrafts; it's a one-stop shop for you to pick up souvenirs from Munnar.

| Munnar's Art of Bicycle Trips organises 10–12 day tours in Kerala

The Vanilla Shop   Spices and Handicrafts
📞**09447209100; Munnar-Kochi Road; 8am–9pm** Away from the bustle of town, The Vanilla Shop lies close to the KRSTC bus stand. Since it's a stand-alone shop (not in the busy market) you have enough time to explore the wooden artefacts and spices with ease.

Srishti   Jams and Welfare Centre   Handmade Paper
📞**04865 230340; www. srishtinatural.com; Srishti Welfare Centre; 8am–4.30pm** The community development wing of Tata Tea, Srishti assists differently abled family members of tea plantation workers to make home-made strawberry jams, handmade paper and bakery products. These are branded under Aranya Naturals (dyeing unit), Athulya (handmade paper) and Srishti the Deli (bakery products).

Periyar Tiger Reserve

Highlights

❶ Periyar Tiger
 Reserve
❷ Elephant Junction
❸ Green Park

To discover Kerala's wildlife wonder, Periyar Tiger Reserve, head to the small town Kumily (4km from the sanctuary), at the border of Tamil Nadu and Kerala. The small town has capitalised on selling the joys of Kerala: coffee and spices (mainly cardamom and pepper), interactions with elephants and kalaripayattu and Kathakali shows. With a massive spread of plantations and an adjoining reserve forest area, Kumily is a relaxing break amidst verdant surroundings, particularly for wildlife enthusiasts.

❶ PERIYAR TIGER RESERVE

The Eco Tourism Centre run by the forest department in Thekkady organises nature walks, jungle scouting, bamboo rafting, border hiking, overnight stays in the jungle and four trips inside the sanctuary on a motor boat. Of these, bamboo rafting is the most scenic and private. You can float through the day (with stops for meals), gliding between the picturesque dried trees that emerge from the lake, fringed by the forest. Deer, wild hogs and elephants can be spotted along the banks. Others can explore the jungle on foot with armed

A jungle trek is the best way to spot elephants

GETTING AROUND

Kumily is spread over a very small area and one can walk anywhere with ease. If you are not up to it, autorickshaws are huddled in all junctions and charge ₹20 as minimum fare. If you plan on covering a lot in a day and want to hire a taxi, Anshad's fleet of Indigos and Swifts are clean and comfortable (✆09495216817).

guards and guides for 2½–3-hour treks. For an overall feel of the place, the 1½-hour funeral-paced motor-boat ride is ideal. Large double-decker metallic beasts purr down the lake four times a day. Though you are grouped with 300 others split over four boats, it's a novel experience. Bookings should be done well in advance, even for short trips into the jungle. ✆**04869 224571; www.periyartigerreserve.org; Ambadi Junction, Thekkady; adult/child/foreigners/foreigners' children ₹25/15/310/110; Nature Walk/ Green walk ₹800 for 4; 7am, 10am, 2pm, 2½–3 hr; Jungle Scout ₹1500 for 2; 7pm, 10pm; Bamboo Rafting ₹3000 for 2; 8am–5pm; Border Hiking ₹4000 for 4; 8am–5pm; Tiger Trail ₹6000 for 1, overnight stay; boating ₹150 for 1, cameras ₹25**

❷ **ELEPHANT JUNCTION**

In typical Kerala style, Kumily is full of advertisements of 'elephant interaction' at every corner. This can be best experienced with Elephant Junction, which offers a multitude of ways to spend some pachyderm time. If riding atop an elephant around a coffee-cardamom plantation is still not enough, you can spend time bathing and feeding them. ✆**04869 224142; Murukkady PO; packages for half hour–full day₹350– 5000 per head**

❸ **GREEN PARK**

The heady smell of spices lures you through the Kerala-styled door of Green Park, which packs in 5-acres of a mixed organic spice plantation with

✓ *Top Tip: Kumily-Thekkady confusion*

Kumily, 4km from the sanctuary, is a growing strip of hotels, spice shops and Kashmiri emporiums. While Thekkady is the sanctuary-centre with the KTDC hotels and boat jetty. When people refer to the sanctuary they tend to use Kumily, Thekkady and Periyar interchangeably, which can be confusing for travellers who are unfamiliar with the area.

☑ *Top Tip: Packing essentials*

The green surroundings of Kumily also bring with them mosquitoes with a voracious appetite. Pack some heavy-duty mosquito repellent for this trip. A flashlight is also a must, as power cuts are frequent in the town. Take comfy walking shoes (preferably sneakers) to walk through the forest trails. Leech socks are recommended in the monsoons.

a few farm animals. If you're travelling with children, this promises an hour of fun and learning, as a guide makes you negotiate large leafy paths to taste, touch and be enthralled by the variety of plants, fruits and spices. You even get to climb a wooden planked hanging bridge.

☎09446806941; Attappallam PO; 9am–6pm; ₹100 per head/hr

☑ *Top Tip: Gavi Eco Tourism Project*

Another access to the sanctuary is through a small village called Gavi, 40km from Kumily, reachable by a four-wheel drive. The **Gavi Eco Tourism Project** (☎04869 223270, www.gaviecotourism.com, 8am–5pm, ₹1000 per head incl of breakfast, lunch, jungle trek, boat

| Gavi is popular among nature and adventure enthusiasts

ride, cardamom plantation visit, hike to Sabarimala View Point; jeep hire ₹1500, call Ann Mariya on ☎04869 222988) run by the Kerala Forest Development Corporation (KFDC) offers a day-long trip into the jungle, inclusive of a jeep ride, walking trail, meals and lovely options to stay. Most visitors start at about 5am from Kumily, passing misty tea plantations, to clear the checkposts at 20km and drive another 20km into the jungle to the Gavi tourism station. Here, after breakfast, a guide is assigned per group to take you for short hikes and a boating trip. There are three well-maintained options to stay the night here; **Green Mansion Jungle Lodge** (₹2200 per person), **Swiss Cottage Tent** (₹2500 per person), and **Jungle Camp** (₹10,000 for 4 persons). Cost includes all meals, boating, jungle walk and guide fee. Bookings need to be done at least a day in advance. Most hotels will do it for you at no cost.

🛏 Accommodation

Green Woods   **Resort ₹₹₹**
📞04869 222752; www.greenwoods.
in; KK Road, Kumily; d ₹10,000–
14,000, villa ₹19,000, ste ₹20,000–
42,000, tree house ₹15,000 (incl of
breakfast) Centrally located, Green
Woods sits atop a low hill, overlooking
the town. There's a multitude of
accommodation choices, a pool, an
in-house restaurant, shop and wi-fi.
Adventurous couples may want to
choose the resort's special treetop
pick, Vanya. This is a single tree house
(no children allowed) that can be
reached by a jeep ride followed by a
half-hour trek. Needless to say, the
view of the neighbouring jungle from
here is excellent.

Aanavilasam   **Plantation House ₹₹₹**
📞04869 263777; www.aanavilasam.
com; Pathumury–Aanavilasam Road,
Thekkady; ste ₹12,949–18,345, pool
villa ₹16,186 (incl of breakfast) If
absolute privacy is what you seek,
Aanavilasam is an ideal choice.
Six luxurious and minimalistic
rooms in the bungalow discourage
overcrowding at this property nestled
in 7-acres of spice plantation. Enjoy
the impeccable hospitality while you
relax by a fireplace in the common
area or grab a good book from the in-
house library.

Mayapott
Plantation Villa   **Plantation Villa ₹₹₹**
📞04868 224271; www.mayapott.
com; Kadamakuzhy, Vallakadavu,
Kattapana, Thekkady; d ₹9500–

Aanavilasam is a bungalow at a
spice plantation

10,500 (incl breakfast and dinner)
Mayapott has an *Alice in Wonderland*
feel about it. A small white door,
camouflaged by drooping creepers,
ushers you into a blend of mammoth
rock-scape, acres of shady spice
plantations and a natural pond. All
four rooms have the same scintillating
view, minus any distraction from TVs.
This boutique plantation stay is run by
a small team, which ensures that your
comfort is their priority.

TOP CHOICE Spice Village   **Boutique Hotel ₹₹₹**
📞04869 224514; www.cghearth.
com; Kumily Road, Thekkady; d
₹18,000–23,700 (incl of breakfast)
The atmospheric, eco-inclined Spice
Village is one of the most celebrated
restored properties of CGH Earth.
Conservation efforts such as solar
panels to generate electricity, non-

chemically treated water in the swimming pool, recycling of water and the usage of locally sourced produce has won Spice Village many accolades. The highlight of your stay will be the interaction with the knowledgeable team of naturalists here. To relax, spend time in the museum-like bar with an antique billiards table and many well-documented photographs. The pub is a reminder of the time when AW Woods (the first ranger of the region) lived here.

The Elephant Court Hotel ₹₹₹

📞04869 224696; www. theelephantcourt.com; Thekkady-Kumily Road; d ₹9000–13500, ste ₹19500–41500 (incl of breakfast)

The heritage ambience of Elephant Court, cheerful staff and comfortable rooms are a pleasant choice for families. The Kerala-style architecture is particularly charming for first timers in the state. There is free wi-fi in the lobby and a pool, along with other modern amenities.

Niramaya Retreats Plantation
Cardamom Club Resort ₹₹₹

📞04869 223905; www.niramaya. in; 66th Mile, Spring Valley, Kumily; d ₹14,000 (incl of breakfast)

Set amidst a vast 16-acre thicket, Niramaya is home to just six luxury cottages, overlooking the breathtaking Spring Valley and away from the bustle of the town. The resort offers a relaxing atmosphere with top-notch spa facilities (both Ayurvedic and Western). Cottages have thatched roofs made of bamboo leaves that ensure enough insulation and are aesthetically furnished; you never feel the need of an airconditioner. The resort is perfect for those who want solitude, but if that gets too much you can always meet other guests at the bar or the evening bonfire.

Thekkady Wild Corridor Resort ₹₹₹

📞04869 224414; www. thekkadywildcorridor.com;

A plush Jacuzzi villa at Carmelia Haven Resort

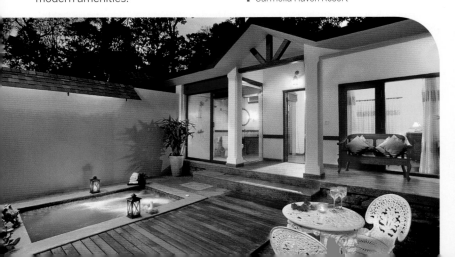

✓ *Top Tip: KTDC properties*

All Kerala Tourism Department Corporation (KTDC; ☎04869 222026; www.periyarhousethekkady. com; Thekkady, Idukki) properties are easily accessible, and three of them lie within the forest premises. Choose one to suit your pocket. Since the sanctuary gates close at 6pm, you need to return to the hotels in time. If informed in advance, the guards at the sanctuary gate can give you a levy.

• **Lake Palace** (d incl of breakfast & dinner ₹20,000–25,000): Lake Palace is the plushest of the three and lies by the edge of the Periyar River. It can be reached only by boat. Enjoy the vintage feel of the refurbished building and stunning views from your room.

• **Aranya Nivas** (d incl of breakfast & dinner ₹6000–7000, ste ₹8000): Though Aranya Nivas is the medium budget option, it has a sunny pool area and a pub. The rooms are slightly musty so it's best to choose the airy ones on the first floor.

• **Periyar House** (d incl of breakfast & dinner ₹1990–3565, ste ₹4465): Periyar House is aimed at budget travellers but has reasonably good basic facilities. The rooms are slightly cramped so you can opt for the suite for more space. There is an in-house restaurant so you don't have to step outside to eat.

Murrikkady PO, Kumily; d ₹7000–9000, villa ₹14,000–20,000 (incl of breakfast) A stay at the Thekkady Wild Corridor will avoid the bustle of the town and give you fantastic views of the undulating forest-covered hills. The three-storey brown buildings of the resort emerge from the middle of a thick plantation with an inviting central pool. A spacious balcony from where you can see a marvellous sunrise amply makes up for the average aesthetics of the rooms. The hotel has an in-house restaurant, spa and wi-fi facility in the common areas.

Carmelia
Haven Resort   Plantation Resort ₹₹
☎04868 270252; www.
carmeliahaven.com; Vandamedu,
Thekkady; d ₹6000, tree house

₹9000 (incl of breakfast) Twenty five kilometres from Kumily, Carmelia, a plantation resort, is nestled between cardamom and tea plantations. Vandamedu town is far from the tourist rush. Apart from the interesting mix of rooms (including a cave), there are enough activities that will keep you busy. Boating in the 4-acre personal lake of the resort tops the list vis-a-vis plantation visits, swimming pool and jeep safari. The resort has wi-fi as well.

Pepper County   Homestay ₹₹
☎04869 222064; www.
peppercounty.com;
Kizhakkethalakkal, 1 Mile, Kumily; d
₹3500 (incl of breakfast and taxes)
Pepper County offers the company of lovely hosts, Mr Cyriac and his wife, in their newly built house bordering

a 7-acre spice plantation. Since there are only four rooms, it never gets too crowded, so you can enjoy a peaceful stay, strolling around the plantations.

The Wildernest   Bed & Breakfast ₹₹
☎04869 224030; www.wildernest-kerala.com; Thekkady Road; d ₹4500 **(incl of breakfast)** Ten simple and tasteful rooms of The Wildernest lie around a lush jackfruit tree. The red oxide floors of the rooms, green metal spiral staircases and stone walls blend in perfectly with the forest nearby. The property lies on the main Thekkady road, which leads up to the sanctuary gate and is walking distance to the key places in town.

TOP CHOICE Chrissie's   Hotel ₹
☎04869 224155; www.chrissies.in; Bypass Road; , Thekkady; d ₹2000

| True to its name, Pepper County sits on the edge of a spice plantation

(incl of breakfast) Chrissie's is a well-kept secret, snugly situated behind a coffee plantation bordering Forest Department land. You would never guess how peaceful the place is as you enter through a small white door. The 16 rooms are brightly lit and have a balcony each (choose the first floor for a better view). They are warmly furnished and have no TVs. If you are a yoga enthusiast, feel free to use the studio. Simple continental and Middle Eastern food is served in a common area; do not expect room service. There is wi-fi in the lounge area.

El Paradiso   Guesthouse ₹
☎04869 223351; www.goelparadiso.com; Ambadi Junction, By Pass Road, Thekkady; d ₹1500 **(incl of breakfast)** All 15 rooms of El Paradiso are tucked away behind Babu Elias' main house. The rooms are sparkling clean and overlook a small green

patch. First-floor rooms are more airy and some of them have their own balcony with hanging chairs. Families can book the family room with four beds (₹2500). You will get plenty of home-style local food and warm hospitality.

 Eating

Kalavara

Silver Crest **Multi-Cuisine ₹₹₹**
📞04869 222481; Thekkady Road; mains ₹500–750; 7.30am–10pm The Kalavara restaurant at Silver Crest hotel overlooks the pool and serves decent multi-cuisine (Indian and Chinese) fare. It's a good place to relax in after a tiring day of sightseeing.

Kripa **Multi-Cuisine ₹₹**
📞04869 222972; Lake Road; mains ₹250–500; 7.30am–10.30pm The large glass windows of Kripa allow you to watch the slow-paced life of Kumily

> The Wildernest is on the road that leads up to Periyar Tiger Reserve

pass you by as you enjoy delicious Kerala fish curry. Try the karimeen, meen polichathu and fish moilee. You can ignore the soups.

The Mirage **Multi-Cuisine ₹₹₹**
📞04869 224800; KK Road; mains ₹500–750; 7am–10.30pm A spanking new restaurant at Holiday Vista hotel, serving a long list of multi-cuisine dishes, though it's safest to stick to their north Indian preparations. The restaurant is just off the main Thekkady Junction and a welcome respite from the heat and grime of the marketplace.

Sri Krishna Gujarati Marwari Restaurant **Vegetarian ₹₹**
📞09 349601434; KK Road; below ₹250; 8am–10.30pm Always buzzing at meal times with hungry visitors, this

📷 *Snapshot: Cardamom auction*

Twenty kilometres from Kumily, the Spice Board at Puttady organises e-auctions on Sundays, Tuesdays, Wednesdays and Fridays at 11.30am (through the year). A unique addition to your itinerary, it gives you a chance to understand the commercial importance of cardamom in Periyar. The auction master starts the bidding with a base price, raising it only by ₹2 for seven seconds. Traders come here to participate in e-bidding, and the winning party gets the displayed stock. You can watch this with prior permission from the Deputy Director of the Spices Park (call on 9400622348 between 9am–5.30pm) at Puttady.

is a truly popular pure veg option in town. You have to reach early to grab a seat and enjoy the south and north Indian dishes.

🤸 Activities

Since entry into the jungle is prohibited after 6pm, your best diversion is a cultural programme. Kathakali and kalaripayattu performances are most popular. Hour-long shows are packed with abridged dance-drama stories and short martial art demonstrations.

Mudra Cultural Centre
📞 09446072901; www.mudraculturalcentre.com; ₹200 per head/show; 5–7pm Though Mudra's evening cultural extravaganza is held in a bare kalari rink, the performances are quite thrilling. These are organised by students of a Kottayam-based dance school.

Kadathanadan Kalari Centre
📞 09961740868; www.kalaripayattu.co.in; ₹200 per head; 6–7pm Although not as atmospheric as other centres in Kerala, the Kadathanadan

Kalari Centre stages a kalaripayattu show for an hour every evening. The athletic agility of performers will leave you speechless.

🔒 Shopping

Spices   **Market**
Lake Road; 8.30am–8.30pm A variety of aromatic spices in easy to carry packs are available on the shopping street in Thekkady. The quality, variety and prices are more or less similar in all shops.

Gitem   **Clothes and Accessories**
04869 222794; Ambady Junction; 9am–10pm Numerous Kashmiri shops line the road that leads up to the sanctuary gate. Of these, Gitem offers a bit of boho fashion with colourful harem pants, silver jewellery, loose tops and wildlife-themed T-shirts.

                Organic Spices,
Red Frog   **Art & Antiques**
📞 04869 224560; www.redfrogindia.com; 8.30am–9pm This neat white shop is an exception among the cluster of those selling Kashmiri clothes and Kerala handicrafts. It

offers self-branded organic spices and tea and also some antiques, masks, DVDs and other curios. An art gallery by the same name stands on the opposite side of the road and displays the work of local artists.

Chocolate World   Home-made Chocolates

📞09947082999; Thekkady Junction; 9.30am–9.30pm You might need to squeeze your way to the counter to order some home-made chocolates, as Chocolate World is a hot local favourite. It offers a variety of flavours like dark chocolate, milk and orange in take-away packs.

Via Kerala   Contemporary Curios

📞0484 2312392; near Periyar Tiger Reserve, Cardamom County; 8am–9pm Via Kerala ticks with people looking for fun and thoughtful souvenirs. It specialises in Kerala-themed curios like cushions, bags and stuffed toys, and Malayalam-lettered packs of cards.

Konark   Kerala Handicrafts

📞04869 223508; Lake Road; 8.30am–8pm A zoo (quite literally) of wooden elephants is what strikes you first about this shop. Then comes the intricate mass of carved goodies that make great souvenirs for friends back home. What's even better is that you can take a quick peep into the workshop in the basement where all these handicrafts are made.

Carved handicrafts available at Konark make for great souvenirs

Palakkad

Palakkad is known for its unique geographical status – it lies in an unusual break of 27sq km within the Western Ghats. This little town is the perfect base to access south India's evergreen forests. It is also the most convenient stop from where you can visit two pockets of pure nature: **Parambikulam Tiger Reserve** at the Tamil Nadu border and the **Silent Valley National Park**. Palakkad has also earned itself the sobriquet of 'Granary of Kerala' owing to its vast fields of paddy.

Highlights

❶ **Parambikulam Tiger Reserve**
❷ **Silent Valley National Park**
❸ **Kalpathy Heritage Village**
❹ **Tipu's Fort**

❶ **PARAMBIKULAM TIGER RESERVE**

The Parambikulam Tiger Reserve constitutes 285sq km of wildlife-spotting territory. The reserve can be accessed only via the Sethumadai Checkpost in Tamil Nadu, 62km from Palakkad. From here, make a secluded 10km climb through bamboo clumps and thick jungles to a junction at the top of the ridge known as Top Slip. The junction is a popular stop for local tourists but you can avoid it and head straight to Parambikulam, 2km further to the south. Here, you formally re-enter Kerala's borders.

A biodiversity hotspot, the tiger reserve is home to a variety of flora and fauna. Among its residents are elephants, bison, gaur, sloths, sambar, crocodiles, tigers and panthers. The major attractions are spread over large distances; the most popular, **Parambikulam Dam** is 23km from the entry gate. The forest reserve is also famous for the **Kannimara Teak**, one of the oldest and largest living teak trees in the world. A favourite photography spot, the tree is 18km from the gate. A trip here warrants an entire day. If you like the proximity to wildlife, you can choose to stay in tented accommodation for the night (₹4500 full board).

Sethumadai Checkpost: ☏04253 245025; Eco Care Centre, Anappady; entry/cameras/light vehicle/heavy vehicle ₹15/25/50/15; 7am–4pm; Parambikulam Tiger Reserve: ☏04253 245024; www.parambikulam.org; Annappady,

GETTING AROUND

Since the two main attractions lie more than 40km away from the main town, it's best to hire a taxi in Palakkad. The rates are a minimum of ₹2000–3000 for every 150km, depending on the car type. If you are planning on taking an auto, the fare is ₹15 per km.

Thunakavadu; adult/child/foreigners/camera/heavy vehicle/ light vehicle ₹15/5/200/25/200/50; 7am–3pm

❷ SILENT VALLEY NATIONAL PARK

The verdant rainforests of the Western Ghats are best seen in the Silent Valley National Park. To get here, you need to reach a small village called Mukkali (60km from Palakkad), via Marakkad. The forest office at Mukkali grants entry into the forest for a maximum of five hours. Only jeeps are allowed inside the park and can be hired with a guide. The rainforest is brimming with a large variety of reptiles, mammals and birds. Such a profusion of beauty is bound to leave you speechless. The park closes in February and March

Lazy moments in the sun at Parambikulam

as the forest is prone to fire. Closing and opening times are sporadic so it's best to call before going. ☎04924 243225; www.silentvalley. gov.in; Mukkali, Mannarkad; entry Indian/foreigner/jeep ₹35/220/1100 (incl of guide); 8.30am–1pm

❸ KALPATHY HERITAGE VILLAGE

With a view to conserve the ancient architectural features of a typical Brahman village, a small hamlet off Palakkad was declared a heritage site by the state. You can drive through the area, which has been – and still is – inhabited by the same sect for centuries. The Kundambalam Temple organises an annual chariot festival in this part of town. It is said that the festival dates back to 1425.

Tipu's Fort is an interesting place to visit for its history

❹ TIPU'S FORT

Tipu's Fort, also known as the Hanuman Swamies Kotta or Palakkad Fort lies in the centre of the city and is a famous landmark. It was built by Tipu Sultan's father, Hyder Ali, in 1766. The fort's high walls are encircled by a moat and a sprawling garden; a favourite hangout for locals and visitors. The fort itself, however, is not of great aesthetic interest.

📷 Snapshot: Ramaserry idli

A quick detour is worth your while to grab a bite of the famous ramaserry idli. The **Saraswathy Tea Stall** is situated 8km out of Palakkad and serves this spongy soft delight that has put this nondescript village on the food map for travellers. This idli is flatter and bigger and served with podi (dry spicy mix) and coconut oil; of course you have to develop a taste for the dish. The recipe has been handed down through generations and now only four families in this village keep the tradition on. The subtle whiff of woodfire on which it is cooked lingers wonderfully after the idli emerges from a claypot covered with cloth.

Accommodation

TOP CHOICE Kandath Heritage Tharavad Homestay ₹₹₹

 04922 284124; www.tharavad. info; Thenkurussi; d ₹7600–12,600 (incl of full board) Set amidst lush paddy fields in Thenkurussi village, Kandath Tharavad is over 200 years old. Earthy architecture, embellished with carved teak pillars, a cool flooring coloured with natural dye, all ensure that this place is a treat to stay in. You must spend time with Mr Bhagawaldas, the owner, to understand the interesting nuances of Vaastu (architectural science) that have been used in the house. The four rooms have en suite facilities and are simple, airy and comfortable

Sri Vatsa Regency Hotel ₹₹

04923 251119; www. hotelsrivatsaregency.com; Pittupeedika, Main Road, Koduvayur; d ₹4000, ste ₹6500 (incl breakfast) This new luxury hotel in town is situated 13km off the city centre, but is worth the drive. Besides all modern facilities in the rooms and an in-house restaurant, there is a travel desk and wi-fi. Sri Vatsa also has an Ayurvedic treatment centre called Saukya.

Palakkad Heritage Heritage Hotel ₹

04923 252143; www. palakkadheritagehotel.com; karuvannurthara, Bypass Road, Koduvayur; d ₹1500 (incl of breakfast) The name says it all – Palakkad Heritage provides an atmospheric vintage ambience with its typical Kerala architecture; tiled roof and wooden pillars. There is also a modernised courtyard with a swimming pool and snug rooms with old furniture. The 93-year-old house comprises only five rooms, ensuring that you savour your fill of uninterrupted leisure. It is 13km from the city and that adds to the tranquillity of the setting.

 Eating

Hotel Indraprastha Vegetarian ₹₹

0491 2534641; www. hotelindraprastha.com; mains ₹250–500; 24 hr open One of the oldest hotels of Palakkad, Indraprastha still buzzes with visitors during lunch and dinner hours. The circular wooden-roofed restaurant just outside serves delicious Indian cuisine at any time of the day.

Pulari Cafe Multi-Cuisine ₹₹

04923 251119; www. hotelsrivatsaregency.com; mains ₹250–500; 7am–10pm Pulari Cafe in Sri Vatsa Regency is a small brightly-lit place that serves a variety of cuisines, though with an emphasis on Indian food. There is also a smattering of seafood if you want.

Lakshadweep

Why Go?

It's not until you've been to this palm-fringed cluster of islands, 250km off the coast of Kerala, that you realise just how many shades of blue really exist. The ferociously blue waters are strangers to pollution, the silver sands have never seen a plastic bag and the villages haven't been turned into tawdry tourist traps. Whether you swim, scuba-dive, or just stare, the incandescent water will be the undisputed star of this story.

Getting There & Away

Air: The only airport with access to Lakshadweep is Kochi. Air India has a regular service from Kochi to Agatti. However, check for flight availability since the schedules keep changing. From **Agatti**, other islands are accessible only by high-speed crafts or Pablo boats, with the exception of **Kavaratti**, which can be reached by helicopter. There are direct flights to Kochi from Mumbai, Bengaluru, New Delhi, Kolkata, Chennai and other main cities.

Cruise: SPORTS (Society for Promotion of Nature Tourism and Sports) – the government organisation – offers cruises all year around, which combine one to three islands in one package. These all-inclusive package tours depart from Kochi to the islands of **Kadmat**, Kalpeni, **Minicoy** and **Kavaratti**, depending on which tour package you opt for. For more details see p219.

■I An aerial view of one of the islands of Lakshadweep

Top Highlights

1 Diving & Snorkelling

No matter how beautiful you find the islands, always remember that it's nothing compared to what lies beneath – four thousand and two hundred square kilometres of pristine archipelago lagoons, unspoiled coral reefs and psychedelic colours of marine life are a diver's dream. The best news is that you don't need to be a certified diver to enjoy the singular experience of swimming with gigantic sea turtles.

2 Lighthouses

Zooming into the stratosphere amidst a dense palm cover, each island offers a pristine white, lovingly maintained lighthouse (p221) and all of them come with stories of shipwrecks. All the history of these islands, all of their spectacular vistas come rushing to you as you stand on top of the world, at 50m above a piercing blue sea.

3 Cruise

At a time when every destination is more or less a two-hour flight, the idea of taking a long ship journey may sound exhausting. But once you're on board the ship (p219), you're transported to a different time. Without phone signals or television, days on board are about spectacular sunsets, evening deck walks and morning tea accompanied by an endless sea.

Expert Recommendation
Diving in the ocean

Sumer Verma, CEO of Lacadives, has over 7000 dives to his credit and has worked for over 15 years in the diving industry. He is also an underwater photographer.

• **Diving Course:** It is mandatory to know swimming for a diving certification course. A course with PADI (Professional Association of Dive Instructors) will help complete your confined water and theory requirements before heading to the islands. Choose a reputed diving school/centre for learning.

• **Scuba Diving Course:** Those with limited time can go on a DSD (Discover Scuba Diving) experience. This involves a hand-held diving one-on-one experience with an instructor under water. You may be taken for half an hour down to 10m underwater.

• **Equipment:** These are included in the price offered by all dive shops and will include masks, fins, and a scuba cylinder with compressed air. The equipment will weigh 15kg on land,

but feel luxuriously weightless under water. Choose a reputed dive shop.

• **Instructors:** Diving is always done in pairs or with buddy-instructors for safety. Follow instructor's directions to convey any discomfort.

• **Fitness:** Diving is suitable for all from 10 years onwards. It's best to consult the doctor for those with medical problems like heart ailments, epilepsy, asthma or any recent surgeries before diving.

• **Best Time:** Mid-October to mid-May.

• **Dive Sites:** Kadmat Island – North Cave, the Wall, Jack Point, Shark Alley, the Potato Patch, Cross Currents and Sting Ray City. Bangaram – Manta Point, Life, Grand Canyon and the sunken reef at Perumal Par.

Lakshadweep

Best Trips
1 Kavaratti
2 Minicoy
3 Kadmat

On arriving at this aquamarine paradise that has more palm trees than people, you feel surprised and grateful in equal measure that this tropical island system is a part of India. The distance from the mainland and the efforts of a vigilant government have placed these virgin islands in a time capsule. The simple village folk, whose main sources of income are fishing and coir production, welcome tourists with open arms. While the sea at **Kavaratti** introduces a kaleidoscopic underwater world, the **Minicoy** throws up ancient shipwrecks and lighthouses. **Kadmat** speaks only of serenity.

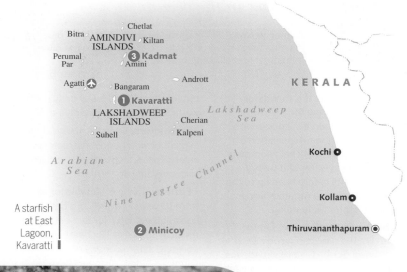

A starfish at East Lagoon, Kavaratti

Kavaratti

❶ MAIN BEACH

The administrative headquarters of Lakshadweep, Kavaratti, accommodates the tourist lodge, water sports centre and lone restaurant. Kavaratti may not make the best beach getaway but it's a fantastic diving location. Of the many world-class dive sites that the professionally managed **Lakshadweep Diving Academy** will take you to, the **Wall of Wonders** is the best. This gigantic wall of soft coral goes deep into the sea, ablaze with the colours of exotic marine life.

Visit Kavaratti as part of the Taratashi package or a combination package with Kadmat which allows for a stay on the island; the Coral Reef/ Samundram package offers only a day trip; Helicopter service from Agatti to Kavaratti costs ₹8500 per tourist (refer to box below).

❙ Off the Kerala coast, Kavaratti

☑ *Top Tip: The island trip planner*

Be prepared for a whole new tourism experience at Lakshadweep. Here, the government pretty much decides your holiday. While they are eager for tourist traffic, they keep travel to Lakshadweep a state secret. This lack of clarity bullies most people into booking government cruises, which are all-inclusive packages. Choose the **Coral Reef** package if you don't mind travelling with a crowd on a strict schedule. Choosing from the island stay packages like **Taratashi** or the **Swaying Palms** will provide a gentler experience. You should decide on your islands first (only Kadmat, Kavaratti and Minicoy have lodgings since the resorts at Bangaram and Agatti have been closed) and contact the SPORTS office (p215) who will work out an itinerary keeping ship schedules in mind. Most inter-island transport leaves from Kavaratti but be aware that the trip will involve long journeys in a small motorised fishing boat (₹15,000) in the event the speed crafts (₹2000) are not available.

📞**0484 2668387; www. lakshadweeptourism.nic.in; IG Road, Willingdon Island, Kochi**

❷ MARINE AQUARIUM

One of the few 'sightseeing' options at Lakshadweep. A visit to the aquarium gives you a reason to get off the beach and explore the island. While autos are available, it's highly recommended that you take the short walk through the lovely village lanes. As you enter the dingy aquarium-cum-museum with its range of pickled tropical fish specimens you may wonder why you're seeing them dead in jars when you have the opportunity to meet them alive underwater, but it's interesting enough nonetheless. There is also a shark pool on the premises with a couple of impatient sharks, which may be worth a look if you don't plan to dive deep enough to meet one.

A visit to the aquarium is included in all packages for Kavaratti.

❸ UJRA MOSQUE

The ancient mosques in Lakshadweep are white limestone cottages with cheerful red terracotta roofs, reminiscent more of coastal temples than mosques. Of the 300 the mosques here, Ujra is the most famous. This collection of three structures, including a dargah, is housed in a courtyard of white sand. It does not hold regular namaaz. The beautifully designed pillars and elaborate verandah with carvings of plants and leaves are a celebrated attraction here.

Minicoy

Highlights
❶ Thundi Beach
❷ Lighthouse Visits
❸ Townhall

❶ THUNDI BEACH

The beauty of Thundi Beach at Minicoy is nothing short of striking. The translucent emerald waters stretch endlessly in all directions, undisturbed except for a lone bobbing fishing boat. The shallow lagoon on the southern tip of the island extends over a kilometre into the sea, not unlike a personal swimming pool. With its white seabed, that gives the water the appearance of liquid glass, the lagoon is swarming with enormous sea turtles. While the diving facility here is smaller in scale than Kavaratti, this crescent-shaped island offers world-class shipwreck dives as shallow as 8m into the sea. Ancient steamer ships lie on the seabed and local accounts place their sinking as far back 1862.

Visit Minicoy on a Swaying Palm package; Coral Reef/Samundram offer only day trips

❷ LIGHTHOUSE VISITS

For lighthouse lovers, Lakshadweep is the Holy Grail. Each island has a beautiful and well-kept white lighthouse surrounded by palm tress. The lighthouse at Minicoy, one of Asia's tallest, going well above 47m, is believed to have been constructed in the wake of several shipwrecks in the 1800s. Don't let the steep 200-step climb deter you. Once you reach the top, the island lies spread out below you from one end to the other, and all the shades of blue come together in one spectacular sweep. Look out for the antique oil canister and equipment on display as you climb.

A stunning view from Minicoy Lighthouse

Minicoy lighthouse is walking distance from the tourist lodge; Entry ₹10; camera ₹25; 4pm–5.30pm; Sun closed

❸ TOWNHALL

Minicoy may be in Lakshadweep, but its heart is in Maldives. The cultural practices of this little gem of an island are worth witnessing and Falassery village is the place to do it. Rooted as a matrilineal society, the village operates as a family led by the moopan. At its beautifully decorated Townhall you will see the entire village descend to discuss important matters and celebrate special occasions like Republic Day and Independence Day with giant communal meals. Displayed at the Townhall is the star 'jhaldhoni' of the village, crafted by ace boat makers, which is rowed by the males of Falassery in boat races or to welcome dignitaries.

Kadmat

When you're in Lakshadweep you have to constantly remind yourself that you are still in India. On Kadmat, the island most frequented by foreigners, this feeling is more acute. With scenic beauty that parallels Minicoy and a dive facility that rivals Kavaratti, Kadmat has the best of Lakshadweep. It offers a great stretch of beach and endless lagoons on both sides that teem with all varieties of marine life. However, the highlights here are the range of spectacular dive sites that go from 9 to 40m and cater to all levels of divers. Boasting of brilliant water visibility, dive sites like **Shark Alley** or **Turtle City** make for unforgettable experiences. If you're ever plan to get a diving certification, Kadmat is the place to do it. **Transport from Agatti via high-speed ferry (₹2000) or a private Pablo boat (₹15,000) is managed by SPORTS; Alternatively, Kadmat can be visited as part of the Marine Wealth Awareness Package**

A beachside resort at Kadmat

 # Accommodation

Kadmat Island

Beach Resort **Cottages** ₹₹₹

📞0484 2668387; www.
lakshadweeptourism.com; IG Road,
Willingdon Island, Kochi; 3 night/4
day package including meals and
water sports ₹26,400 The white AC
and non AC cottages ,spread out on
the beach, meet your requirements
adequately. Expect the basics to be
covered, the hot water to run, the
phone to dial and the views to be
spectacular, but nothing more.

Twenty Bedded

Tourist Lodge, Minicoy **Cottages** ₹₹

📞0484 2668387; www.
lakshadweeptourism.com; IG Road,
Willingdon Island, Kochi; ₹6000 per
night including meals and water
sports The compact but incredibly
pretty 10 cottages are spread out on
the beach and come with open-air
bathrooms and a modest sit out,
perfect for taking in the sunset. The
open-wall restaurant facing the beach
makes for a romantic dinner venue.

Paradise Hut,

Kavaratti **Tourist Lodge** ₹₹

📞0484 2668387; www.
lakshadweeptourism.com; IG Road,
Willingdon Island, Kochi; ₹6000 per
night including meals and water
sports Paradise Hut is not a hut at all

but a small building on the beach with
a restaurant alongside. It offers two
double rooms in one unit, which gets
a bit awkward if you happen not to
know the couple in the second room.
Scrupulously clean, the facilities here
are adequate but hardly luxurious. The
highlight of the lodge is that it offers
generous balconies in every room and
a rooftop that transports you from the
bustle below.

 # Eating

Food is not a high point in
Lakshadweep, mainly because it's not
easy to get. Whether you choose to
do a cruise or stay over at the islands,
your package will come inclusive of
meals. The restaurants in the area,
most of which only cater to locals,
are open only in the evenings. What
you will find in plenty are 'cool bars'
which serve strictly non-alcoholic cold
drinks. At Kalpeni, you can visit the
little eatery of Koya where you can try
the rice pancake rotis and the crispy
reef fish (₹60) stuffed with spices. In
Kavaratti, try Al Bake for the parathas
and chicken masala (₹90) or the
octopus fry (₹50) at Sandy Beach.
In Minicoy, tuna is the star of the
meal. If you visit Falassery try some
delicious tuna samosa and a steamed
sweetmeat called fonivara bondi made
of coconut and jaggery.

GET TO KNOW KERALA

◼I Fishermen hauling in nets at the Chowara Beach

Kerala Today

Kerala has been labelled 'the most socially advanced state in India' by Nobel prize-winning economist Amartya Sen. Land reform and a focus on infrastructure, health and education have played a large part in Kerala's success. Despite the changes that come with growth and development, Kerala has managed to hold on to its vivid mosaic of culture, scenic beauty and customs with tenacity.

Political Scenario

The political evolution of Kerala has straddled two major fronts during the last four decades: the Left Democratic Front (Communist Party) and the United Democratic Front (Indian National Congress). No other major party has made any inroads into the state, which is politically very active with a high level of awareness amongst the people. In fact, Kerala was the first state where left leanings were first appreciated and voted for. It's no wonder that you will find Che Guevara posters peeping from every corner and *The Communist Manifesto* often being referred to in conversations. The trade unions of Kerala are famous for holding strikes frequently; for travellers, this could mean being stranded due to taxis refusing to function or unexpected bandhs blocking roads and other services.

Economic Scenario

Kerala's economic health is mainly due to a thriving service industry, agriculture, remittances from the Gulf countries and, now, an IT boom. Tourism plays a major role in employment and is a key earning factor in the economy. Kerala's extensive paddy fields and spice, coffee and tea plantations are other major contributors to the self-sufficiency of the state. The Kerala Gulf boom has been a major shot in the arm for the state's economic well-being as millions of Gulf migrants have repatriated their earnings over the last decade. The Kerala government is also investing heavily in building IT parks and Special Economic Zones (SEZ), giving the sector a big nudge. Above all, Kerala's outstanding literacy rate (the state ranks first in the country) has made an indelible contribution to boosting the economic environment.

Tourism

The moniker, 'God's Own Country' needs special recognition when discussing tourism in India. The expression is prominently used by Kerala Tourism and has catapulted the state to an internationally sought-after holiday destination for decades. One of the fastest growing tourism hubs in the country, Kerala's allure lies in its tremendous diversity of landscapes, from rolling hills to tranquil backwaters and pristine beaches to dense forest reserves. Then, of course, is its vibrant cultural identity – with music, dance, festivals and rituals.

Tourism has rapidly permeated the lives of the locals, as well. Some have responded by opening up their homes to travellers. The concept of homestay was first introduced in Kerala and it has been a successful experiment. Also popular are the burgeoning Ayurvedic centres, which combine natural treatments with luxury living. The state is now also making forays into specific travel initiatives like medical tourism and projects inclined towards eco tourism.

Given Kerala's heartening cosmopolitan environment, art festivals like Kochi-Muziris Biennale are bound to set a trend in the coming years. Such initiatives will broaden Kerala's appeal, establishing it as much more than just a beach destination.

Bird's-eye view of the cosmopolitan hub of Kochi

History

Kerala's history finds resonance in Hindu mythology and is supported by archaeological findings dating back to the Neolithic period. The relics of Kerala's past are reasonably well preserved, giving travellers a glimpse of the influences that shaped its character.

Prehistoric Kerala

Laterite rock caves, tombs and burial urns can still be found in various parts of Kerala. Marayur, near Munnar, has a handful of burial chambers (dolmenoids) from the megalithic period. The Ezhuthu Guha (cave) in the sandalwood forest in Idukki district, houses several rock art paintings and carvings, some of which have been assigned to the late Mesolithic era. Similarly, the engravings of the Edakkal caves point towards a rich Neolithic era around 5000 BC.

3000 BC–AD 500

The spices of Malabar drew Babylonian, Assyrian and Egyptian traders to the Malabar coast, setting the tone for the future transformation of the coastal cities of Kerala into major international ports. Roman vessels loaded with gold are recorded as having crossed the rough seas to exchange it for spices with the Dravidian kings of Kerala. With every passing century, the trade links grew stronger, even as internal leadership shifted from the Pandya to the Chera and Chola dynasties. Along with the traders came new religions. Arabs, Persians, Christians and Jews arrived in quick succession, giving rise to communities like the Mappilas and Syrian Christians.

500–1400

A number of dynasties rose and fell during this period. The Cholas largely reigned over Kerala during the 11th and 12th centuries. It was after the short-lived sovereignty of Ravi Varma Kulashekhara of the Venad kingdom in the 14th century, that Kerala became an aggregate of warring chieftains. The Zamorins (hereditary rulers) of Kozhikode pushed out other rulers and established a stronghold in the central part of the state. They also developed strong alliances with Muslim, Arab and Chinese merchants.

A portrayal of Vasco da Gama's meeting with the Zamorin of Kozhikode

1400–1663

Vasco da Gama's arrival in 1498 opened the floodgates to European colonialism as Portuguese, Dutch and English interests fought Arab traders, and then each other, for control of the lucrative spice trade. Even though the Zamorins initially encouraged trade, soon conflict between traders spread to the local inhabitants, and the rift led to fights between the Portuguese and the Zamorin forces with a decisive victory for the latter in the Battle of Chaliyam Fort in 1571. It was the Dutch, however, who expelled the Portuguese in 1663.

1663–1795

After the Portuguese exit, the Dutch East India Company began to take control, though constant battles with the Travancore royal family debilitated their forces. The Battle of Colachel in 1741 with the Venad kingdom led to the Dutch detachment from the region. The Mysorean invasion of Kerala in 1766 gave the English East India Company an opportunity to ally with the local forces. They gradually reduced Travancore to a mere protected ally in 1795 during the Third Anglo-Mysore War.

1795–1947

The British converted Kochi and Travancore to princely states in the late 18th century. By 1812, they were in control of Kochi, Malabar and Travancore. Local kings and communities opposed this as anti-British sentiments spread across the country. A notable feature of the freedom struggle was the involvement of peasants and workers in the 1920s and 30s, which gave the movement a unique social momentum. It later led to the formation of a strong left wing in the state. After independence in 1947, the princely states merged with the Union of India.

1947–1957

Kerala, as it is today, was created in 1956 from Travancore, Kochi and Malabar. In 1957, Kerala got the world's first freely elected communist government.

Late 1970s–Early 1990s

Political power alternates between the Left Democratic Front led by the Communist Party of India (CPM) and the United Democratic Front led by the Congress. Ranked as the most literate state of the country, Kerala achieved universal literacy by 1991.

1990s–2012

In social and economic spheres, Kerala performs better than most Indian states. One of the most talked about things is the initiative to decentralise power and give more teeth to the grassroots. An aggressive campaign to promote tourism puts Kerala in the spotlight. In 2012, Kerala even overtook Taj Mahal as the most searched destination on Google.

Vasco da Gama – the game changer

Portuguese explorer Vasco da Gama was a game changer for the trade empire of coastal India. Having survived shipwrecks and almost fatal sea journeys, he landed in Kozhikode in 1498. His discovery of the land of spices resulted in a strong ripple effect, eventually adding to the multi-culturalism that is an inherent part of India today.

Kerala Cuisines

You could say that it was the intoxicating aroma of spices that lured traders long ago to Kerala. The same heady concoctions make the cuisine a delicious enough reason to travel to this part of India today. So, expect a generous use of coconut, chilli and spices, in mouth-tingling local recipes that differ with region and community.

Culinary Influences

With Greek, Roman, Chinese, Portuguese, Arab and Dutch traders making their way to the port towns of Kerala, it is no wonder that the food has been cast with a spectacular range of culinary influences. Though there are differences in the taste and style of preparations between north and south Kerala dishes, both use similar vegetables and ingredients. Plantains, coconut, gourds and yam are commonly used. Additionally, north Kerala has a large array of non-vegetarian dishes, given its Arab lineage. Mappila food (p158), as it's called, is especially famous for biryanis. In the southern districts, Syrian Christians sway the menu towards appams, chicken stew, duck roast and other non-veg delights. The Hindu population of Kerala is known for serving a delightful veg banquet, called the sadya. In this, 24–28 kinds of dishes are served in a specific order on a banana leaf.

Seafood Specialities

Kerala is a seafood-lover's paradise. A wide variety of catch, fresh from the Arabian Sea, can be found stacked in restaurants, especially the seaside joints of Kovalam and Varkala. You can choose from an array of snapper, rockfish, spotted pearl, prawn, lobster and squid amongst others.

Food Today

Don't worry if you don't have an adventurous palate. Travelling in Kerala will still not be a problem. There are plenty of multi-cuisine restaurants in most cities where you get a fair mix of north Indian and 'Chinese' food. Speciality restaurants offering Thai, continental and other cuisines are also available in larger cities. In fact, there is a growing influx of fast-food chains like Dominos and McDonalds in these cities. Since Kerala is accustomed to western travellers, it is never

difficult to get salads or lighter dishes as well.

Favourite Dishes

• **Avial** – A must on the sadya menu, avial is a thick curry of coconut, curd and an assortment of vegetables. Given that the seasoning is cooked in coconut oil, avial is mild in taste and is best eaten with rice.

• **Appam and Stew** – A staple in Nasrani (Christian) households, the appam-stew combo is a favourite with travellers. It's light on the tummy and the stew can be made with chicken, mutton or vegetables. This is usually a breakfast option.

• **Biryani** – A Mappila biryani is something you must try in the Malabar region. The lamb biryani is an aromatic rice dish with plenty of ghee, dry fruits and a generous helping of meat.

Puttu is eaten with steamed bananas or with a spicy gram curry

• **Puttu and Meen Curry** – This is usually served for breakfast. Puttu is rice powder and coconut, steamed in a metal or bamboo holder. This dry white bread is then served with meen (fish) curry or black gram for vegetarians. The meen curry is made with regular Indian spices like garlic, mustard, turmeric, chilli powder, ginger and curry leaves.

• **Kappa** – Tapioca is boiled, cut into slices and then mixed with grated coconut, chilli, salt and turmeric and works wonderfully as a salty snack, especially with the local toddy. This is usually an acquired taste.

• **Paal Payasam** – The most popular sweet of Kerala is paal payasam or milk kheer. Rice is cooked slowly in milk with coconut extract, sugar, cashews and dry fruits. Sometimes jaggery is used instead of sugar.

Festivals & Events

The energy, colours, traditional ceremonies and the enthusiasm amongst locals make Keralite festivals nothing short of fabulous — be it Onam, the snake boat races, or the numerous temple festivals. For travellers, the chance to participate in local life and to get an opportunity to click great pictures is reason enough to plan a trip keeping these dates and seasons in mind.

Nishagandhi Dance & Music Show

A week-long music and dance extravaganza unfolds in the thick of the tourist season in January at the Kanakakunnu Palace in Thiruvananthapuram. Traditional art forms are brought alive to the audience with regular performances of Bharatnatyam, Kuchipudi, Mohiniyattam and Kathakali by renowned artistes.

January

| Mohiniyattam is a dance form native to Kerala

Swathi Sangeethotsavam

There couldn't be a more appropriate place than the central courtyard of Kuthiramalika Palace in Thiruvananthapuram – built by King Swathi Thirunal Rama Varma – to hold this festival. The old palace complex resonates with the sounds of classical music every year in January. The festival was begun by the royal family of Travancore to commemorate the late ruler and his passion for music. Performances are free of cost and open to all.

January

Paragliding Adventure Carnival

The first of its kind, the paragliding carnival was held in Vagamon

(62km from Kottayam) from 23 February to 3 March 2013. Equipped with safety gear, an ambulance and expert paragliders from around the world, Fly Vagamon offered a lifetime experience of soaring in the sky in tandem with an instructor, to more than 300 people. Hopefully it will become a regular event in the future.

February/March

Vishu

Vishu refers to the Malayalam New Year celebrated by the Hindu community of the state. Kani Kanal, or the 'first sight of the day', includes an arrangement of new clothes, ornaments, rice, flowers, mirror, fruits, coconuts and a yellow cucumber. Usually the elders of the family take young ones with their eyes closed to a room where this symbolic representation of prosperity is kept. It is said that one's fortune in the New Year depends on what one sees first on Vishu day.

April/May

Thrissur Pooram

A cluster of towering, heavily decorated elephants are the main characters of this fascinating spectacle. Ensure that you get a good spot to see the switching of the caparisons between competing elephant teams, and stay on late into the night when the fireworks start at the venue. The festival brings together 10 participating

| Elephants lined up at the spectacular
| Thrissur Pooram festival

❚ Onam is synonymous with ornate flower
❘ decorations and traditional lamps

temples to pay obeisance to Lord
Vakunnathan (Shiva).
April/May

Spice Coast Open

The first surfing festival in India
was held in Kovalam from 3rd to
5th May 2013, adding more action
to the already lively beach. Crowds
of surfers, swimmers and excited
adults and children watched as
enthusiasts rode the near-perfect
waves of this coastal stretch, a
surprisingly unlisted surfing hot
spot. The event is likely to be
organised annually.
May

Snake Boat Races

The cheering crowds and frenzied
environment at the snake boat
races in Kerala cannot but infect
the most sober visitor. This lively
rowing showdown involves teams
of hundreds, rowing vigorously
on elegant 125ft-long canoes
on the watery racetracks of the
backwater canals. There are over
20 such races held in the state, of
which the Nehru Snake Boat Race
of Alappuzha (second Saturday in
August) is the most famous.
August

Onam

The Hindu harvest festival
is steeped in strong mythical
history. Onam commemorates
the annual visit of the legendary
King Mahabali, under whom
Kerala experienced a golden age
of prosperity. It is said that the
wrongly banished king returns
annually to visit his kingdom, and
this occasions a celebration every
year. A modern interpretation of
the festival also credits a successful
harvest as reason for celebration.

Flower decorations, lamps, and the traditional feast, sadya, are the norm in every household.
August/September

Kovalam Lit Fest

Literature enthusiasts get a chance to listen to and interact with famous authors from all over the world and buy signed copies of their books at this annual festival held in Thiruvananthapuram and, quite strangely, Delhi. It is second to India's Jaipur Lit Fest in terms of new releases, discussions, quizzes and readings.
October

International Film Festival of Kerala

Alternative cinema takes centre stage at the annual film festival in Thiruvananthapuram each year. World-renowned movies get a chance to enthrall Indian audiences at this forum, along with outstanding entries from India.
December

Kochi–Muziris Biennale

The resounding success of the first Indian Biennale held from December 2012 to March 2013 at the Kochi islands indicates that this cauldron of artistic expression is likely to return soon. The various works of international and Indian artistes were showcased in unusual venues like broken-down buildings, abandoned warehouses and walls along the streets.
December–March

Grand Kerala Shopping Festival

To avail massive discounts, freebies, gift certificates and more, travel to Kerala during the Grand Kerala Shopping Festival. Discounts and deals are available in jewellery, clothing, tech products and almost anything that you can find in the shopping hub of Kochi, MG Road. Many brands also showcase their goods in this annual festival.
December

Snake boat races see long canoes in a lively rowing showdown

Customs & Culture

Kerala's diverse religious composition has resulted in a fascinating melding of customs and traditions, even though Hindus, Muslims and Christians continue to follow distinct cultural practices. The state has a vibrant performing arts scene that has kept alive age-old art forms. Here is a rundown of the state's cultures and customs.

Customs

Drummers are an important part of any religious festival in Kerala

While different communities have varying customs, there are some that are common throughout. Hindu households (and often hotels) in Kerala greet you with an oil lamp made of bell metal, known as nila vilakku. Simply put, because fire symbolises purity, lighting a lamp signifies sanctity in the household. Do not be surprised to see the lamp at Christian functions too – many of the practices have permeated religious boundaries over the years.

However, some barriers still remain. Most important Hindu temples have a strict religious policy: only Hindus can enter, and then too, men have to be bare-chested and women dressed in a sari or similar garment.

Where food is concerned, it is customary to eat with your right hand. Do not hesitate to use your hands to eat – that's how most people tuck in here and the food tastes better!

Culture

Kerala has an intensely rich culture of performing arts that lives on in daily life. Dance forms like Kathakali and Mohiniyattam, along with kalaripayattu are performed especially for tourists in many tourist centres like Fort Kochi and Thekkady. To some this may feel like an overexposure, but this also means that the state has helped these ancient forms and their artistes to survive.

North Kerala has held onto the tradition of Theyyam performances with great tenacity and organises performances from October to the end of April. Kerala celebrates its festivals with great vigour; key events like Onam, Snake Boat Races and various temple poorams throw the state into a celebratory frenzy. In the field of art, Kerala's most eminent artist, Raja Ravi Varma, has left a rich legacy, which can be seen in museums, and in prints, postcards and souvenirs.

Society

A cosmopolitan culture has always existed in the state, given the rapid and long-term influx of foreigners via the spice trade. The religious ambience is largely peaceful. Though a patriarchal system has always been deeply entrenched, a high literacy rate for both genders has made a huge impact on establishing a gender balance; the state is not overly conservative. However, an earlier longstanding system of marumakkattayam (matrilineal) society in some regions has altered in modern times making the husband the ultimate guardian of the family.

Marriages

Hindu, Christian and Muslim weddings follow unique customs except in the case of a tali (equivalent to a mangalsutra). It is common practice in both Hindu and Christian weddings to tie one on the bride. As in the rest of India, 24–25 years is considered an apt marriageable age for girls and slightly older for young men. Inter-religious marriages are also becoming more common than ever before.

| Kalaripayattu, a ritualistic discipline
| taught throughout Kerala

TRAVELLERS' HELPDESK

◗ Public transportation is a safe and convenient way to get around in Kerala

Travellers' Helpdesk

Before You Go

As a first stop, it is advisable to go through the state's official tourism website, www. keralatourism.org. Important festivals, top sights, suggestions on where to stay and maps on this site will help you draft your itinerary. There are specific websites for wildlife parks, for instance, which give you valuable information if this is the focus of your visit. Another helpful resource is the property listings on www.ktdc. com, the **Kerala Tourism Department Corporation** website.

Arriving

AIRPORTS

• **Kochi** (📞0484 2610115): Cochin International Airport lies 30km from Ernakulam and is well connected with major Indian cities, Sri Lanka and the Gulf countries.
• **Thiruvananthapuram** (📞0471 2500283): The Thiruvananthapuram International Airport is suitable if you are travelling to the southern side of the state. It is 5km from the city centre.
• **Kozhikode** (📞0483 271 2630): This international airport is the nearest air node to the northern regions of Kerala. Middle East nations and important cities

Train journeys provide an excellent opportunity to explore the real Kerala

of India are well connected to this airport, which lies 27km from the city.

RAILWAY STATIONS

Major cities in Kerala are well connected to the metros of India. The state has 13 major rail routes, of which the most scenic one runs along the coast from Kasaragod to Thiruvananthapuram. The following are the important railheads of the state. Visit the official railway website www.irctc.co.in for more information.
• **Ernakulam** (📞0484 2376131): This is one of the largest stations of Kerala with connectivity to most parts of India and is also known as Ernakulam South to make a distinction between another satellite station known as Ernakulam Town.
• **Thiruvananthapuram** (📞0471 2334680): Thiruvananthapuram is the largest and busiest railway station of the state and is connected to places as far as Jammu in north India, Bhubaneswar in the east as well as other cities.
• **Alappuzha** (📞0477 2238465): The Alappuzha station lies 4km from the city and is great for tourists who want direct connectivity to the backwater destinations of Kerala. Though it's small, it is connected to Mumbai, Bengaluru and Chennai, amongst other important cities.

• **Kannur** (☎0497 2705555): Kannur is an important junction that connects north Kerala to major cities in India. Platform 1 here is the second-longest platform in the state. Be ready to walk a long distance.

• **Palakkad** (☎0491 555245): One of the main rail nodes of Kerala, Palakkad services trains from Thrissur and Coimbatore.

• **Thrissur** (☎0487 2423150): This connects to the temple city of Guravayur amongst other places near the city. It has three other satellite stations.

• **Kozhikode** (☎0495 2701234): This important junction is well connected to Thiruvananthapuram, Kochi, Coimbatore, Chennai, Mumbai, New Delhi, Bengaluru, Mangalore, Pune and Jammu.

GETTING INTO THE CITIES

Ernakulam

There are many agencies you can book a taxi with for airport pick- up and drops and also day-long tours. **Cel Cabs** (☎0484 60609090) is a 24-hour-service. Tariff is calculated for a minimum of 3km (₹75) and each additional km costs ₹9. **Kerala Prepaid Taxi** can be reached on

| Most autorickshaws ply by meter except if you are travelling by night

☎9995205828; www.keralaprepaidtaxi. com. Daily tariffs for a Tata Indica are around ₹1500 for 150km and ₹10 for each additional km. You can also strike a deal with private operators. Contact **Nasir** (☎944 7347476) in Kochi.

Thiruvananthapuram

Cel Cabs (☎0471 60609090) also operate here but the tariff is slightly different. The minimum of 4km costs ₹120 with an additional charge of ₹13 per km. Cel Cabs have a range of tariff combinations, which can be seen on www.celcabs.com. You can also use **Trivandrum Taxi** (☎9995419998, www. trivandrumtaxi.com). Charges for eight hours or 80km are ₹1250. Each additional km costs ₹8.50.

Kozhikode

Taxi Metro (☎9995729242) charges ₹1500 for eight hours or 80km and an additional ₹200 for 10km or an hour.

Thekkady/Munnar

A & A Tours and Travels run by Anshad (☎9495216817) are extremely reliable and have a clean fleet of cars. Tariff includes ₹1600 for 100km, ₹10 for each additional km and ₹100 for driver bata.

Note that if you are hiring the same taxi for several days, you might have to pay a driver bata (daily allowance ranging from ₹200 – ₹300) but it will be simpler to strike a better deal for the entire package.

Autorickshaws: Getting around most cities in autos is a comfortable option. Distances are small and the fare starts at a minimum of ₹20. Most auto drivers ply by meter except if you are travelling late at night, in which case you can bargain a little. If arriving late night or early morning at the railway station, you should get an auto from the pre-paid stand.

ℹ️ *Major trains*

ROUTE	TRAIN NO. & NAME	DEPARTURE
Delhi to Thiruvananthapuram	Kerala Express 12626	11.30
Delhi to Thiruvananthapuram	Trivandrum Rajdhani 12432	05.10
Mumbai to Thiruvananthapuram	Netravati Express 16345	11.40
Mumbai to Thiruvananthapuram	Kanyakumari Express 16381	15.45
Bengaluru to Thiruvananthapuram	Bengaluru-Kanyakumari Island Express 16526	21.40
Bengaluru to Thiruvananthapuram	Bengaluru Kochuveli Express 16315	17.15
Chennai to Thiruvananthapuram	Chennai Thiruvananthapuram SF Mail 12623	19.45
Kolkata to Thiruvananthapuram	Guwahati Trivandrum Express 12516	06.30
Delhi to Ernakulam	Mangala Lakshadweep Express 12618	09.20
Delhi to Ernakulam	Kerala Express 12626	11.30
Mumbai to Ernakulam	Mangala Lakshadweep Express 12618	08.50
Mumbai to Ernakulam	Kanyakumari Express 16381	15.45
Bengaluru to Ernakulam	Intercity Express 12677	06.15
Bengaluru to Ernakulam	Bengaluru-Kanyakumari Island Express 16526	21.40
Chennai to Ernakulam	Chennai-Egmore-Guruvayur Express 16127	07.40

Most trains stop at Ernakulam, Thiruvananthapuram and other major junctions en route.

Money

CREDIT & DEBIT CARDS

All hotels and most of the bigger restaurants accept Master and Visa credit and debit cards. However, the smaller shops and homestays may not take cards. It is best to have sufficient cash when shopping and check out in advance the payment option with homestays.

COSTS & BUDGETS

Kerala is very susceptible to differential pricing according to season, which varies up to 30–40% between peak and off-season. The best weather to travel is between December and February. However, if you like the monsoons, you can be assured of great discounts on your stay (in addition to a more peaceful, non-touristy time).

• **Tight budget (daily budget of below ₹3000):** Accommodation consumes a significant part of your budget in Kerala, so if travelling in season, it will be difficult to get anything in this range except for Fort Kochi, Varkala and Kovalam, which attract a lot of foreign travellers and offer cheap and clean places to stay. Food is easier on the pocket as meals are available for less than ₹100. You are also not likely to spend too much on travel within cities, unless you are indulging in houseboats.

• **Mid-range (daily budget of ₹3000–6000):** Mid-range hotels in cities offer services like wi-fi and if you are lucky, even pools. You may even get a heritage place within ₹4500 with breakfast included. If this is your budget per day, you can include better restaurants, but will still not be able to include houseboats, which start at ₹9000 (unless you are travelling during low season, in which case you can bargain for a cheaper rate).

• **High-end (daily budget of ₹6000 and above):** Most top-end accommodation with classy interiors or scintillating views will cost you more than ₹6000 per day if you are travelling during high season. On such a budget, houseboat/plantation stays will not be an issue. There are many heritage properties and five-star hotels in Kerala which may be far flung but offer full board facilities or, at least, complimentary breakfast. You may have to shell out an extra ₹300–350 per head for lunch and dinner.

❶ *ATMs*

There is no dearth of ATMs in the tourist towns of Kerala, especially Federal Bank ones. You will find these frequently along with HDFC, ICICI, SBI and AXIS banks. However, do carry enough cash if you are staying in homestays or plantations that are far from town centres.

Health

Hospitals and medical shops are not difficult to find in Kerala, but for emergency services Thiruvananthapuram, Kozhikode and Ernakulam are the most reliable. If you are on an overnight trip in a houseboat or a distant plantation stay, it's best to keep a medical kit handy.

Practicalities A–Z

BUSES

Kerala State Road Transport Corporation (www.keralartc.com) offers regular and a few Volvo buses

| A colourful bus in the streets of Palakkad

between destinations. If you are travelling from Bengaluru (or any other city from Karnataka), use the **Karnataka State Road Transport Corporation** Volvos, which you can book on www.ksrtc.in. Many private operators are listed on www.redbus.in, of which Kallada is the most popular within Kerala.

BUSINESS HOURS

• **Restaurants:** Stand-alone restaurants are usually open 11am–3pm for lunch and 7–10.30pm for dinner. Restaurants in hotels serve breakfast from 7–10.30am but smaller joints are open even earlier at about 6.30am. You will not find a lot of nightlife in Kerala after 11pm except for a few pubs in Ernakulam.
• **Shops & Markets:** The larger markets in all cities open around 11am and usually close by 8pm. Most markets are shut on Sunday. General stores and chemists open by 7.30am and close around 8pm.
• **Historical Sites:** Forts, palaces and museums open at 9am and close by 4.30pm in most cities. Some places close half an hour earlier during winter. Check with the specific site before visiting. Mondays are often closed so do check before planning your day.
• **Temples:** Temples open as early as 4.30am but shut down for the afternoon from noon–4pm. They reopen at about 4pm and close at 8pm. Larger temples like Sree Padmanabhaswamy Temple and Guruvayur Sree Krishna Temple open even earlier and have short darshan timings in between.
• **Banks:** Nationalised banks are open 10am–2pm and private banks 10am–4pm for transactions. Many banks operate uptil noon on Saturdays but are closed on Sundays.
• **Government Offices:** All government offices are open 10am–5pm. Saturday and Sunday are holidays. They are also closed on public holidays.

DISABLED TRAVELLERS

Kerala, like most Indian cities, is not easy for the disabled but several hotels have comfortable lift services and ramps for wheelchairs. Monuments, museums, forts and other sightseeing options often do not have facilities for disabled travellers.

EMERGENCY NUMBERS

• **Police Control Room:** ☎100
• **Fire Station:** ☎101
• **Ambulance:** ☎108
• **Crime Stopper:** ☎1090
• **Women Helpline:** ☎1091
• **Tourist Information Toll Free:** ☎1800 425 4747

HOLIDAYS

Kerala follows government public holiday rules; nevertheless, check the local calendars for festivals which may be declared as holidays. What is more important is being aware of strikes during your trip, as these may cause you to waste a day or two along the way.

INTERNET

There are several internet cafes in tourist-heavy towns of Kerala, which are mostly frequented by western backpackers. Though, you are more than likely to find wi-fi in hotels and guesthouses now. The charge per hour for internet usage in a cafe starts at ₹20; hotels usually offer free wi-fi facilities.

NEWSPAPERS

Malayala Manorama is the most famous Malayalam daily circulated in the state. For English language newspapers, you are likely to find *The Hindu, The Indian Express, Times of India* and *Hindustan Times.*

TOILETS

The state of public restrooms is as dismal as any other place in the country. Highway stops, museums and historical sites have restrooms but these may not be in top-notch condition. It is recommended to carry your own toilet paper roll and hand sanitiser.

TOURISM OFFICES IN KERALA

• **Thiruvananthapuram:** (☏0471 2315397); DTPC, Vellayambalam.
• **Ernakulam:** (☏0484 2351015); Tourist Information Officer, Dept of Tourism, Boat Jetty.
• **Alappuzha:** (☏0477 2260722); Tourist Information Office, Near Boat Jetty.
• **Kozhikode:** (☏0495 2720012); DTPC.
• **Kannur:** (☏0497 2706336); DTPC, Near Civil Station.
• **Wayanad:** (☏04936 202134); DTPC, Kalpetta.
• **Thrissur:** (☏0487 2320800); DTPC, Palace Road, Chembukkavu.
• **Kollam:** (☏0474 2750170); DTPC, Near Boat Jetty.

KERALA TOURISM OFFICES IN METROS

• **Mumbai:** (☏022 22153393); 74 World Trade Centre, Cuffe Parade.
• **New Delhi:** (☏011 23382067); Travancore Palace, Kasturba Gandhi Marg.
• **Kolkata:** (☏033 65367190); Kolkata Malayali Samajam, 22 Chinmoy Chatterjee Sarani.
• **Chennai:** (☏044 25382639); TTDC Complex, Walajha Road.

POLICE CONTROL ROOMS

• **Thiruvananthapuram:** ☏0471 2331843

• **Ernakulam:** ☏0484 2359200
• **Kozhikode:** ☏0495 2721831
• **Kollam:** ☏0474 2746000
• **Alappuzha:** ☏0477 2251166
• **Thrissur:** ☏0487 2424193
• **Wayanad:** ☏04936 205808

WOMEN TRAVELLERS

Kerala is by and large safe for women travellers, barring a few smaller towns where isolated incidents of sexual harrassment have occurred (on the streets). The Kerala police have become more vigilant recently in high tourist traffic areas such as Fort Kochi and Kovalam. It is recommended not to be out after 8pm (most cities close down by then anyway).

 Hospitals

THIRUVANANTHAPURAM

• **Apollo Clinic** (☏0471 2303010, www.apolloclinictvm.com, Law College Junction, Kunnukuzhi)

KOCHI

• **Lake Shore Hospital** (☏0484 2701032, www.lakeshorehospital.com, NH 47 Bypass, Maradu, Nettoor)

• **Amrita Institute of Medical Sciences** (☏0484 2801234, www.aimshospital.org, Ponnekara)

KOZHIKODE

• **Malabar Institute of Medical Sciences Ltd** (☏0495 3911400, www.mimsindia.com, Mini Bypass Road, Govindapuram)

• **Fathima Hospital** (☏0495 2766630, www.fathimahospital.com, Bank Road)

Index

PICTURE CREDITS

Placement key: T=Top, TC=Top Centre, TR=Top Right, TL=Top Left, C=Centre, B=Bottom, BC=Bottom Centre, BR=Bottom Right, BL=Bottom Left.

Although we have done our best to credit all the copyright holders of the photographs used in this book, we apologise for any unintentional omissions. If informed of any further acknowledgements we will definitely include them in future editions of the book.

Lonely Planet would like to thank the following photographers, organisations and picture libraries for permission to reproduce their photographs:

Aanavilasam Luxury Plantation house: 203TR.

Ambady estate: 194B.

Amruthum Ayurvedic Village Resort: 58BL.

Art of Bicycle Trips: 199B.

Carmelia Haven Resort: 204B.

Coconut Creek Farm & Home Stay: 103TR.

Emerald Isle: 92B.

Eros International: 39B.

Getty images: AFP/ Raveendran 47TR; Dorling Kindersley/ Tim Draper 132T; Flickr 84TL; Flickr Open/ Madhu Kannan 156B; India Today Group 23C; Lonely Planet Images 96BL\ 160B\ 209B\ 236C\ Christer Fredriksson 22C/ 32C\ Peter Ptschelinzew 238 – 239; Robert Harding World Imagery/ Stuart Black 224 – 225; The Image Bank/ Keren Su 40 – 41\ Peter Adams 10 – 11/ 112.

Harivihar Heritage Homestead: 30C, 159B.

Indiapicture: Alamy/ Anders Blomqvist 19C\ 46T\ 63B\ 115TR, Angus McComiskey 188B, Anne-Marie Palmer 36B, Arvind Balaraman 232BL, Cephas Picture Library/ Diana Mewes 161T,

Charles Stirling (Diving) 21TR\ 216T, CuboImages srl/ Renato Valterza 35T, Daniel J. Rao 18TR, dbimages 54T\ 73TR, Dennis Cox 78T, ephotocorp/ Mihir Sule 218B, Gavin Mather 72B, Imagebroker/ Olaf Krüger 152TR, Imagery India 123B, India view 127T, Jamaway 241B, Joan Swinnerton 217TR, Kazimierz Jurewicz 2 – 3B, Kevin Schafer 200B, Mahadevan Sankar 185TR, Maurice Joseph 17B, Melvyn Longhurst 102B, Mohamed Abdul Rasheed 168BL, Muthuraman Vaithinathan 234T, Neil McAllister 243B, Norma Joseph 214, Pete M. Wilson 23TR, Pictures Colour Library/ Travel Pictures 20C\ 106C, Pumkinpie 235BR, Raj Singh 151T, Ruby 116T, Simon Reddy 13T\ 48T\ 105TL\ 231T, Steve Davey Photography 122T, Stuart Forster 176T, Subhash S.L 18B, Travelib Asia 15B\ 124B\ 109B\ 169BR, Travelstock44 69B, Universal Images Group Limited/ Education Images 219TR, Yadid Levy 12B; Dreamstime 116BR\ 142B; IP-Black 101BR\ 114T\ 134TL; Monkey Business 117B; Robert Harding World Imagery/ Tuul 71B.

Kerala Tourism board: 8C, 16T, 17TR, 24B, 27T, 29B, 48B, 50B, 53B, 56T, 57B, 85TR, 86C, 88B, 91B, 98 – 99B, 100T, 111T, 115B, 121T, 144B, 148, 151BR, 152B, 157TR, 167BL, 174T, 177B, 181B, 182, 184T, 186T, 187B, 192B, 202BL, 211B, 212TL, 233B, 237BR, 240T.

Mayura Residency: 146BL.

Nattika Beach Resort: 147T.

Nature Zone Resort, Munnar: 196B.

Neeleshwar Hermitage: 170BL.

Pepper County: 206B.

Swati Srivastava: 216B, 221TR.

Sheema Mookherjee: 74B.

Shutterstock: AJP 153B; Copit 173B; Curioso 185B; Jayakumar 6 -7; Pawel Pietraszewski 21B; Pikoso.kz 82C; Rafal Cichawa 80; VLADJ55 227B; WITTY234 128TL.

Somatheeram Ayurveda Group: 76C, 77T.

Spice Tree Munnar: 195T.

Supriya Sehgal: 64B, 83T, 84B, 150B, 163T, 186BL.

Taamara: 95T.

Tharavad Heritage Home: 104B.

The Residency Tower: 59T.

The Wildernest: 207T.

Tom's Old Mansion: 136B.

Tranquil - A Plantation Hideaway: 178B.

Travancore Court: 126B.

Turtle on the Beach: 75T.

Villa Jacaranda: 67B.

Villa Maya: 60B.

Wikipedia: Creative Commons Attribution 2.0 Generic license/ Aruna Radhakrishnan 135B\ Mehul Antani 44; Creative Commons Attribution-Share Alike 2.0 Generic license/ Challiyil Eswaramangalath Vipin 143\ Manvendra Bhangui 222B\ Suresh Krishna 190C; Creative Commons Attribution-Share Alike 3.0 Unported license/ കാക്കര 191B\ Nisheedh 164B\ TEMS.VT. 38T; Public Domain 47B\ 118C\ 228B.

COVER IMAGES: Front – INDIAPICTURE: Alamy/ Imagery India; **Back** - SHUTTERSTOCK: f9photos.

Supriya Sehgal would like to thank the following people for their guidance and support :

Joseph Sham, Fort Kochi

Geethaa Oommen Mathen, Ernakulam

Kence Georgey, Kumarakom

Jagannath Chirakkara, Bekal

Tayil Sadanan, Mahe.

LONELY PLANET INDIA TEAM

Commissioning Editor Kavita Majumdar
Design Manager Kavita Saha
Designer Harpreet Wadhwa
Layout Designer Arun Aggarwal
Picture Researcher Shweta Andrews

Although the authors and Lonely Planet have taken all reasonable care in preparing this book, we make no warranty about the accuracy or completeness of its content and, to the maximum extent permitted, disclaim all liability arising from its use.

PUBLISHED BY

Lonely Planet Publications Pty Ltd
ABN 36 005 607 983
1st edition – August 2013
ISBN 978 1 74321 964 5
© Lonely Planet August 2013   Photographs © as indicated 2013
10 9 8 7 6 5 4 3 2 1
Printed in India